'Christi van der Westhuizen has pushed the bou[...]
the current scholarly discourse, and opened up [...] possibility of a much richer
understanding of not only the persistence of the problem of racism; her reflection on
how racism and patriarchy interact in the social construction of Afrikaner women's
identity is a compelling vision of how these two systems of domination are critical in our
understanding of the oppression of all women. Her unique articulation of the concepts
"Sarielese", "*ordentlikheid*", "intersectional shifting", interwoven with the narratives
of the women in her interviews, show a much deeper, darker and shameful side of
racism. Only someone with the talents of Van der Westhuizen could weave an analysis
of racism with such profound insights. Yet her last word on this most urgent problem
of contemporary South Africa is a transformative vision. She closes her book as she
opened it – with Nelson Mandela's reading of Ingrid Jonker's poem – by gesturing
towards the transformative potentialities of the experience of shame.'

— **Pumla Gobodo-Madikizela**, professor and research chair,
Historical Trauma and Transformation, Stellenbosch University,
and author of *A Human Being Died That Night: A Story of Forgiveness*

'*Sitting Pretty* offers a path-breaking, nuanced and insightful reading of white, middle-
class, heterosexual "Afrikaner" women in postapartheid South Africa. Van der
Westhuizen's analysis of popular culture draws on poststructuralist theory to provide
insight into how key signifiers work to fix meaning and shape everyday life. Through
her analysis of the discursive production of identity, she shows how *ordentlikheid* –
ethnicised respectability – works as an aspirational mode of whitening and as a gender-
sexual regime, seeking not only to re-infuse identity with moral worth in the aftermath
of apartheid, but also to in-form enclave neo-nationalism, a retreat into private micro-
apartheid geographies. *Sitting Pretty* crucially also explores the redemptive possibilities
of dissenting Afrikaners, bringing home the implications of the role of shame in the
transformation of relations and the restoration of ties to others. Van der Westhuizen's
mapping of struggles to fix meaning in popular culture makes a serious contribution
to our understanding of the complexities of the postapartheid order, and to what is
demanded from us if we are truly to realise that order.'

— **Aletta Norval**, professor of Political Theory, University of Essex,
and author of *Deconstructing Apartheid Discourse*

'Christi van der Westhuizen is one of South Africa's most incisive analysts of "the
social". In *Sitting Pretty*, she mobilises her intellectual dexterity to bring into the open
the project of becoming *ordentlik* as the key objective of Afrikaans women's responses to
the democratisation of the country. The task of *ordentlikheid* is performed within two
modes: materially as middle-class women, and physically to express the gender, class
and race criteria of the *volksmoeder*; that is, to sit pretty. Piercing the modes by which
Afrikaans women re/constitute themselves as moral agents through an *ordentlikheid*
that is furthered by its guardians, the *volksmoeder* and her patriarchal overseer, Van der

Westhuizen skilfully reveals the discursive strategies at play. Van der Westhuizen's work is simply superb, courageous and sophisticated. It provides productive ways for making sense of our social reality; and points to a "mutual humanisation through a consciously driven politics of recognition" that can open new vistas of social imagination.'
— **André Keet**, professor, Critical Studies in Higher Education Transformation, Nelson Mandela University

'Offering an incisive analysis of the complex nexus between race, gender, sexuality and Afrikanerdom and surfacing various ways in which social asymmetries are perpetuated in contemporary South Africa, this book makes for compelling reading. Christi van der Westhuizen's examination and use of the notion of *ordentlikheid* as both "a normative and analytical concept" is inspired and captivating. This book can be considered essential for scholars with an interest in the politics of othering and inequality in South Africa.'
— **Norman Duncan**, professor of Psychology and vice-principal, University of Pretoria

'Van der Westhuizen offers an important contribution to the growing field of critical whiteness studies and one that is urgently needed in the context of ongoing pressures from Global Northern neoliberal heteronormative masculinist discourses. A well-established critical commentator on the rise of white nationalist governance in South Africa, in this volume she turns her "dissection knife to the centres of power" in postapartheid South Africa. Through this careful and provocative dissection, she offers challenging observations as to the ways in which white ethnic recuperation operates via aspirations to moral worth in the face of widespread global critique of a spoiled form of whiteness. There is also sophisticated insight into moments of possibility for white Afrikaans subjectivities to contribute to anti-racist resistance through practices of the self, which engage in an honest reckoning with shame before the eyes of the black subject. This is a significant book with much to offer for an analysis of neoliberal racialising discourses in South Africa and beyond.'
— **Shona Hunter**, associate professor of Sociology and Social Policy Governance, University of Leeds, and author of *Power, Politics and the Emotions: Impossible Governance*

'For those inclined to think of racism and discrimination as problems best solved by anti-racist laws and policies, post-apartheid South Africa offers a sobering challenge. As Van der Westhuizen provocatively argues, culture, discourse and affect in the more private, domestic realms of gender, ethnic and sexual identity can elude and resist the reach of public policy, providing spaces for white privilege and power to reconfigure themselves and continue their pernicious, dehumanising work.'
— **Matt Wray**, associate professor of Sociology, Temple University, and author of *White Trash: Race and Class in America*

Sitting Pretty

White Afrikaans Women
in Postapartheid South Africa

Christi van der Westhuizen

UNIVERSITY OF KwaZulu-Natal Press

Published in 2017 by University of KwaZulu-Natal Press
Private Bag X01
Scottsville, 3209
Pietermaritzburg
South Africa
Email: books@ukzn.ac.za
Website: www.ukznpress.co.za

ISBN: 978 1 86914 376 3
e-ISBN: 978 1 86914 377 0

Managing editor: Sally Hines
Editor: Alison Lockhart
Proofreader: Cathy Munro
Typesetter: Patricia Comrie
Indexer: Christopher Merrett
Cover design: Marise Bauer, M Design
Cover image: *Madonna Blank met Rosegloed* by Lizelle Kruger, oil on canvas, 40 × 30 cm.
© 2010 Lizelle Kruger. Reproduction under licence. All rights reserved.

This book has undergone a double-blind independent peer review process.

Print administration by DJE Flexible Print Solutions, Cape Town

For Melanie, for wild imaginings

Contents

Acknowledgements

Thank you to the respondents in this study for sharing their time(s) and narratives. Thank you to Debra Primo and Kholeka Mabeta at UKZN Press for making the book happen, enthusiastically, and to Sally Hines, Alison Lockhart and Adele Branch for relatively painless and even joyful production and marketing processes. Special thanks to the irrepressible Louis Gaigher, who set the ball rolling, and to Lizelle Kruger for generously agreeing to the use of her wonderful art. Lastly, thank you to the anonymous reviewers for their comments and insights.

Introduction

In the Shadow of Ingrid Jonker

MANDELA'S INVITATION
After almost 350 years of Dutch, British and Boer colonialism and Afrikaner nationalist apartheid rule, the first democratic parliament of South Africa opened on 24 May 1994. In his inaugural 'State of the Nation' address as the new South African president, African National Congress (ANC) leader Nelson Mandela extended an invitation to South Africans who identify as 'Afrikaner women'. The invitation was in the form of a forward-looking memorialisation: Mandela re-remembered Afrikaans poet Ingrid Jonker (1933–65) and poignantly proffered her 'glorious vision' of possibilities of identification:

> She was both a poet and a South African. She was both an Afrikaner and an African. She was both an artist and a human being. In the midst of despair, she celebrated hope. Confronted by death, she asserted the beauty of life. [. . .] She instructs that our endeavours must be about the liberation of the woman, the emancipation of the man and the liberty of the child.[1]

He quoted the poem that Jonker is best known for: 'The Child Who Was Shot Dead by Soldiers at Nyanga', which speaks about black resistance and humanity in the face of apartheid state brutality. Jonker was the daughter of a National Party Member of Parliament who chaired the committee in charge of apartheid censorship. There was an attempted excision of the poem before its publication in her collection of poems *Rook en Oker* (Smoke and Ochre) (first published in 1963) and she suffered public humiliation at the hands of her father.

Jonker was writing against apartheid at the time when Mandela was incarcerated for his activities in opposition to the regime of which her father was a part. She envisaged a future when resistance against apartheid would bring liberation. 'The Child Who Was Shot Dead by Soldiers at Nyanga' reads as follows:

> The child is not dead
> the child raises his fists against his mother
> who screams Africa   screams the smell
> of freedom and heather
> in the locations of the heart under siege
>
> The child raises his fists against his father
> in the march of the generations
> who scream Africa   scream the smell
> of justice and blood
> in the streets of his armed pride
>
> The child is not dead
> neither at Langa nor at Nyanga
> not at Orlando nor at Sharpeville
> nor at the police station in Philippi
> where he lies with a bullet in his head
>
> The child is the shadow of the soldiers
> on guard with guns saracens and batons
> the child is present at all meetings and legislations
> the child peeps through the windows of houses and into the hearts
> of mothers
> this child who just wanted to play in the sun at Nyanga is everywhere
> the child who became a man treks through all of Africa
> the child who became a giant travels through the whole world
>
> Without a pass (Jonker 2007: 85)

It was a moment rich with meaning: a leader celebrated as the father of the freshly minted 'New South Africa' speaking in an institution representing the fledgling democracy, welcoming an Afrikaner woman into the ranks of a newly imagined, inclusive community. Significantly, she had been marginalised by the whites-only *volk* (people or nation) for recognising its black other.

Mandela's invitation could be read as so compelling as to be a hailing of subjects, or interpellation, to use Louis Althusser's term. His hailing of 'Afrikaner' women was an invocation of the democratic potentialities for subject positions amid the ruins of the apartheid imaginary. This is the focus of this book: to what extent has Mandela's offer of identification been taken up? Do Jonker's contemporary counterparts – at least in terms of the structural classifications of gender, sexuality, class and race (A.M. Smith 1998) – step into the subject positions that democratic discourses have prepared for them? Jonker was subsequently awarded the democratic state's Order of Ikhamanga in Silver in 2004 for 'her excellent contribution to literature and a commitment to the struggle for human rights and democracy in South Africa' (Republic of South Africa 2004: 10). Since the 1990s, several commemorative films and plays about Jonker have been made. Are her present-day structural counterparts as readily absorbed in and absorbing of postapartheid discourses of democracy and humanisation of apartheid's others? Do they, in turn, produce these discourses?

These questions are especially pertinent since the end of official apartheid, precipitated by a weakening in hegemonic articulations (Norval 1996; Laclau 1990). What arose was what Antonio Gramsci calls an 'organic crisis', 'a dramatic collapse in popular identifications with institutionalised subject positions and political imaginaries' (A.M. Smith 1998: 164). South Africa is not only in the throes of attempting to reimagine a politics that does not marginalise and oppress, but is also being reincorporated into the global economy (Habib and Bentley 2008). The transition from apartheid coincided with seismic global shifts as Communism came to an end, sparking neo-liberal triumphalism. South Africans are embroiled in sense-making processes within a radically dislocated postapartheid field and with renewed exposure to a 'global postmodern', characterised by massive upheavals in identifications (Hall 1997a, 1997b). As identities proliferate globally, so they do locally.

It is common cause that the postapartheid social field is in tumultuous flux (Carton, Laband and Sithole 2008; Hadland et al. 2008; Chipkin 2007; Distiller and Steyn 2004; Wasserman and Jacobs 2003). Transitioning from apartheid to democracy holds differential effects for women (Gunkel 2011; Du Toit 2009; West 2009; Samuelson 2007) and men (Shefer et al. 2007). Democratisation troubles whiteness (Van der Westhuizen 2007; Salusbury and Foster 2004; Steyn 2001), masculinity (Ratele 2016; Morrell 2001) and heterosexuality (Steyn and Van Zyl 2009; Judge, Manion and De Waal 2008; Van Zyl and Steyn 2005).

Specifically, the disarticulation of Afrikaner nationalism as discourse catapulted the identity of 'the Afrikaner' into states of confusion and defence (Van der Westhuizen 2016b, 2007; Blaser and Van der Westhuizen 2012; Verwey and Quayle 2012; Vestergaard 2001; Steyn 2004).

This book finds that, with regard to white Afrikaans women's response to the turmoil of democratisation, they are engaged in one project above all: to become *ordentlik*, or respectable, again. 'Afrikaners cannot escape the fact that the system was put in place *in their name*' (Steyn 2003: 222). They seek to rescue their identities from the moral abyss that apartheid and its official ending tipped them into, and to re-infuse their selves with moral worth. The words 'sitting pretty' in the title of this book capture the dimensions of *ordentlikheid*: the promise of its accomplishment is through adherence to specific forms of femininity, heterosexuality, whiteness and middle-classness. Materially, these middle-class women are sitting pretty, which is the legacy of a century of colonial and apartheid upliftment of Afrikaners in South Africa. To embody the gender, class and race criteria of the *volksmoeder*, or mother of the nation, these women are required to 'sit pretty', that is, physically organise their bodies in accordance with certain prescriptions. In pursuit of both of these meanings of 'sitting pretty', white Afrikaans women have to re-establish *ordentlikheid* as the sign of this identity's moral worth amid the upheavals and upsets of the intense contestation that is democratisation.

RAISING A *VOLK*

The 'Afrikaner' identity was historically forged in reaction to white Afrikaans-speakers' status of being marked as just-about-white in relation to hegemonic whiteness, represented by British colonialists and later white English-speaking South Africans (WESSAs). In the first half of the twentieth century, the 'Afrikaner' was regarded as at risk of deteriorating to 'the station and class' of 'the coloured' (Du Toit 2003: 172; see also Adhikari 2005: 11–15 and Erasmus 2001: 17–18). The threat of disqualification from whiteness was particularly intense during the 'poor white' scare of the 1930s. Impoverished Afrikaans whites in the cities were positioned in a way akin to the American phenomenon of 'white trash', a liminal and 'dangerous threshold state' (Wray 2006: 2). The 1910 pact between the two settler groups was capitalised on to shake off the colonial stigma of being just-about-white and to secure Afrikaner whiteness, a process that culminated in apartheid. As global whiteness jettisoned direct colonialism, Afrikaner whiteness was stigmatised yet again, this time due to its implication in apartheid, instrumental in the political, economic and social ascendancy of Afrikaners. From the 1960s, the moral question of apartheid injustice started to bear down heavily on Afrikaners. This was shown by, among other factors, intensifying political contestation in Afrikaner ranks from the 1960s onwards, including conflict about the sociopolitical and economic degrading of culturally similar coloured people. It was also seen in intra-Afrikaner reflection on the effects of apartheid on black people – exemplified by the success of Jonker's poetry and books such as Elsa Joubert's *Die Swerfjare van Poppie Nongena* (first published in 1979), translated as *The Long Journey of Poppie Nongena* – and writings on 'the Afrikaner identity crisis' (for example, De Klerk 1984). Rising black resistance and international opprobrium collapsed apartheid as the supporting scaffolding of Afrikaner identity.

AFRIKANER NATIONALISM, *ORDENTLIKHEID* AND THE *VOLKSMOEDER*

The official inauguration of the 'New South Africa' in 1994 heralded the end of the country's reputation as international exemplar of a particularly intransigent colonial whiteness named apartheid, which had been elaborated throughout the national realm. The Afrikaner nationalists who had come to power in 1948 devised and instituted hierarchical racial and ethnic divisions with borrowed features from British colonial indirect rule (Mamdani 1996), which sutured a specific and wholly new imaginary as symbolic horizon (Norval 1996).

The interpretation of Afrikaner nationalism by the Gesuiwerde Nasionale Party (GNP or Purified National Party, which later simply became the National Party) was the strand that wrested power from 'South Africanism', the ideological formation that brought the previously warring settler groups together in their white pact. The United Party, in its party-political manifestation by the 1930s, had emphasised reconciliation between the two English- and Afrikaans-speaking 'white races' on the basis of segregationism aimed at black people. Aletta Norval (1996) finds that the GNP discourse not only advanced racial exclusivity, but also a version of whiteness that differentiated internally on the grounds of race (43). Immigration, for example, was only open to 'appropriate' white elements. In the social field of the 1930s and 1940s, characterised by intense contestation among identities (Dubow and Jeeves 2005; Hyslop 1995), the GNP increasingly distinguished ways of being 'properly Afrikaans' (Norval 1996: 44). It manufactured the *volkseie* (literally the *volk* or nation's 'own'), deployed as particularist demands and creating political frontiers that were inscribed both racially and ethnically and that became socially generalised (9). Norval criticises Marxist revisionism's class reductionism. She points out that apartheid and segregation discourses 'structured *all* social relations [. . .] delimiting the sphere of the thinkable, setting the boundaries within which all social practices had to take place' (27). Moreover, Norval notes, apartheid was effected not only through exclusion, but also through inclusion: these were simultaneous operations.

As Norval argues, apartheid manufactured multiple others, both internal to the *volkseie* and external. However, the predominant theoretical debates in South African social sciences place the emphasis on either race or class. What happened to apartheid's *other* others after 1994? This book seeks to bring into focus its gendered internal other – 'Afrikaner' women – at the interfaces with race, sexuality and class. It is an investigation into how the radical dislocation of the apartheid imaginary (re)configured subject positions caught in these categories' generative reciprocities.

NORMATIVITY AND INTERSECTIONALITY: *ORDENTLIKHEID* AND THE *VOLKSMOEDER*

The subjects under investigation are individuals who self-identify as women, Afrikaans-speaking, white, heterosexual and middle class, a group about which little research exists, from either the apartheid or postapartheid eras. The study's delimitation means black and/or lesbian and/or working-class women and men have not been included. Firstly, lest the scope becomes too unwieldy, any research study is necessarily restricted and therefore exclusionary of some categories. Secondly, a primary consideration serving as rationale for this study is to turn the dissection knife to the centres of power, the less analysed social positions of whiteness, heterosexuality and middle-classness. It is only over the past two decades that researchers have focused their attention on understanding categories of normativity that hold the hegemonic power to construct the social in their image. This book contributes to a critical understanding of these normative modalities, with a view to problematising and counteracting their oppressive effects. Applying the project of decentring hegemonic identities to South Africa is all the more essential because of the confluence of whiteness, middle-classness, Afrikaansness and heterosexuality in a notably pernicious form of colonialism. Mobilised as 'the Afrikaner' by Afrikaner nationalism, this identity drew on particular productions of racial, gender, sexual and class hierarchies to entrench colonial exclusions and marginalising inclusions at the same time as direct colonialism was being forced to an end elsewhere. This assemblage of markers served as nodal hooks for the apartheid imaginary that exerted hegemony over all identities for a half-century. In postapartheid South Africa, Afrikaans-speaking white people continue to command considerable material assets and economic power. Studies on postapartheid identities find various strategies aimed at rehabilitating Afrikaner identity, of which the majority involve revamping *oppressive* power relations of yesteryear (Steyn 2004, 2001). Including femininity as one of the objects of this study, constructed as other in relation to hegemonic masculinity, allows an unpicking of the strands of othering *internal* to Afrikaner identity. It also allows for an investigation of subjects occupying the dual position of both oppressors and oppressed: these subjects were advantaged by Afrikaner nationalism and apartheid, but simultaneously radically undermined by gender subjugation. Including femininity provides the possibility of uncovering dissidence amid conformism. Lastly, this book provides insights into the process of subjectivation (Butler 1997) and can be drawn upon to examine the specificities of the co-construction of postapartheid identities.

In investigating the mutually productive relationalities between social asymmetries, the concept of intersectionality, grown from black feminist theory, proves particularly useful (McCall 2005; Collins 2000a; Crenshaw 1995). Intersectionality assists in taking apart intertwined formations of inequality, in this case 'Afrikaner' identity as a minority, or 'subaltern' whiteness (Steyn 2003; Gabriel 1998), pursuing a masculinist and bourgeois agenda (Du Toit 2003; Du Pisani 2001; Vincent 1999; Hyslop 1995; Brink 1990).

Being mindful that race should not be conflated with ethnicity, despite their overlaps (Cornell and Hartmann 2007), the intersectional nexus at which the identity is (re)crafted is captured in this book with the key term '*ordentlikheid*'. *Ordentlikheid* is an Afrikaans word used here to reference ethnocultural features associated with a certain bodily comportment. It can be translated with a conglomerate of related words, ranging from respectability, presentability and good manners to politeness and Calvinist humility. *Ordentlikheid* works as both a normative and analytical concept in this book. It acts normatively as productive dynamo set on recruiting subjects, newly absconded from Afrikaner nationalism, for an ethnic project to make a particular white, bourgeois, heteromasculinist power formation respectable again. This book also applies the term analytically as nodal category to dissect the social practices at identity intersections that produce subject positions in a postapartheid context where Afrikaner nationalism is in disrepair. *Ordentlikheid* is particularly useful as analytical concept, given that the shift from official apartheid to democracy in South Africa uprooted subjects' sense of the self as 'moral'. 'The Afrikaner', the hegemonic identity in the apartheid 'matrix of domination' (Collins 2000a), finds itself troubled. Democratisation, combined with admission into the 'global postmodern', creates a sense of being catapulted into moral ambiguity. *Ordentlikheid* becomes even more important as a stabiliser of Afrikaans white subjects' sense of self and to rinse away the pollution of apartheid.

The other key term in this book is *volksmoeder* or mother of the nation. Ample historiographical examinations exist of the *volksmoeder* discourse in the cauldron of contending Afrikaner nationalisms before 1948 (Du Plessis 2010; Viljoen 2008; Brink 2008, 1990; Swart 2007; Du Toit 2003; Bradford 2000; Vincent 2000, 1999; Kruger 1991; Gaitskell and Unterhalter 1989). This book takes a path less trodden: it explores the postapartheid dislodgement of the *volksmoeder* as a nodal point previously suturing both Afrikaner nationalism and apartheid. The *volksmoeder*, as a nodal point, or privileged signifier, represents the most revered femininity of normative *ordentlikheid*, a hegemonic femininity in relation to which white, Afrikaans-speaking, female-bodied subjects are produced, policed and disciplined, in iterations that activate failures, disruptions and refusals. Thus this book answers the call for examinations of hegemonic femininity: Rosalind Gill and Christina Scharff (2011: 2) question why 'there is no investigation of "hegemonic femininity", yet a wealth of writing on "hegemonic masculinity"' exists. The idea of hegemonic femininity suggests a plurality of femininities in which some are dominant and others subordinate. Patricia Hill Collins (2004: 193) describes a 'pecking order' with 'middle-class, heterosexual, White femininity as normative', used as a yardstick for femininity in opposition to men, 'sexual outlaws (prostitutes and lesbians)', girls and unmarried women. Black femininity, she says, is at the bottom of the hierarchy of femininities. So this book springs from a curiosity about what happens to the *volksmoeder*'s hegemonic femininity in the face of democratisation. Does this femininity find ways of recognising its historically denied racial, sexual and gender non-conforming others? As part of this investigation of postapartheid (dis)continuities in the *volksmoeder*'s purchase on subject positions, a discourse analysis is conducted of *Sarie* women's magazine as a purveyor of a contemporary, officially sanctioned discourse creating hegemonic white Afrikaans femininity.

SUBJECTIVITY: FAILING TO SUCCEED

The transition from apartheid to democracy unstitched the hierarchical unity of the national family of Afrikaner nationalism, making 'the Afrikaner woman' available for reconfiguration. Identities have proliferated in what has been variously called the postmodern, postsocialist, postcolonial age – also in South Africa, as apartheid's divisions are rearranged, overturned or re-upholstered. This book approaches the 'post' in 'postapartheid' circumspectly to avoid 'easy triumphalism': as has been cautioned with the terms postmodernism and postcolonialism, I am alert to the 'problematics of temporal sequence and transcendence [. . .] continuity and rupture' in relation to the second term, apartheid (Quayson 2005: 89). The end of official apartheid does not signal the end of its effects: postapartheid 'signifies a mode of being which goes beyond, yet remembers, the logic of apartheid. This beyond cannot be a pure beyond. Apartheid cannot simply be left behind' (Norval 2003: 265). Elaborating on this point, 'postapartheid' is understood using Achille Mbembe's (1992: 3) insight on the postcolony to understand postapartheid as 'a given historical trajectory – that of societies recently emerging from the experience of colonisation'; it is a distinctive system of signs in which 'identities are multiplied, transformed and put into circulation'.

Poststructural discourse analysis is adopted here to chart a way out of 'oversimplified and deterministic analytical frameworks' to study ideology, politics and culture on their own terms (Chipkin 2007: 18) and to deepen democracy as 'an academic-cum-political task' (Alexander 2002: 27). Norval (1996: 27, 139) proposes analysing the discursive construction of identities, which exposes the relationship between apartheid and capitalism as contingent, rather than necessary, while showing how apartheid shaped all social relations. This would carve a way to studying the still (relative to race and class) under-examined gender relations that underpinned apartheid and continues to shape postapartheid identities, not to speak of interconnected and mostly unexamined sexuality (Shefer 2010).

An 'either race or class' debate about inequality dominated the South African social sciences in the latter decades of the twentieth century. Both strands of thinking – emphasising race and class, respectively, as the master category organising relations in South Africa – made important contributions, but collapsed into reductionism. The discord over whether race or class should enjoy precedence in analysis continues in postapartheid South Africa, now as a result of conflicting interpretations of the deracialisation of the upper echelons of society and the rise of the black middle class (Seekings and Nattrass 2005; Erasmus 2005). Narrowly focusing on 'either race or class' is to the detriment of understanding the consequences of various social markers mobilised by apartheid and how these categories continue to interact with each other to produce inequality. Linzi Manicom (1992: 441–3) comments that women were invisibilised and othered within 'the very epistemological assumptions and analytic strategies' of South African social sciences. Therefore gender did not feature in the race-class debate 'despite very fundamental categories of state and politics – like citizen, worker, the modern state itself – [being] shot through with gender; they were in fact historically constructed and reproduced as masculine categories, predicated on the subordination of women' (444). The 'sexual apartheid' of conceptually separating women and family 'from the "important" domains of men' misrepresented colonialism. For example, families were dismissed as 'mere' feminine spheres when, in fact, they were core sites of class construction (Bradford 1996: 352, 357) and racialisation (Du Plessis 2010). This 'conceptual denial' of women mirrored their status in South African social and cultural structures (Bradford 1996: 354–7; see also Penzhorn 2005). While gender only became 'a more respectable concept in southern African studies' in the early 1990s, its position within social analysis had still not been resolved (Bradford 1996: 351–2; see also Walker 1990: 3). Subsequent scholarship started to fill the lacuna (for example, Baderoon 2014; Worden 2012; Gunkel 2011; Du Toit 2009; West 2009; Samuelson 2007; Keegan 2001; Dagut 2000; Lester 1998).

It would not suffice to tack on 'patriarchy' to break through the 'sterility of the race-class debate' (Manicom 1992: 463). Rather, Manicom proposes a theoretical shift to a poststructuralist focus cognisant of the temporally and spatially contingent meanings of 'woman' in relation to 'other significant markers of social power' (Walker 1990: 26):

> There is no pre-given, historically 'true' 'woman' or 'women' that can be ferreted out from beneath [. . .] racial and class versions of womanhood [. . .] To assume a fixed opposition between men and women suppresses the diversity within each of those binary categories, invariably allowing normative or essentialist gender definitions to infuse our understandings. It removes from investigation that which has to be explained, namely, the meanings of those gender categories relative to their histories, relative to other social constructions (Manicom 1992: 454).

This book takes Manicom's argument as a starting point and examines the specific production of white Afrikaans womanhood in relation to its history and relative to other social constructions. It further adopts Manicom's insight that the line of enquiry should change from 'who rules and why' to questioning modes of subjection. This means investigating how state and non-state sites manufacture 'women' as objects for rule. I unpack how normative gender meanings of 'domination and subordination in relation to specific historic regimes' (Manicom 1992: 456, 458, 463) construct Afrikaans white women.

To achieve these ends, I apply Ernesto Laclau, Chantal Mouffe, Michel Foucault and Judith Butler's theories on the discursive formation of subjectivity, that is, how individuals adopt identities and are turned into subjects. To make it clear, identities are approached as constructed in particular historical and institutional sites, produced by subjects through 'specific enunciative strategies' and within 'the play of specific modalities of power' (Hall 1996: 17). Of interest is the positioning of subjects within a discursive structure, a result which Laclau and Mouffe call 'subject positions' (Carpentier and Spinoy 2008: 5). As every discourse has an open character, subject positions are never totally fixed (Laclau and Mouffe 1985: 113) and a subject can occupy multiple subject positions or identities. These positions have no hidden 'deep' origin, as they are outcomes of articulation and therefore contingent (Critchley and Marchart 2004: 4; Laclau 1990: 184). Identities are formed through subjects continuously and repetitively 'presuming and enacting' differences/exclusions/antagonisms from other identities (Butler 2000: 12, 31), which involves processes of sexing, gendering, racialising and so forth. Butler (1990: 23, 33) explains identity as 'a culturally restricted principle of order and hierarchy, a regulatory fiction': what seems like the coherence or continuity of a 'person' is in fact a 'normative ideal', a 'socially instituted and maintained [form] of intelligibility'.

However, the subject is only partially determined by its structural position, charting a path between structure and agency: 'while human beings are constituted as subjects within discursive structures, these structures are inherently contingent and malleable' (Laclau 2004: 322). Foucault (2004) argues that individuals are not some 'multiple inert matter [. . .] struck by power': while they are effects of power in that power allows 'bodies, gestures, discourses and desires to be identified and constituted as something individual', individuals can 'both submit to and exercise this power' (29–30). Laclau (1990: 41) similarly contends that the subject is an 'effect of power': 'the constitution of an identity is an act of power and [. . .] identity as such *is* power' (31).

Every identity depends on an exterior that both denies it and produces its conditions of possibility (Laclau 1990: 39). This constitutive outside 'can never become fully inside': identity's efforts at self-closure never succeed (Butler 2000: 12, 30-1). 'The incompleteness of the structural identity constitutes the subject as the locus of a decision about how to establish itself as a concrete subjectivity with a fully achieved identity' (Torfing 1999: 149). These decisions to fill identity's lack – its inability to achieve self-closure due to the radical subversion by its constitutive outside – manifest in acts of identification with the hegemonic projects in the discursive structure. Therefore, 'there is no source of the social different from people's decisions in the process of the social construction of their own identities and their own existence' (Laclau 1990: 193). The antagonising outside's prevention of the full suturing of the identity is a condition that Laclau dubs 'dislocation'.

However, as the outside's threat also works as an affirmation (27), dislocation is not only negative but opens up new possibilities, as no course of historical action is set in advance (171–3). With the accelerated tempo of dislocations in a postmodern context, the subject grasps that contingency is a characteristic of the world and therefore other options and choices become available (Howarth 2004: 268; Laclau 2004: 323). Deciding to take a certain course of action, rather than another, is how subjects constitute themselves (Laclau 1990: 171–2). Thus, even merely surrendering to the position still requires my decision to do so. The failure and contingency of identities creates the space for subjectivity, agency, freedom and particularity of human behaviour: 'I am *condemned* to be free,' says Laclau (44).

Dislocation opens different possibilities for the subject. In a dislocatory situation, discursive structures' 'undecidability' becomes visible and they 'no longer function to confer identity' (Howarth 2004: 264). In these moments, 'subjects become political agents in the stronger sense of the term, as they identify with new discursive objects and act to reconstitute subjects'. The end of official apartheid is such a dislocatory situation. The terminal crisis in apartheid in the 1980s came about as a result of the 'horror of indetermination': 'a situation in which the dominant discourse is unable to determine the lines of exclusion and inclusion according to which the identity of the social is constructed' (Norval 1996: 133). The deeper the dislocation, the more structurally profound the rearticulations will be, which expands the role of the subject and holds the possibility of a polyphony of voices and radically democratic struggles, such as anti-sexism, anti-racism and anti-capitalism, to emerge (Carpentier and Spinoy 2008: 11–12; Mouffe 2005).

Foucault (2002: 342) also emphasises that power can only be 'exercised over free subjects' and that freedom is a prerequisite for the exercise of power. His work shifted from investigating the processes of objectivisation that turn an individual into a subject, to 'the way a human being turns him- or herself into a subject' (327). He posits that the self can be formed as an 'ethical subject' in relation to systems of prescription 'explicitly or implicitly operative in [her] culture, and of which [she is] more or less aware' and in 'the way in which the individual establishes his relation to the rule and recognises himself as obliged to put it into practice' (Foucault 1992: 26–7).

This notion of the ethical self can be usefully applied to *ordentlikheid* as an organising principle, especially as the subjects under review seek to cleanse themselves from the moral pollution of apartheid. For Foucault (1992: 28), the proviso for an action to qualify as 'moral' is that 'it must not be reducible to an act or a series of acts conforming to a rule, a law, or a value', that is, morality is not equal to normativity. This is a tall order, so to speak, as always-incomplete identities derive their seeming stability from abidance by norms. Butler (2004: 41–2) provides a useful elucidation of the power of norms and their invisibilisation through normalisation:

> A norm operates within social practices as the implicit standard of *normalization*. Norms may or may not be explicit, and when they operate as the normalizing principle in social practice, they usually remain implicit, difficult to read, discernible most clearly and dramatically in the effects that they produce. [. . .] The norm governs intelligibility [. . .] imposing a grid of legibility on the social and defining the parameters of what will and will not appear within the domain of the social.

However, while normalisation has a smoothing effect that may render subjects blind to their own conformism to oppressive and exclusionary structures, the end of official apartheid served to rip away whatever cloaking veil might have remained over South African racism and heteropatriarchy. This is the moment of dislocation in which subjects are condemned to be free, as Laclau says, insofar as it compels decisions about (re)constituting their identities. The question is: do they embrace the liberating possibilities of the democratic moment to achieve ethical subjecthood?

Foucault (1992) distinguishes between two different modes of achieving such ethical subjecthood. Subjection is either achieved through adherence to specific rules to avoid punishment or through 'practices of the self' (29–30) where adherence to rules is no more important than the relations with the self. In the last scenario, the individual endeavours to form the self as an ethical subject through methods and practices for self-knowledge and transforming the self (30). This Foucault (1990: 68) refines as a 'cultivation of the self', in which the ethical subject is forged out of processes of self-examination – discovering 'the truth concerning what one is, what one does and what one is capable of doing'. In answering criticism that Foucault had merely shifted into liberal individualism, Margaret McLaren (2002) points out that he regards cultivation, or 'care of the self', 'as social practice, giving rise to relationships between individuals' (Foucault 1990: 45). So my question is: have white Afrikaans women embraced the possibilities of this moment to cultivate self-knowledge in relation to racialised, sexual and gendered others, to problematise the normativities that govern 'the Afrikaner' and to transform themselves, drawing on the new potential for self-reflective non-conformism?

POSTSTRUCTURALIST DISCOURSE ANALYSIS: 'THE TALE TELLS THE TELLER'

The findings of the research presented here flow from a discourse analysis probing ways of making meaning in texts from a popular women's magazine and from focus group and individual in-depth interviews. To probe culturally sanctioned discourses, the Afrikaans women's magazine *Sarie* was selected for its continuing success: despite targeting a comparatively small section of the population – Afrikaans-speaking, middle-class women – it remains among the top-selling women's magazines in South Africa, with a total readership of 904 000 in the period under review. Twelve *Sarie* editions from its sixtieth anniversary year, 2009, are examined. Its success is remarkable because of its origins as a product of the formerly Afrikaner nationalist media company Nasionale Pers (Naspers), one of the cogs in the *volksbeweging* (people's movement) that brought the National Party to power in 1948. Its significance is bolstered by Naspers's growing prominence since its capitalisation on the re-admission of South Africa into the global economy after the official end of apartheid. Naspers transformed into a multinational company and became the largest media company in South Africa and Africa and the second largest in the southern hemisphere.

The other source of data in this book is focus group and in-depth individual interviews. Respondents were selected on the basis of self-identifying as women, Afrikaans-speaking, white, middle class and heterosexual. Purposive sampling was used to find the interviewees. The focus group interviews took place in Johannesburg and the northern suburbs of Cape Town with 25 respondents between the ages of 30 and 65. The individual in-depth interviews were with six respondents selected from the focus groups. The interviews were conducted in 2011 and 2012.

The texts gleaned from *Sarie* and from the interviews were subjected to poststructuralist discourse analysis (Carpentier and Spinoy 2008; Butler 2004; Jørgensen and Phillips 2002; Laclau and Mouffe 1985). The approach adopted here concurs with Stephen Whitehead and Frank

Barrett's (2001: 20) emphasis on identities as fluid, unstable arrangements. Thus the 'I' is here understood as a power effect of discourses, a subject both producing and being produced by discourses (Foucault 2004; Laclau and Mouffe 1985). Discourse is 'a differential ensemble of signifying sequences in which meaning is constantly renegotiated' (Torfing 1999: 85). Identities are constantly under construction, processes taking place in specific and concrete social occasions of negotiation and entextualisation that produce constellations of identifications, rather than individual monolithic constructs (De Fina, Schiffrin and Bamberg 2006: 2). Language use is therefore understood as a social phenomenon in which structures of meaning are fixed and/or challenged through conventions, negotiations and conflicts (Jørgensen and Phillips 2002: 25). This books's aim is not to unearth the 'truth behind' discourses, but rather to work with what is said or written, 'exploring patterns in and across the statements and identifying the social consequences of different discursive representations of reality' (21). As Hall (1997b: 44) points out: 'You can only say something by positioning yourself in the discourse. The tale tells the teller, the myth tells the mythmaker, etc. The enunciation is always from some subject who is positioned in and by discourse.'

Consequently, respondents are not approached as 'simple repositories from whom information can be extracted'; rather, the focus group and in-depth interviews are read as situated productions of knowledge (Puttergill and Leildé 2006: 15) and, particularly, of selves. Foucault's notion of knowledge/power is applicable, simply meaning that 'the power to define is the power to create' (Distiller and Steyn 2004: 1). Discourses as knowledge/power regimes form normative truths which subjects produce, draw upon and are interpellated by to constitute and verify their identities. Antjie Krog (1998: 99) asks and answers: 'Is truth that closely related to identity? It must be. What you believe to be true depends on who you believe yourself to be.' To this, I would add the corollary: 'What you believe to be true makes who you are.'

The struggle to fix meaning is the entry point for this analysis, with the aim to map out the processes in which signs are fixed and 'the processes by which some fixations of meaning become so conventionalised that we think of them as natural' (Jørgensen and Phillips 2002: 24-6). Normative assumptions of the master categories of inequality - race, class, gender and sexuality - are detected and examined, alongside an investigation of the possibilities for 'a politics that is at once more complex and inclusive' (McCall 2005: 1777). My research sought to detect micro-level, taken-for-granted constructions. This approach is fruitful when studying race and racism: the 'routinisation of race' in racial states suffused the ordinary and invisibilised race (Goldberg 2002: 245). Philomena Essed (2002) analyses racism as imbricated in everyday discourses. In South Africa, the apartheid state relied on 'common-sense' understandings of race to deploy apartheid in everyday situations (Posel 2001a). The complementary angle on gender and sexuality, which similarly problematises normalisation of oppressive relations, is that 'acts and gestures, articulated and enacted desires, create the illusion of an interior and organising gender core, an illusion discursively maintained for the purposes of the regulation of sexuality within the obligatory frame of reproductive heterosexuality' (Butler 1990: 31).

OUTLINE OF CHAPTERS

Chapter 1 shows how claiming 'the Afrikaner' became a risky business after the fall of official apartheid, leading to disavowal of the identity, even as it became overdetermined with clashing meanings. To describe the white, Afrikaans-speaking subject position, I propose the intersectional concept *ordentlikheid* as an ethnicised respectability that conveys the elements that constitute the white, Afrikaans-speaking subject – whether identifying as Afrikaner or not, racist or anti-racist, feminist or not. Historicising the identity, I find *ordentlikheid* to work as an aspirational mode of whitening and as a gender-sexual regime. Afrikaans white subjects attempt to restabilise the discursive field after the rupture of apartheid's official end, especially to re-infuse their identity with moral worth. Their strategies of change are detected at two frontiers of identification: the racialised other and the WESSA other. The research shows a 'becoming', the attempted achievement of whiteness and middle-classness as continuous processes, in concert with a racial naturalisation of the master/servant division. Class serves as a vehicle for race, particularly to re-assert black inferiority after the advent of democracy disturbed race as validation of unequal social and material relations. The frontier effects with the black other reveal the deployment of race as a class-based service relation to naturalise a 'lesser' status for people racialised as black. In response, moral equivalences are fabricated between the apartheid and the democratic dispensations to paint black people with a colonial brush as inherently morally corrupt, while saving apartheid's creator, 'the Afrikaner', from ignominy. Various strategic reversals are mobilised to rescue much-vaunted 'white goodness'. Some of these reversals are paradoxical, as whiteness seeks to draw on the newly acquired moral capital of blackness to re-upholster itself even as it casts moral suspicion over blackness. Turning to the identity frontier with WESSAs, I find manoeuvres to overcome the double stigma of being both just-about-white *and* ejected by global Anglo whiteness. *Ordentlikheid* is unfurled as a moral script to recoup this ethnic whiteness or to hold on to the privileges of whiteness by subsuming Afrikaner identity in global Anglo whiteness, which operates as an invisibilised, or incognito, identity.

Chapter 2 further explores the recuperation of *ordentlikheid* by looking at culturally sanctioned discourses on white Afrikaans heterofemininity in the form of the *volksmoeder*. *Sarie* magazine offers such a discourse. It is a technology of normativity, conveying 'preferred meanings': taken-for-granted 'everyday knowledge of social structures, of "how things work for all practical purposes in this culture", the rank order of power and interest and the structure of legitimations, limits and sanctions' (Hall 2006: 513). In *Sarie*, eight discursive strategies are identified that cast a lifeline at the *volksmoeder* and, with that, enable the recuperation of *ordentlikheid*. Notably, tailor-made versions of neo-liberalism and postfeminism are applied in the quest to rejuvenate a particular version of white Afrikaans heteronormativity for the contemporary moment. *Sarie*'s technologies of femininity interpellate its subjects with the following discourse: 'Be good to yourself to be good to (white) others.' Therefore, the *Sarie* subject accesses both community and femininity through the consumption of *Sarie*: the self-for-others woman-as-wife/mother is the 'I' created through *Sarie*'s 'we'. This 'we' excludes black people and sexual and gender non-conforming others, except those that are positioned as 'good blacks' and 'good homosexuals'. *Sarie* creates a virtual white, heterosexual world, kept in check by a panoptical male gaze, here called the patriarchal overseer.

In Chapter 3 I investigate whether the Afrikaner nationalist nodal point of the *volksmoeder* retains its purchase on the women under review and, if so, how. The findings show that reports of the death of the *volksmoeder* are premature. This identity mode finds new leases on life in reworkings of the old props of silence, service and sexuality purposed for white reproduction, here called 'white sex'. Perhaps unexpectedly, I find that postfeminism and neo-liberalism provide succour to these mainstays of the *volksmoeder*.

As is also found in *Sarie* discourses, the *volksmoeder* receives a revivalist injection from postfeminism's depoliticising effects and its naturalisation of motherhood, which hinders subjects in grasping how the *volksmoeder* imaginary continues to impose compulsory motherhood in postapartheid South Africa. As with the *Sarie* discourses, *ordentlikheid* is revitalised through the normalisation of the woman/wife-as-mother and the abjection of its racialised and sexual and gender non-conforming others. Therefore, white reproduction as the key to these women's access to whiteness is legitimised and actively pursued.

In Chapter 4 the examination moves to the discursive possibilities for 'manhood' in the ethnosexual compound of Afrikaner identity, as generated by the subjects under review. The previous two chapters show the *volksmoeder* to be the pre-eminent organiser of Afrikaner gender relations. As this nationalist creature is born from a colonial logic that hinges on Cartesian co-constructive binarism, questions arise as to the outline and content of its masculine other. More specifically, what are the implications for Afrikaner manhood of the *volksmoeder* directives of silence, service and white sex? Also, how does the intensified postapartheid work on Afrikaner male identity relate to the recuperation of *ordentlikheid*? Interest in Afrikaner masculinity has grown in recent times – see, for example, Falkof (2016); Nadar (2009); Du Pisani (2001) and Swart (2001), – but much remains to be understood. Therefore, building on the previous chapters, this chapter brings into further visibility this other gender pole of the 'Afrikaner'. The analysis approaches Afrikaner male identity as it emerges in the discourses of Afrikaans white women, an approach not taken before. I discern a neo-nationalist configuration of Afrikaans white heteromasculinity after the collapse of official apartheid, when seen from the vantage point of its heterofeminine other. Female subjects' talk surfaces the most dominant or revered form of Afrikaner manhood – what is here termed 'the patriarchal overseer' of the *volksmoeder*. Gender non-conforming, 'lesser' male positions arise, but only to be struck down. The postapartheid identity work attempting to buff this particularist masculinity to its former glory reveals the extent of its organising force field for subjects interpellated as 'Afrikaners'.

In Chapter 5, the penultimate chapter, I attempt to answer the question 'So what?' What are the aims of the refurbishments of Afrikaner identity, using *ordentlikheid* and the *volksmoeder*, as described in the previous chapters? Does becoming *ordentlik* again manifest in space? How might race interact with other social categories, such as gender, class and sexuality in postapartheid spaces? And what does this mean for the family? I argue that a neo-nationalist political form has developed to recuperate 'the Afrikaner' and retain power and privilege. In what I call Afrikaner enclave neo-nationalism, *Blank Suid-Afrika* (White South Africa) is privatised and recreated on microcosmic scale in white, Afrikaans enclaves. The home – specifically an ethnoracial, heteronormative domesticity – forms the heart of the enclave. In an echo of the *Sarie* mode of self-actualisation, the Afrikaner neo-nationalist space constitutes itself and the subjects within it through the neo-liberal mode of consumption as self-production.

In the conclusion, I draw together the strands of the argument before contending that, among emotions, shame most presents opportunities for transformation. It is the primary social emotion and makes available disruptive moments in processes of identity formation. But a distinction is necessary between acknowledged and unacknowledged shame. White subjects' shame before the eyes of black subjects opens the possibility of restoring and creating social ties in ways that breach apartheid categorisations. With shame as affective practice, dissident white subjects work against the psychosocial degradation of whiteness to overturn colonial denial of humanity to black people. This could contribute to the dismantling of the 'apartheid Afrikaner'. However, unacknowledged shame involves subjects clinging to and retreating into normative defensive whiteness, thereby foreclosing the possibility of mutual rehumanisation that shame as recognition of the other holds. This line of argument resonates with Mouffe's (2005) idea of mobilising affect, or passions, in the service of democratic values. I also bring in Butler's (2004) notion of a politics of recognition – indeed, a politics of *humanisation*, which is very much needed in the face of a locally rising white, masculinist hubris, egged on by New Right discourses from 'big men' in the global North. White Afrikaans-speaking women and men must adopt an active position of directed dissidence to turn *ordentlikheid* into a truly ethical position, aligned with values of humanisation, as opposed to the values of dehumanisation of apartheid and colonialism.

A NOTE ON TERMINOLOGY

In this book 'postapartheid' is not hyphenated to emphasise that no radical break occurred between apartheid and what followed. Insistent colonial and apartheid legacies and continuities enter the social fray in competition with liberating and egalitarian instances. That said, *post*apartheid serves as an alert that this epoch is *not* apartheid.

South Africa's colonial and apartheid history has left a minefield of racial terms, further complicated by postapartheid revisions. The term 'black' is here used to refer to apartheid's racialised others, that is, the categories of Indian, coloured and black. 'Brown' is a translation of the Afrikaans *bruin*, which is a postapartheid term for people classified as 'coloured' in apartheid statutes. Lastly, in this book 'Afrikaner' may be placed in quotation marks, where appropriate, to underline that this identity is both constructed and contingent.

1

'We'll Put an Extra Little Sauce on'

Ordentlikheid, an Ethnicised Respectability

THE TROUBLE WITH 'THE AFRIKANER'

'The Afrikaner *volk* [people or nation] does not exist,' announced the anti-apartheid Afrikaans newspaper *Vrye Weekblad* in a headline as early as 24 August 1990.[1] The article added: 'The Afrikaners simply do not exist as a separate identifiable group any longer. There are, however, different groups or fragments of Afrikaners, or Afrikaans-speaking whites. Some regard themselves as the Afrikaner *volk*, others simply as *Boere* [Boers], others as South Africans and others again as Afrikaans-speaking Africans' (in Cloete 1992: 42–3). Writing a few years after the first democratic election of 1994, Dan O'Meara (1997: 7) agreed that

> white Afrikaans-speakers in South Africa today do not define themselves in the same way as they did in the early 1950s [. . .] this shifting definition (or perhaps even abandonment) of Afrikaner identity is not explained by some collective coming to its senses [. . .] Rather, the conditions of existence which underpinned the framing of 'Afrikaner' identity in nationalist discourse have changed, as have the social position and roles of much of the white Afrikaans-speaking population.

These texts are among the many over the past 40 years describing the mounting crisis of Afrikaner identity, as godfather of the *verligtes* ('enlightened' Afrikaner nationalists) Willem de Klerk (1984) called it in the mid-1980s. It confirms what we know about identities: like any other, the Afrikaner identity is precarious and historically contingent. Its beginnings were marked by intense contestations, which were mostly stayed when apartheid managed to install its temporary hegemony over the South African social sphere. With the dual crumbling of apartheid and Afrikaner nationalism, the identity lost its moorings. While previous battles were about divergent claims on Afrikanerhood, another position has joined the fray: those who shun Afrikaner identity, as this book shows. The disavowal of the identity demonstrates the extent of its dislocation. Afrikaner identity's implication in the globally maligned system of apartheid restigmatised it as morally suspect because it was instrumental in the political, economic and social ascendancy of those who called themselves Afrikaners. With the apartheid imaginary in tatters, 'Afrikaners cannot escape the fact that the system was put in place *in their name*' (Steyn 2003: 222). As my research shows, renouncement is one of the attempts people make to erase the apartheid stain. I also find that whiteness is dislodged as a category for identification, with subjects opting for contradictory strategies to still the resultant upheavals in making meaning. Gender is troubled, but less so than race, while class is the steadiest anchor in these tumultuous waters. Divergences among strategies militate against neat divisions, in that subjects cling to Afrikanerhood to claim white supremacy, just as others renew 'the Afrikaner' using discourses of egalitarianism. Conversely, some relinquish Afrikanerhood to continue their claim on white supremacy, while others discard it to venture towards a more inclusive 'South Africanness'.

Claiming 'the Afrikaner' identity has become a risky business. How, then, does one describe the white, Afrikaans-speaking subject position, given that 'the Afrikaner' is overdetermined with clashing meanings? An ethnicised respectability, captured by the Afrikaans word *ordentlikheid*, is proposed here as the conveyor of elements that constitute the white, Afrikaans-speaking subject – whether identifying as Afrikaner or not, racist or anti-racist, feminist or not.

In this chapter I argue that a historical identity configuration that can be called *ordentlikheid* serves as a panacea to current Afrikaner identity woes; indeed, it is the glue that holds the identity together as it adapts to changing historical conditions. *Ordentlikheid* is difficult to translate: its meanings are embodied and include presentability, good manners, decency, politeness and humility with a Calvinist tenor.[2] These terms collectively all speak to the idea of respectability, which is therefore the primary English translation I use in this book. In the postapartheid context where Afrikaner nationalism is in disarray, the identity is (re)crafted at the intersectional nexus of *ordentlikheid*, which is here understood as both normative and analytical. The term acts normatively as a disciplinary and generative identity dynamo, demarcating a space for this particularist whiteness at the intersections of gender, sexuality, class and race to recruit subjects for an ethnic political project of white, bourgeois, heteromasculinist power, adapted from its former permutation as purveyed by Afrikaner nationalism. Analytically, the term is applied as a nodal category to examine the discourses at specific intersections of identity where white, Afrikaans-speaking subjectivities are produced.

The concept of *ordentlikheid* allows for an intersectional examination of the identity in question. Intersectionality is defined as 'the relationships among multiple dimensions and modalities of social relations and subject formations' (McCall 2005: 1771). As a transdisciplinary term, it allows the researcher to draw on various theoretical paradigms (Styhre and Eriksson-Zetterquist 2008: 571). Using *ordentlikheid* as an intersectional lens addresses Pamela Scully's (1995: 341) criticism that analysis of colonial and metropolitan histories is insufficient if these are not approached as multilayered processes in which sexuality, gender, class and race function as co-constitutive markers and 'referents to each other'. Racial classification, for example, was conjured from 'a complex identification of class, sexual and racial markers'. Keeping in mind the historicity of *ordentlikheid*, as an analytical concept it allows for new postapartheid formations to be examined in their 'overlapping, mutually determining and convergent fields of politicisation' (Butler 1997: 37). The anti-categorical analytical approach to intersectionality (McCall 2005), as utilised here, deconstructs the assumptions of the master categories of inequality – for example, race or gender – to liberate individuals and groups from the 'normative fix of a hegemonic order and to enable a politics that is at once more complex and inclusive' (1777). Analytically, the concept of intersectionality assists in untangling 'the way in which power has clustered around certain categories and is exercised against others', subordinating some while privileging others (Crenshaw 1995: 375). It aims to dismantle the 'matrix of domination' in which socially constructed differences of sexuality, gender, class and race function as devices to manufacture intertwined systems of inequality, which are always present, even when not noticeable (Collins 2000b: 559–60). 'The Afrikaner', arguably the hegemonic identity in the apartheid matrix of domination, finds itself troubled and in a state of heightened contestation. Seeking to cleanse themselves of the stain of apartheid, Afrikaans white subjects revert to *ordentlikheid*.

ORDENTLIKHEID AS AN ASPIRATIONAL MODE OF WHITENING

Examining 'Afrikaner' identity through the lens of *ordentlikheid* surfaces a key co-generative relationality. Afrikaner identity works as a subaltern whiteness at a mutually productive interface with white English-speaking South African (WESSA) identity. In its turn, WESSA identity, as normative South African whiteness, draws on global Anglo whiteness (Salusbury and Foster 2004). Unpicking *ordentlikheid* reveals a double movement: *ordentlikheid* derives from and elaborates on WESSA respectability, but is also, paradoxically, what sets Afrikaner whiteness apart from WESSA identity. It articulates the femininity under scrutiny with a just-about-white identity's aspiration of parity with hegemonic Anglo whiteness, while still retaining its ethnic particularity.

Subalternity is a Gramscian concept associated with postcolonial studies, but is used here to denote a non-dominant, marked, particularist or racialised identity 'different from [any] of several competing identities' (Howard 2000: 386).[3] John Gabriel (1998) distinguishes subaltern whiteness as one of several modes of whiteness, which all share 'a point of privilege, a position of power from where it has been possible to define, regulate, judge as well as accrue material and symbolic awards' (184). The conditions of subaltern whiteness arise from whiteness never being denied or conferred 'once and for all' and being characterised by changing boundaries of exclusions and inclusions along patterns of domination and subordination (185). These processes of racialisation are hidden and involve 'the strategic use of one version of whiteness against another'. Groups belonging to 'minority whiteness' have been both 'the object of racism as well as colluding in it' (5).

Between the British seizure of the Cape in 1795 and the formation of the Union of South Africa in 1910, British imperialism, as English nationalism writ large, was predominant. By the time of the founding of the Union, it was vying with fledgling Afrikaner and African nationalisms (Johnson 2012: 3). In the British Empire, Englishness held sway as 'a strongly centred, highly exclusive and exclusivist form of cultural identity' (Hall 1997a: 20), which claimed for itself the right to 'command [. . .] the discourses of almost everyone else [. . .] the colonised other was positioned in its marginality,

devised in relation to the metropolitan centre. The British Empire worked
to employ differences across its localities to contribute to one system' (37).
British imperialists active in Africa in the nineteenth century projected
themselves as a race-based aristocracy, in a discourse where 'race' denoted
'nation'. For example, Cecil John Rhodes regarded the British as 'the finest
race in the world [. . .] the more of the world we inhabit the better for the
human race' (Barber 1999: 27). Victorian scholar Lord Acton described
'other races' as constituting 'a negative element in the world; sometimes the
barrier, sometimes the instrument, sometimes the material of those races
to whom it is given to originate and to advance'. The latter included the
British who had the 'duty' to rule over 'child-like natives', 'not unlike the
obligation that decent Englishmen owed to women, children and animals'
(Fryer 1988: 31). This view conjures the British bourgeois hierarchy – with
its deployment of race, gender, age and the Christian idea of 'man' lording
over nature – that was projected onto colonised peoples and, as is argued
here, lesser whites, such as the Boers.

Discursive hints at *ordentlikheid* can be traced to historical writings about
the Dutch settlers in the eighteenth century, which resonate with the early
colonial racial construct of 'the noble savage'. David Johnson (2012: 45–7)
finds the application of French philosopher Jean-Jacques Rousseau's notion
of racialised others as 'children of nature' in French travellers' descriptions
of both the 'Hottentots' *and* the Dutch settlers.[4] The 'Hottentots', in their
pastoral 'state of nature', are constructed as illustrating the benefits of
'incultivation'. Similarly, the distance from European civilisation and the
'pernicious influence of luxury' nurtured virtuousness in the Dutch settlers,
as their proximity to nature and rural life meant they were 'neither stimulated
by artifice nor false decencies' (in Johnson 2012: 46). Colonial racialisation
shifted to less favourable stereotypes: European travellers depict the *trekboers*
of the late eighteenth century as 'miserable and lazy', differing from the
Khoikhoi only in respect of 'physiognomy and colour', as their mode of
land use and living was the same (Fredrickson 1981: 36). Johnson (2012:
116–39) discerns a British imperialist myth of the Dutch settlers as 'rural
degenerates' in his analysis of the Graaff-Reinet and Swellendam rebellions
of 1795–9. By the late 1800s, the Boers had become 'an inferior or degraded
class of colonist' (Keegan 2001: 460), with depictions of an indolent, slow-
witted, 'simple race', ignorant and dirty (Giliomee 2004: 150; Barber 1999:
18). Lord Kitchener concluded that the Boers were 'uncivilised Afrikaner

savages with a thin white veneer' (Pieterse 1992: 104).[5] Such discursive constructions exemplify the racialisation of 'subaltern forms of whiteness [. . .] as part of a process of constructing and anchoring a more dominant version or set of interests and identities' (Gabriel 1998: 98), in this case Anglo whiteness and, later, WESSA identity.[6]

Nancy Charton's normative 1975 essay summarises the 'empirical evidence' of WESSA attitudes to 'the Afrikaner' and lists positive and negative clichés, such as simple, warm, uncultured, superstitious and lacking in efficiency. Pejorative terms for Afrikaners included 'Dutchman', 'hairyback', 'rock spider', 'mealie muncher', 'takhaar', 'bywoner', 'backvelder' and 'plank'. These 'mocking' terms show 'the element of cultural and social superiority' of WESSA identity, that Charton admits to (45–6). She adds: 'Fifty years ago rural stereotypes were justified in the reality of the situation [. . .] there was also some justification for socially superior attitudes on the part of the English', as Afrikaners were lagging behind in education and business (46). Disparaging depictions of Afrikaner civil servants were 'not misplaced', given Afrikaners' preponderance in the state bureaucracy (47). The racialisation of Afrikaner whiteness is confirmed in Charton's noting the WESSA concern that Afrikaner nationalist 'semi-barbarous political parvenus' endangered white supremacy during apartheid (47). Such apprehensions echo racial anxieties in the eighteenth century over the lack of apparent European-style evolution among the Dutch settlers, with European visitors questioning whether white expansion into Africa would indeed promote 'civilisation' or lead to white degeneration into barbarism (Fredrickson 1981: 36). This fear was also expressed about British settlers (Lester 1998: 521) in southern Africa, confirming contestation between these two local settler ethnicities in claiming whiteness (see also Lambert 2012).

As late as the 1980s, reformist Afrikaner nationalist intellectual De Klerk (1984: 21) identified the root of 'negative Afrikaner nationalism' as a collective 'inferiority syndrome' and 'feelings of humiliation' due to 'the great offence of the English' in the South African War of 1899–1902. The longevity of this productive 'syndrome' remains apparent in an objection in 1990 by Afrikaner nationalist newspaper *Beeld* (6 September 1990) to the historically WESSA-owned *Financial Mail*'s refusal to use what was then the official name of Spoornet for the state-owned railways, because the word *spoor* (Afrikaans for 'rail') was 'not good enough' for them. Antjie Krog

(2007: 31) quotes an excerpt from J.M. Coetzee's 1990 book *Age of Iron* to describe how middle-class Afrikaners believed their WESSA others saw them during apartheid:

> They know all too well how they were perceived by the English: 'I have only to see the heavy, blank faces . . . The bullies in the last row of school desks, raw-boned, lumpish boys, grown up now and promoted to rule the land. They with their fathers and mothers, their aunts and uncles, their brothers and sisters: a locust horde, a plague of black locusts infesting the country, munching without cease, devouring lives. Why in a spirit of horror and loathing do I watch them? . . . Heavy eyelids, piggish eyes, shrewd with the shrewdness of generations of peasants. Plotting against each other too: slow peasant plots that take decades to mature . . . Cetswayo, Dingane in white skins . . . Huge bull testicles pressing down on their wives, their children, pressing the spark out of them . . . Their feat . . . to have raised stupidity to a virtue. To stupefy . . . The Boar War.'

Thus 'the Afrikaners' were constructed as an intermediate group mired between their aspirations to the material and cultural power and affluence of the British/WESSAs and their fears of competition with black people and of group depletion through miscegenation (Van der Westhuizen 2007: 60).

These observations demonstrate the importance of keeping ethnicity in sight in critical whiteness research, as Victoria Hattam (2001: 66) cautions. Following the intersectional approach, ethnicity is analysed here as situational, a 'plastic and malleable social construction, deriving its meaning from those who invoke it and the relations of power between individuals and groups' and from its articulation with other differences (A.D. Smith 1998: 204). Aletta Norval (1996) insists that ethnicity and race cannot be reduced to one category when discussing apartheid. By 'simply collapsing ethnicity into whiteness', questions remain unanswered, such as what the cultural and political significance of ethnicity is or why a separate language of ethnicity was required, if racial assimilation was the prime objective (Hattam 2001: 66). Differentiating between whiteness and ethnicity allows us to discern their 'interactive effects' (68) and the redistributional conflicts within and between ethnic collectivities (Rattansi 1994: 58). Race and ethnicity function as political resources for both dominant and subordinate groups to advance their identities and related claims, which means race and ethnicity are not only imposed, but can also be devised as resistance (Goldberg and Solomos 2002: 4).

Ethnicisation happens as social formations are nationalised; indeed Etienne Balibar (1991: 96) argues that the fiction of ethnicity is crucial for nationalism, which wields it as a double inscription of belonging, 'what it is that makes one belong to oneself and [. . .] to other fellow human beings'. It provides the 'nation' – or the *volk*, in this case – with a 'pre-existing' unity and allows interpellation in 'the name of the collectivity whose name one bears'. This is exemplified by the conjuring of 'the Afrikaner'. For Deborah Gaitskell and Elaine Unterhalter (1989: 62), Afrikaner nationalism was about rebuilding Afrikaans white 'distinctiveness for parity with or even domination of the English'. Anglo ethnicity claims for itself the unmarked position that marks and places other ethnicities (Hall 1997a). Afrikaner nationalism was an assertion of a particularist ethnicity against an invisibilised ethnicity, an assertion of an ethnicised whiteness against a hegemonic whiteness. Normative whiteness, particularly that of Anglo whiteness, builds itself into coded discourses of universalism in denial of its ethnic particularity (Gabriel 1998: 184, 185). While the 'whiteness of the Afrikaner has been always already marked' (Steyn 2003: 218), WESSA identity draws on global Anglo whiteness, its unexamined and normalised operation securing its 'disproportionate influence' in the South African symbolic order (Salusbury and Foster 2004: 108). WESSAs claim normalcy by masquerading as 'cultureless' and without collective political aims, which they contrast with other South African identities. It is a subjectivity that has historically been British-identified and, after 1994, retains symbolic ascendancy from 'a transnational culture of whiteness'.

Afrikaner whiteness 'defied' and 'resisted' WESSA hegemonisation (Steyn 2003: 218) through a counteracting discourse of Afrikaner *volkstrots* (people's pride), noble suffering and Calvinist decency (Van der Westhuizen 2007: 59). Afrikaner nationalist discourse recuperated the eighteenth-century discourse of Boers-as-unspoilt-children-of-nature to reinscribe simplicity, ignorance and child and nature analogies as signs of Afrikaner innocence, uncorrupted mentality and closeness to God, as Johnson (2012: 126) finds in the 1930s in the midst of Afrikaner nationalist mobilisation.

Afrikaner nationalist histories written in the 1960s overhauled and relaunched the 'rural degenerate' of the 1795–9 rebellions as hospitable, brave and fair Christians – salt of the earth (130).[7] Self-manufactured Afrikaner *ordentlikheid* in the twenty-first century continues to draw on these descriptors – see, for example a Ph.D. dissertation that argues for the primordial origins of the Afrikaner nationalist 'character' (Van Rensburg 2012). Such deployments have succeeded in installing a dominant trope in South African discourses, which, if not historicised, seems like a seamless and monolithic continuation from the rural Dutch or *trekboer* settlers of the eighteenth century to the twenty-first-century 'Afrikaner'. Despite 75 per cent of Afrikaners being urbanised by 1960, up from 29 per cent in 1910, and the mostly white commercial farmers having dwindled to 35 000 by the 2010s, this image hangs in postapartheid South African embassies abroad:

Source: Photograph by Christi van der Westhuizen

Conduct a search for 'the Afrikaner' on Google and the predominant visual association is found to be rural, with a woman (unusually) next to her *bakkie* (pickup truck) with chickens on the back.

The 'salt of the earth' reworking, with its implication of simplicity and ignorance, has become the internationally projected image. In an article in the *Wall Street Journal*, the authors provide the following description: 'Afrikaners have been characterized in South Africa as salty country types who like their khaki shorts short and their beige wool socks long. Some of their urban brethren are known for crude tattoos, gold teeth and their colorful pronunciation of expletives' (McGroarty and Bischof 2014). Interestingly, this image is complicated by its co-construction with 'coloured identity', brought about by the appropriation of Cape coloured street culture by Die Antwoord (The Answer), an internationally successful techno rap band consisting of a WESSA male and an Afrikaner female.

This salt of the earth stereotype is also deployed by the ruling African National Congress (ANC), as illustrated by the following contemporary example emanating from South Africa's president, Jacob Zuma (2009 to the present). It exhibits elements articulated to produce the trope of Afrikaner *ordentlikheid*, particularly its co-production with a hidden, 'untrustworthy'

WESSA identity. Zuma expressed appreciation at 'a meeting with representatives from Afrikaner groups' for 'the Afrikaner's honesty' and added:

> When the Afrikaner says, 'you are my friend' [or] 'you are my enemy', they mean it [. . .] Up to this day, they don't carry two passports, they carry one. They are here to stay. [. . .] Of all the white groups that are in South Africa, it is only the Afrikaners that are truly South Africans in the true sense of the word. [. . .] It is the only white tribe in a black continent or outside of Europe which is truly African, the Afrikaner.[8]

In this text, the 'absent but present' co-constitutive white counterpart to 'the Afrikaner' is 'the WESSA'. Afrikaner honesty is manufactured in two ways. First, WESSA identity, by inference, includes 'carrying two passports', which precludes 'true' belonging to South Africa and Africa, as 'two passports' signify impermanence and foreignness. An equivalence is invoked between dual citizenship and dishonesty, or duplicity, the co-constitutive flip side being 'the Afrikaner's honesty'. Afrikaner nationalism historically wielded 'belonging' to claim entitlement to rule over South Africa. Zuma's postapartheid intervention posits an inversion in which Afrikaners' intermediate position between black and WESSA others is implicitly maintained, and where the claim of Afrikaner 'belonging' is extended to democratic South Africa. Second, 'you are my friend, you are my enemy' can be read as a euphemistic reference to racism: Afrikaner nationalism was operationalised through racial oppression, among other things, and Afrikaner nationalists' enemy was black people with political aspirations. Black people did know exactly where they stood with the Afrikaner rulers: they were on the receiving end of a plethora of dehumanising measures, justified with a blatant rhetoric of racism. Ironically, Zuma suggests that the crudeness of the Afrikaner nationalist form of racial othering makes these subjects honest, and confirms their claim to belonging.

ORDENTLIKHEID AS GENDER-SEXUAL REGIME

Before the South African War, the Boers lived 'on the margins of respectability', a cultural non-conformity posing the danger of racial degeneration (Keegan 2001: 464). After the war, *ordentlikheid* became mobilised as a bourgeois gender project to manufacture an Afrikaner *volk*.

This was done by interpellating (especially female) subjects to 'save' them from the 'uncertain edges of whiteness' in multiracial urban slums (Du Toit 2003: 173). *Ordentlikheid* as a mode of whitening, and therefore as a generator of 'Afrikaner' identity, became infused with a sexual charge. We are dealing with an attempt to set apart, to differentiate. As is the case with nationalisms generally, women serve as the bearers of respectability, imprinted on their bodies through comportment and dress. Their bodies demarcate the nation.

Respectability is a nineteenth-century bourgeois European invention, exhibiting longevity partly as a result of its absorption by nationalism – later also by twentieth-century South African nationalisms, in reaction to British imperialism as nationalism writ large.[9] Respectability's usual articulation is as a 'sexual ideology' (Hull 1982: 265), with an emphasis on sexual control, restraint and prohibition. However, Michel Foucault (1998: 10–49) points out the limitations of the 'repressive hypothesis', as sexuality as a technology of power does not stymie, but multiplies sexual heterogeneities. Historically, deriving from Victorianism (Steinbach 2017), respectability is invoked to demarcate the bourgeoisie as the dominant class (Hull 1982: 248–9), thus this book's intersectional application fits well, since sexuality is analysed in co-constitutive operations with other normative categories, such as class. George Mosse (1982) describes the elements of respectability as dichotomisations such as normalcy/abnormalcy, man/woman, masculinity/femininity, heterosexual/homosexual and white/black, in which the second, lesser term degrades 'the nation' (226–8). This was the stuff of the 'absolutely hierarchised world defined by polarities' generalised by British imperialism, which privileged adult over child, masculine over feminine, modern over primitive, normal over abnormal (Nandy 1983: x).

The Cape Colony, similar to other British imperial localities, saw the imposition of British ideas of respectability, particularly in relation to gender regulation (Ross 2009). Lynn Thomas (2006: 466–7) places 'the highly malleable ideology of respectability' as arising in the Cape Colony during the 1870s and 1880s, when the colonists identified Victorian virtues such as industriousness and cleanliness as synonymous with Englishness. Alan Lester (1998: 518–9) places class-as-respectability even earlier as the primary demarcation: after the British settlers' arrival in 1820, when the gentry and middle classes, as 'respectable' settlers, sought control over the lower orders. A crisis of class relations developed, leading respectable British male settlers to install 'their' women as a boundary against the subversion of the class and gender order (520).[10] Class divisions gave way to an invented, transplanted Britishness and shared settler 'character', which included industry and enterprise. Women were central to the latter: tightly bound in domesticity, their provision of familiar domestic appearances and household routine reproduced settler identity (526–9).

'Sex in the colonies was a political act with repercussions' since colonial control hinged on the racial hierarchy fixed through inclusions and exclusions of persons as 'white' or 'native' (Scully 1995: 343). This charted the course of people's lives, as it fixed the status of being either a citizen or a subject (Mamdani 1996). Against the backdrop of a malaise in Victorian masculinity, and given the indivisibility of racial dominance and male power, white domination in South Africa was justified by the 'threat of [black] sexual invasion [. . .] as white men attempted to impose their authority over the forces that threatened racialised patriarchy' (Keegan 2001: 461). British women's proper place was construed to be 'mothers in the home'. Laws in the Boer republics in the late nineteenth century forbade sex between white women and black men, rendering the inviolability of white womanhood as much a prescription to white women as to black men, in that the former could not transgress racial mores any more than the latter could (464). No similar prohibitions existed for white men. In the same way that early twentieth-century eugenicist admonitions to British women as reproducers were to prevent the deterioration of nation and race, Afrikaner women were instructed to preserve 'the level of civilisation' of the *volk*, a shrouded euphemism for 'racial purity' (Vincent 1999: 65).

After the South African War, a discourse of moral panic arose about imagined sexual violation of white women by black men. Sexual danger and racial contamination were metonyms for less precise fears about chaos and social disintegration at the time of the founding of the Union of South Africa in 1910, with its attendant seismic economic and social changes, including in gender relations (Keegan 2001: 474). White men felt undermined as patriarchs and bolstered their masculinity by policing white women: 'Defilement of white women threatened the purity of the race, it was unthinkable that respectable women could ever consent to black men being familiar to them'. Racial othering facilitated 'a unity of conception of the world' between Afrikaner women and men about how the social should be organised and the boundaries of 'proper behaviour' (477).

Historians distinguish the 1920s and 1930s as a period of heightened contestation over gender relations across the continent (Thomas 2006: 461). Respectability as a key element in constructing middle-classness was central in the Afrikaner middle-class production of Afrikaner heterofemininity, as several authors show in analyses of Afrikaner nationalist interpellation of 'Afrikaners' from the 1910s to the 1940s. Afrikaner culture was defined in middle-class terms and 'belonged to "whites" [. . .] and the uncertain edges of whiteness had to be assiduously protected. The threat was poorer whites "forgetting" their true, Afrikaner identity, "losing" a "natural" race-consciousness and assimilating with their black inferiors' (Du Toit 2003: 173). Therefore, Louise Vincent (1999: 55) finds that middle-class *volksmoeders* (mothers of the nation; see Chapter 3) approached white poverty as an oxymoron in their upliftment work: 'Poor whiteism was regarded as a temporary irregularity which had arisen as a result of a lack in the moral and political structure of society.'

Therefore, those positioning themselves as middle class set out to draw the boundaries of good and bad, to ensure that the 'right' bodies were included to ensure the safety and security of the nation or *volk* (Skeggs 2008a: 37). As is the case with other nationalisms (Erlank 2003: 659; Hull 1982: 254), cultural entrepreneurs tasked Afrikaner women with maintaining 'Boer manners' (Swart 2007: 51) and providing moral strength and care to the Afrikaner *volk* (Du Toit 2003: 162; Vincent 1999: 59). British settler women maintained boundaries between colonised and coloniser, given their assignment as 'colonialism's social border police on subliminal orders from racist patriarchy' (Dagut 2000: 558–9). Similarly, middle-class, Afrikaans-speaking women organised in Afrikaner nationalist associations were concerned with the recruitment and induction of young, working-class women to save them from urban 'dangers', particularly miscegenation (Hyslop 1995; Brink 1990). Growing numbers of young Afrikaner women worked outside their homes in factories and were being forced to 'the station and class of the coloured,' wrote cultural entrepreneur M.E. Rothmann in her column in the Afrikaner nationalist daily newspaper *Die Burger* in the 1920s (Du Toit 2003: 172).[11] Middle-class women's particular concern should be whether these girls 'in factories and shops remain respectable,' Rothmann wrote. The new-found economic power of young, working-class Afrikaans women posed a threat to the patriarchal strictures of Afrikaner families, which manifested in anxieties that they were sexually and socially out of control, with domestic violence increasing in response (Hyslop 1995: 63).[12] As Beverley Skeggs (2008b: 17) indicates, for the working-class woman to become a viable subject who may speak for herself, she has to 'fit into a particular mode of telling'. Therefore, 'helping women stay respectable meant "keeping" them *blank* [white]' (Du Toit 2003: 174) and 'rehabilitating' them into the traditional family structures that 'the middleclasses held dear' (Hyslop 1995: 64). Jonathan Hyslop (1995) shows how white women's whiteness was contingent upon their and their children's 'honour', that is, women had to demonstrate sexual propriety to gain access to whiteness (76–7). Timothy Keegan (2001: 474) regards 'honour' as a keyword yoked into a chain of equivalence with non-sexuality, purity, women's subordination and men's dominance. My research findings on the sexual production of *ordentlikheid* are discussed in Chapter 3 on the *volksmoeder*.

The re-upholstering of *ordentlikheid* happens along two frontiers, with the black other and the WESSA other. At these two fronts, race and class are deployed in mutually reinforcing modes. Drawing on Jacques Derrida, Anna Marie Smith (1994: 24) explains frontiers thus:

> The enclosure of a space within a set of frontiers only comes about when an opposition has been established between that space and some sort of outsider figure. It is, in short, only against an outside that an inside is possible. In this sense, we could say that the inside space – such as the white nation in racist discourse – actually depends on its outsider figures – such as the black immigrant – for its constitution.

The outsider figure serves as a constitutive outside, as discussed in the Introduction. Frontiers are drawn and redrawn, according to the limits experienced by antagonised identities and are therefore constantly displaced (Wang 2008: 229). The next section explores the frontier effects with the others of 'the Afrikaner', the double stigma of the Afrikaner identity and its attempts at rehabilitation.

BECOMING WHITE AND MIDDLE CLASS
Embedded in racial inequality is an equation of 'black as poor', which renders 'natural' the material deprivation of black people. As with gender, perceptions and practices of class were 'refashioned' in the colonial context

'to create and maintain the social distinctions of empire and the cultural boundaries of rule' (Stoler 2002a: 40). 'Racial thinking was part of a critical, class-based logic that differentiated between native and European' in the colonial context (13). The European self-image was of 'well-deserved privilege and priority', with middle-classness as a cultural cultivation aimed at distinguishing the coloniser from the colonised (24–5). Racism drew on middle-class respectability, among other things, as a white defence against the colonised (71). Historically, in South Africa class distinctions were wielded as an integral part of the contested racial paradigm, determining entry into the ruling classes. After apartheid, whiteness discourse renders white culture as 'naturally middle-class' because white people, 'denuded of their previous, legally prescribed material advantage [. . .] redefine what it means in a material sense to be "white" [. . .] within the changing socio-economic landscape' (Salusbury and Foster 2004: 100).

Ordentlikheid is demarcated as an ethnicised whiteness in a confluence of hierarchical inclusions and exclusions. This is done through the creation of frontier effects with blackness and poverty, reconjuring the colonial trope of 'whiteness-as-civilisation' to not only erect unequal binaries of white/black and middle class/poor unequal differentials, but also to install intra-race and intra-ethnic class divisions to produce the 'civilised' white self. With this discourse, subjects aim to whiten themselves by creating interlinked class and race frontiers. A formative impetus can be discerned: whitening through class and race barriers. Sedimented in the discourse is the uncomfortable proximity between 'poor Afrikaners' and black people, who are positioned as 'naturally poor'. The discourse effects distance from blackness-as-poverty, inadvertently revealing a threatening slippage between blackness-as-poverty and 'poor Afrikaners' as racialised whites. The Afrikaner nationalist construction is of 'poor Afrikaners' as an oxymoron, as a result of what is presented as the natural proclivity of Afrikaners towards middle-class-based race purity. This work of whitening belies this elaborate production. In the following interview text, a subject is inducted into whiteness, with a lower-class status serving as marker of blackness. Nerina's tale shows a dissident subject's path to questioning white superiority as starting out without a sense of this superiority, then being interpellated into a comprehension of 'blackness' as equivalent to inferiority and the opposite of 'civilised', then disarticulating these elements as inaccurately attributed.[13]

Nerina (32): We played [. . .] with the black children and I enjoyed it [. . .] My aunt said you're becoming black and then I [called out,] 'I don't want to be be black'[. . .]

Researcher: What were you thinking?

Nerina: I felt superior [. . .] when my aunt pointed it out to me [. . .] It was probably in the back of my mind, but it was the first time that I thought I feel superior towards the black child that I was playing with [. . .] I didn't want to be the same skin colour [. . .] I was white and I believed it was better than being black.

Researcher: What is that 'better'?

Nerina: It was more civilised probably because their houses were poorer and dirtier than ours.

Researcher: I'm hearing a resonance with class.

Nerina: Definitely. For a large part of my life as child I looked down on poor Afrikaners. To be honest, I still don't have the greatest respect for white poor Afrikaners.

Nerina's narrative does not turn her arrival as a child with no understanding of race in a racist context into a mechanism of white denial. Reflecting on the tale, she says:

Nerina: When I think back I feel very ashamed.

Researcher: Why?

Nerina: Because in later years as a teenager I started to understand about the political situation that [. . .] some people did not get opportunities. It is not that they are inferior, it is just that [. . .] you got the right skin colour [. . .] that you are in a very privileged position.

Researcher: Some say it was not that bad for black people under apartheid, that they actually had opportunities and their deprivation is being exaggerated.

Nerina: No, I don't think apartheid is exaggerated [. . .] They did not have opportunties. It wasn't genocide like the Germans and Hitler, but apartheid was very bad. It elevated a certain little group of people over others.

Therefore, Nerina admits shame about wrongfully attributing white privilege to black inferiority and thus rebuts another essentialising, dehistoricising white diversion. The potential of shame in doing this work of rebuttal is further explored in the Conclusion. Suffice to say here that the narrative confirms the co-implication of class and race.

WHITE MASTER/BLACK SERVANT: RACE AS LABOUR DIVISION

Similarly, a master/servant grid overlays the white/black division in the following excerpt from dissident subject, Andriette, with blackness equating to subservience:

> Andriette (56): I could speak [Tshivenda, a local vernacular] when I was little and my gran was very opposed to it [because it was a language of] black people and [because of] a class consciousness [. . .] of a *baas-klaas* [master-servant] relationship. Whoever is black is subservient to you.

Subservience folds into service. In the next excerpt, from an interview with Ansie, blackness as 'natural subservience' hooks onto the apartheid 'presumption that whites were always privileged, always in charge – the *baas* [boss], always serviced, never the beneficiary', underpinned by 'black people work[ing] for whites; the reverse legally prohibited' (Goldberg 2009: 301). The overlapping, mutually reinforcing race-class division is naturalised through 'common-sense' racism (Posel 2001a). At work here is an explicit normalisation of apartheid, transposing a 'confidence in the authority of everyday experience as the site of racial judgment' onto the macro context (Posel 2001b: 56). 'Amnesia' assists obfuscation about the word '*baas*', suggesting shame, but the word 'boy' for an adult black man slips out.[14] The apartheid divisions 'white man/black boy' and 'white master/black servant' are naturalised in the present as 'basic little things':

> Ansie (57): One was always aware that there is hierarchy.
> Researcher: Based on what?
> Ansie: Because of where they stayed [. . .] they were never our neighbours [. . .] geographically [. . .] There was already a natural division, but as child I never thought about it like that [that we] paid them for a service [. . .] My dad had a black chauffeur [. . .] X was his car boy [There were] ways of addressing [. . .] My mom was *Miesies* [Madam]. I can't remember how X addressed my dad [. . .] but there

was that sligtly superior 'we give the orders of what has to be done'. Those basic little things.

Gender cuts across and further complicates the positioning of white and black as class-based relationality in which black serves white. In the persistent apartheid race-gender-class intersectional configuration, Afrikaans white femininity derives power from the racialised service relationality, drawing on 'natural' white entitlement to resist the gendered labour divisions of the domestic realm. Ornamentation is white, middle-class women's paradoxical prize, while invisibilised black women bear the burden of the feminised household labour of cleaning and caregiving:

> Andriette (56): There is the privileging [. . .] white women also carry much guilt for apartheid. We [. . .] were not the main beneficiaries, but we were privileged [. . .] How many white women have this 'someone has to make the beds and wash the dishes and I walk around with my long nails'?

Racialising subjects therefore enables a classed labour division, which places non-bourgeois black bodies as automatically 'there to serve'. This ethnoracial femininity uses a device that I call intersectional shifting, in which 'the reduced status of the category "woman" is counterbalanced with the elevated status of whiteness and middleclassness to gain ascendance. This device enables white women – during and after apartheid – to draw on black women's bodies as resources to lighten their own gender load' (Van der Westhuizen 2016b: 228–9). Interracial social interaction is thereby restricted to a service relationship, occuring only when black bodies can be usefully employed by white, middle-class subjects.

Ordentlikheid enables insistence on a pragmatic colour blindness that denies the effects of race. Pieta (35) insists that her children 'won't really experience colour'. Drawing on *ordentlikheid*, she expands Afrikaner nationalism's age hierarchy to black people by teaching her children to address black people as *tannie* and *oom*, or 'aunt' and 'uncle'. These are familial terms that Afrikaner children have historically been forced to use when addressing all adults, whether related to them or not. Thus an ostensible rearrangement of racial positioning is deployed to reinforce intra-familial disciplining. Age is also deployed to sustain spaces for white supremacy. This positioning differentiates between black people. Acceptable black people adhere to middle-class distinctions of being 'well-educated' and 'speaking good English'. Acceptable black people also essentialise race.

> Pieta (35): My mom and [dad] grew up with that traditional view [. . .] that white people are half superior. It is half part of their DNA [. . .] They don't think about it [. . .] They are not malicious at all though [. . .] my mom bought her maid a little house [. . .] I realised you can't teach old dogs new tricks [. . .] I've got a Zimbabwean [read: black] friend. I told her: I'd like to invite you to my wedding, but my mom and them won't survive it. She laughed [. . .] She doesn't know what her mom would do with a white girl [either].
>
> Researcher: How would your parents respond?
>
> Pieta: My mom will think I'm insensitive [. . .] They won't disinherit me [. . .] but it will upset them.

The unequal white/black dualism is naturalised as 'DNA'. It still fixes Pieta's subject position. Despite her protestations, she colludes with intergenerational racial disciplining and the parent/child hierarchy and enforces monoracial sexual relations. *Ordentlikheid*'s racism is 'mere' paternalism in Pieta's world; *ordentlikheid* is also always already heterosexual. These manoeuvres show a preoccupation with a projection of the self as moral, a whiteness eager to distance itself from racism, and also pinning racism on white others/elders to deny its own complicity.

DOUBLE STIGMA, PRE-APARTHEID AND POSTAPARTHEID
Realising it's wrong

Afrikaner identity failed to shift with global hegemonic whiteness when the latter shifted away from on-the-ground colonialism towards more intricate, but less visible forms of neocolonialism in the mid-twentieth century. The genesis of apartheid was driven by a 'hankering for order' in which race was the primary ordering principle and category for the defence of the social and moral order (Posel 2001b: 52). Afrikanerhood reeled from the moral blow when official apartheid ended under a cloud of condemnation. Especially the international move against apartheid from the 1960s onwards exposed Afrikaans white identity as again 'not good enough' and morally suspect.

Andriette (56): In Europe [. . .] it was terrible to be taken on by school friends [. . .] and suddenly realising it is a very wrong system.

Katrien (42): Sanctions were a huge factor, that we couldn't compete in sport [. . . It was] as if you start looking outside and realising [. . .] what we are doing is actually not right [. . .] Internally you can justify it but externally [. . .]

'Afrikaners' were increasingly an object of 'global rejection' until their jettisoning of apartheid:

Willemien (33): [. . .] after 1994 the world accepted us.

The shift from official apartheid to democracy in South Africa uprooted subjects' sense of themselves as 'moral'. Democratisation, combined with 'liquid modernity', creates a sense of being catapulted into moral ambiguity. Zygmunt Bauman (2001: 137) describes 'liquid modernity' as follows:

There is more change these days than ever before – but [. . .] change nowadays is as disorderly as the state of affairs which it is meant to replace [. . .] Things today are moving sideways, aslant or across, rather than forward, often backward, but as a rule the movers are unsure of their direction.

In the tumult of postapartheid times, subjects intensify their quest for identity moorings:

Daleen (65): When was that earthquaking speech made by [the last apartheid president] F.W. [de Klerk]? [. . .] The whole playing field changed.
Katrien (42): What was presented as morality, as true and right, was suddenly swept off the table.

A sense of 'collapsing morals' and 'confusion' about 'right and wrong' emerges:

Lindie (43): It made us very confused [. . .] there is also more of an openness and a religious collapse in the world because people rebel against everything, against rules and regulations [. . .]

Antoinette (36): What happened after 1994 in South Africa, but also in the rest of the world, [is] people's moral values dove into the ground [. . .] We can't distinguish anymore between what is really right or wrong.

The discourse that emerges in these excerpts confirms the 'horror of indetermination' brought about by the fracturing of apartheid's lines of exclusion and inclusion that constructed the identity of the social (Norval 1996: 133). As the purchase of social categories is disarticulated and relations of subordination rendered illegitimate, structural positions become sites of struggle (Chipkin 2007: 191).

Dissident and conformist subjects adopt different approaches to recoup *ordentlikheid*. In the following excerpt a dissident subject claims greater space for self-production by rejecting Afrikaner identity and its basis as 'groupthink'. Her attempts are refused by a conforming subject's assertion that Afrikanerhood must continue intact, even if its project failed:

Katrien (42): I am much more expansive and larger than [Afrikaner identity] because I believe you figure out for yourself what you believe in, what your religion is, whatever your view is and the dilemma for me comes in the moment when you find those things within a group and you no longer think for yourself. That's when a country can justify certain things [. . .] and that for me is scary because that is what happened with Hitler, that's what happened with apartheid.

Daleen (65): But that doesn't make those people less German, even though Hitler did disgraceful things.

Katrien: But why does something like that happen? Because people find their identity within a group and they don't think for themselves anymore.

Shame upon shame

Shame is elicited about apartheid (Van der Westhuizen 2016b) – a shame that contains traces of an earlier shame. This earlier shame, with regard to occupying a lesser whiteness in relation to 'the English', can be read as sedimented remnants of affect with regard to the South African War and British imperialist anglicisation campaigns in the early decades of the 1900s. Even in twenty-first-century South Africa, it translates into an existential angst about 'having a right to be here':

> Pieta (35): When we go to a restaurant, I will order in English and then [my mom] says, 'Speak Afrikaans to the people.' When she phones [companies], she insists on speaking Afrikaans [. . .] It's not that I am ashamed of Afrikaans [. . .] I can speak English. Those people can most likely not speak Afrikaans.
> Nerina (32): I also speak just about only English also in my profession [. . .] for the sake of convenience [. . .] My mom [says,] 'Afrikaans is our language and [. . .] if somebody can't help you, they should go and find someone that's Afrikaans because we have a right to be here.'

Acquiescence of social space to the 'English' aims at a subjectivity without shame. 'Speaking English' serves as a rebuttal of inferiority in relation to English whiteness.

Baddies trying to be the best

Afrikaner identity is articulated with racism, colonial and apartheid practices, guilt and attempted rehabilitation:

> Leah (49): Don't you think that the Afrikaans people are under pressure after 1994 because [. . .] we are to blame for everything? [. . .] The Afrikaner is the baddie in everything.
> Pieta (35): People perceive us as racist.
> Leah: We [introduced] the tot system – we are the baddies and nobody likes [us].[15]
> Sandra (43): I don't agree with that.
> Leah: You get English people [who go,] 'Eeeugh'.
> Willemien (33): No, I don't agree.
> Nita (62): One doesn't agree with that.
> Leah: Don't you think we are under pressure and that's why we're trying to be the best?
> Nita: I wouldn't say we're under pressure, but sometimes it seems like [. . .]

Willemien: Like guilt.
Nita: That the Afrikaners, if we now talk about progressive and liberal, then we're definitely not in the top ten [. . .] And I think there's something, jeez, I think this 'bare feet across the mountains' is stuck half deep in us.

In this excerpt, respondents deflect questioning about Afrikaner identity in relation to apartheid (hidden as 'everything' and a present-through-absence opposite to 'after 1994'). A 62-year-old respondent representing a dissident position references an Afrikaner nationalist 'Great Trek' myth, about traversing the Drakensberg Mountains with bare feet, which usually serves as metaphor for Afrikaner commitment to political autonomy, irrespective of the cost. This Afrikaner nationalist identification remains 'stuck half deep' – even for this particular subjectivity – and thus hinders alternative interpellation by discourses of progressiveness or liberalism.

ORDENTLIKHEID AS MORAL SCRIPT TO RECOUP AFRIKANERHOOD

With the end of apartheid tipping *ordentlikheid* into doubt as a moral position, Afrikaner identity under duress is recalibrated to remove racism, 'badness' and guilt. A frequently heard colloquial observation is that 'there are no apartheid supporters left in South Africa' after apartheid. The newly aligned moral order of democratic South Africa is met with strategies of subversion through defensive acknowledgement or erasure ('eracism') or, alternatively, claims of verification to share in the newly elevated standing of blackness. To rescue *ordentlikheid*, discourses emerge that still organise subjects behind race as a frontier and in accordance with the colonial logic of racial binarism, but adapted as various dichotomous combinations of good whites, good blacks, bad whites and bad blacks. Some of these discourses are explored in more detail below.

Bad white/bad black: Redirecting the moral stain of racism to all sides

As Afrikaner identity seeks to rid itself of racism, one route is defensive acknowledgement: racism is acknowledged, but personally disavowed and attributed to others, both white and black.

Ansie (57): These far-right-wing guys [. . .] I believe with my whole heart is someone feeling tremendously inferior within himself [. . .]

No normal right-thinking person [. . .] acts like that. You don't grant someone else a place in the sun [. . .] It's shocking that racism is still so deep in our community on all sides.

Ansie's input reveals the extent to which racism is read as spoiling Afrikaner identity, counteracted by an apportionment of racism to 'all sides', implicitly referencing black people.

Good white/Bad black I: Re-encoding racism: Racism without race and without apartheid

For some, *ordentlikheid* is a moral script of postapartheid Afrikaner whiteness encoding racism anew. It distances such subjects from apartheid 'crudities' while allowing white/black ordering that re-elevates whiteness as morally superior:

Pieta (35): In Centurion [near Pretoria] everybody [. . .] is quite *ordentlik* [. . .] they will really never use a crude [racist] word, never mind a swear word [. . . but] they assume you are semi-racist [. . .] they say they aren't [. . . my husband's] brother is an engineer [. . .] he'll say, 'We are doing a project again with the Groenewalds [common Afrikaans surname] so it is taking long.'
Researcher: Meaning?
Pieta: That is the black people [. . .] green for Groenewald [. . .] in that sense I don't want to be Afrikaans, it's half our traditional image [. . .] looking down on, you know, other people.

The narrative above surfaces the deployment of language games to cloak race, paradoxically rendering it hyper-visible. In this game, the wordplay is with 'green people', that is, people who for the white gaze possess 'noticeable' skin pigmentation. The colour green, which does not appear naturally in the human skin, is used to denote black, with the effect of rendering blackness even more other – to the point of being alien, in multiple senses of not being from here and even being extraterrestrial. This is done in the mode of *ordentlikheid*, as an elaborate word game is used instead of 'crude' racial slurs. The paradoxes of this manoeuvre include that the common Afrikaans surname Groenewald, with *groen* translating as 'green', is used to indicate black people. The 'cleverness' of the word game, as opposed to 'crude' racism, functions to further elevate the player of the game in relation to her/his object.

Colonial racisms contained 'racially cued comportments, moral sentiments and desires' [that] were invariably "about" bourgeois respectability and culture and less explicitly "about" race' (Stoler 2002b: 381). This is also true for *ordentlikheid*, positioned as inherently moral to produce worthy subjects:

> Ansie (57): It is about integrity, honesty, punctuality. You get up for an older person, you greet someone who enters your house. I have friends who [. . .] teach their children it is no longer necessary to greet older people.
> Yvonne (47): Those basic things that we learnt at home, of you say 'please' [. . .] and 'thank you' and you call an older person oom [uncle] and *tannie* [aunt]. I come from a stalwart Afrikaans family [. . .] You greeted everybody with a kiss, whether you knew the people or not.
> Katrien (42): But is that about moral standards?
> Yvonne: It's where your moral standards start [. . .]
> Katrien: Don't you think moral standards are really very subjective to a particular culture and group?

In the excerpt above, previous Afrikaner nationalist age- and gender-based hierarchies and social norms are equated with morality, which is linked in a discursive chain with integrity, honesty and punctuality. A dissident intervention visibilises its particularity.

Good white/Bad black II: The moral reversal of the apartheid and postapartheid orders

In the following excerpt, a moral reattribution of apartheid injustice is juxtaposed with these 'moral standards' to shift culpability from white to black South Africans in a bid to achieve 'cultural blamelessness' (Steyn 2001: 107).

> Antoinette (36): I think what also happened a lot after 1994 in South Africa, but also a lot in the rest of the world, is that people's moral values nosedived [. . .] We can't distinguish between what is really right and what is wrong.

Lindie (43): We were brought up with this is right and this is totally wrong. [. . .]

Daleen (65): It has to do with struggle history, responsibility shifted from your personal responsibility [to] that you blame the [. . .] apartheid dispensation, for everything [. . .] Remember, at the time it was liberation before education. Nobody wanted to take responsibility for their actions. It is always placed outside [. . . Nowadays] even if you're in an executive post, you've been caught for stealing, you're corrupt [. . .] always, structures get blamed [. . .]

Lindie: The people who were oppressed in that era, in their fight [. . .] they were indoctrinated to be lawless and to do many wrong things. And when the new government took over I think many of them struggled to adjust, to become right again [. . .] maybe people are starting to realise [. . .] the people will have to almost be re-indoctrinated [. . .] because [. . .] they [. . .] indoctrinate[d] the children [. . .] to be lawless and cause chaos [. . .] even the new government struggles [. . .] all these strikes and marches [. . .]

'Apartheid' is explicitly mentioned only once in this discussion and 'democracy' not at all, with the temporal reference 'after 1994' serving as the dividing line between moral/immoral. These manoeuvres include a calculated acknowledgement that apartheid amounted to 'oppression', but then use this admission as a springboard to rework 'oppression' as not 'wrong'. The struggle against apartheid is rewritten as an outcome of 'indoctrination' that compels black people to do 'wrong things' and as linked with criminality in postapartheid South Africa. These tactics of delegitimisation therefore reinvent anti-apartheid opposition as the opposite of justice. Rather, blackness is equated with irresponsibility, chaos and lawlessness, perennially. Whiteness derives its content from its co-constructive opposition to 'irresponsible, corrupt, thieving' blackness. These manoeuvres not only refute the basis of the anti-apartheid struggle as being about resistance against injustice, but also reassert a blackness that is unchangingly inferior and, because of its irresponsibility, ultimately immoral. The result is total erasure of white culpability. The above excerpt exposes a rhetoric resuscitating colonial binaries of white/black, right/ wrong, order/disorder, advancement/degeneration and responsibility/ irresponsibility.

Good white/Bad black III: Apartheid as black burden

The following interview excerpt surfaces a discourse in which it is again acknowledged that apartheid was oppressive. 'Oppression', however, excludes the repression of human potential, as the question is raised why a black person would 'think' s/he 'lost opportunities' under apartheid. Admitting to oppression therefore serves as a strategy to legitimate what follows.

> Pieta (35): It's probably because one's white that you half assume as self-evident that everything is now in order, but I don't think it is. I think the overwhelming majority has, if I could say, a chip on their shoulder. It sounds terrible, that's not what I mean, but I think there's still, I think they still carry a burden [. . .] At work there's this Indian woman, X, and she said she doesn't know why the tutors don't greet her and I said, 'It's because you're Indian.' A week later I get called in [. . .] and it's a huge story. How do I explain it's just a joke? And the more I tell her I know it's in bad taste, it is, and I really meant nothing at all by it [. . .] The tutor is racist [. . .] I have no respect for her [. . .] I obviously have a lot of respect for X [. . .] The dean says she could see on X's face that she [X] knew she was overreacting [. . .] X said to me, 'If it should happen again', but I think she should know me well enough to know I'm not at all like that. I'm not spiteful. I won't go on doing it [. . .] We [. . .] as white people are half relieved that all these things are now over. We do not have to carry any more guilt of you know [. . .] oppression or anything, but there's still a burden that is being dragged along [. . .] even though it's how many years later. It's been so many years. I get the idea they feel they haven't had all the opportunities [. . .] I don't know whether it was in *Beeld* or *Die Burger*, but in any case [a woman] at some or other meeting, the cold drink and the sandwiches that remained she loaded into her handbag and the journalist asked her why she was doing that and then she said but it's been paid for and [. . .] she deserves it in any case and I think in the end there is still debt to be paid. It's still not been paid off.

It is instructive that a tale of present-day racism sparked this discourse. Whiteness takes a while to emerge in the narrative, disturbed by an accusation of racism. Denial of white accountability for past injustice is deployed to deny culpability for present-day racism. This is a happy-go-lucky whiteness, having shrugged off guilt and feeling 'relief' at no longer oppressing black people. It expects black people to 'know' its 'goodness' and to exonerate it when it collapses into 'bad taste' – 'bad taste' being the obfuscatingly euphemistic rewording of what is in fact racism. When the focus shifts to the white self, it claims victimhood while obscuring the racist slights delivered to the black other. Folded within the tale are various incidents of racism that every time override black resistance. A black woman's refusal to accept present-day racism is discounted four times in the tale and whiteness is recentred four times. There is the original incident of racism (not being greeted); then the racist dismissal of X's complaint; another racist dismissal (X is overreacting); and the respondent's convoluted white innovation in response to X's complaint. Here, the white refusal that apartheid denied black people 'opportunities' enables the positioning of black people as 'carrying a chip on the shoulder' and 'dragging a burden along'. This 'chip' or 'burden' produces black 'entitlement', as it allows black people to be presented as beset with 'greed'-inflected misapprehensions, such as deserving 'opportunities' and that white people have a 'debt' to pay in postapartheid South Africa.

Good white/Good black I: Black verifier of *ordentlikheid*

Morality and order become equivalent to whiteness. Paradoxically, however, a 'native informant' is conjured to verify this equivalence of whiteness, morality and order. It resonates with the previous excerpt, where the black other causes disappointment for not knowing the inherent goodness of the white self. In the next chapter, the analysis of *Sarie* magazine finds a discourse of 'whitewashing the blackout' in which 'good blacks' are mobilised to acquit whites of culpability for apartheid. In the excerpt below, blackness and 'our coloureds' mentality' are explicitly equated with 'African time' and implicitly with lack of 'respect for property' and 'dishonesty'. Racialisation is effected in that middle-class 'prosperity' is juxtaposed with 'African time'. 'Colleagues' who 'start to move' in corporate (white) spaces, that is, black colleagues, attain characteristics such as 'guts', 'hard work', 'making something of their lives' and 'prosperity'. These versions of whiteness and blackness, *and* the speaking subject producing them, are legitimised by ascribing the source of these versions to a 'close friend' who is coloured. Class ascendancy whitens, as revealed in the interchanging us-them perspective, intermittently positioning the whitened black other as part of 'us'. Divergent questioning by a dissident subject (Katrien) is refused with normalisations ('basic things'; 'universal'):

> Yvonne (47): My black colleagues complain about their colleagues who aren't punctual [. . .] They are there because they've had the motivation and the guts [. . .] I have a close girlfriend and she will say, [. . .] 'You know, I can't understand our coloureds' mentality when it comes to their watches [. . .] We work for prosperity, we don't work on African time.'
>
> Katrien (42): My question will always be: who determines moral standards?
>
> Antoinette (36): There are those standards that are set in the world that are just very important to stick to [. . .] to be honest, to respect fellow human beings, to be considerate, to be helpful. Those types of little things are important everywhere [. . .]

Good white/Good black II: Re-upholstering *ordentlikheid* with innocence and paternalism

Navigating the complex postapartheid terrain with a spoilt white identity can cause unexpected twists and turns, even as subjects insist on colonial schemas. The following narrative emphasises mutuality of care and affection, but is replete with othering talk. Recurrent claims seek to articulate *ordentlikheid* with 'liberalism'. The result is a complicated knot of white ignorance, innocence and righteousness:

> Sandra (43): Our generation that grew up in the apartheid era [. . .] were all raised by nannies [. . .] There was a very close relationship between you and your nanny [. . .] You didn't realise what was going on, the pass books and those things [. . .] We grew up very liberal [. . .] This is a person in front of you [. . .] you couldn't say the k-word [. . .] you speak *ordentlik* to them [. . .] Things happened in a certain way and that's how you had to do it, but I think without knowing it we did rebel [. . .] to do things differently to our parents [. . .] Black people that sort of grew up with us [. . .] know we are part of that era when things went a bit better. We had respect. I cried myself to death when one of them had to go away because you started to love them.

This narrative hints at apartheid once, as an 'era', and then elides it as 'things happening in a certain way'. The Afrikaner nationalist reworking of maligned Boer simplicity as 'innocence' is wielded to deny complicity with apartheid. This move is bolstered by claiming ignorance and effecting an intergenerational distancing by displacing responsibility on the preceding generation: being born into a 'way' where 'pass books and things' 'happen' and that is 'how you must do it'. The trope of innocence culminates in a claim that the respondent's generation 'unconsciously rebelled', linked to black people that 'sort of grew up with us' 'knowing' that her generation is part of 'things going better' and that her generation had 'respect' for 'them'. The notion of black and white people growing up together reclaims the colonial and apartheid intimacies that are usually denied, but also serves to minimise the dehumanising differentation of apartheid. Therefore, the colonial intimacies assiduously disavowed during Afrikaner nationalist ascendancy are surfaced and embraced as a badge of righteousness.

Notably, the word 'them' is used throughout, as in the exclusionary, co-constitutive dichotomy 'us/them', even as Sandra claims to have loved 'them'. This reverses her claim of the attribution of personhood – of humanity – to black people. The attempted rehabilitation is undermined by the othering talk, including the reference to 'one of them going away', an objectification that evokes an image of faceless figures passing through. The 'going away' links to the unheard-of pass books, but is left unexplained and therefore its effect as racist apartheid policy is erased. It is rewritten as an opportunity to present the white self as victim, crying herself 'to death', rather than an acknowledgement of the pain, losses and actual deaths that apartheid movement control caused in black people's lives. This manoeuvre can be read as an insertion of the postapartheid trope of white victimhood to displace the reality of pain and loss experienced by black people during apartheid.

The claim that black people's humanity was acknowledged sheds light on apartheid-era legitimation of institutionalised racism: from this discourse, it can be gleaned that a personal distancing from the system was effected through *ordentlikheid*, which exonerated the 'liberal' white. This vaunted exoneration is now claimed in the postapartheid context to again demand that the black subject dispenses its newly accrued moral value to validate white innocence.

In the next section 'respect', 'warmth' and 'caring' are singled out as the affective elements constituting *ordentlikheid*. *Ordentlikheid* works with racist paternalism, in the vein of: 'We are not racist, we look after our blacks.' This paves the way for the resurrection of the 'salt of the earth' colonial-era myth of 'Afrikaners' as 'straightforward', 'honest' people.

Good white/Good black III: 'We'll put an extra little sauce on'

Sandra (43): You started to love them, they did everything with you. I see it in my household. I have a Maria [. . .] We can't get by without Maria [. . .] the children love her [. . .] I told her, you teach my children to speak Zulu because I want them to be part of the new cosmopoli . . . what is it? Cosmopolitan [. . .] There's a mutual respect between me and the petrol attendant that is my age because we grew up together and things improved from that time [. . .] Politically it didn't improve [. . .] that only came after 1994, but I think it's inherent in us in that growing up together [. . .] that things are perhaps a bit easier.

Pieta (35): We are a warm culture.

Willemien (33): We'll make you cookies and put an extra little sauce on [your food].

Pieta: I see it with my mom [. . .] she has Lena [. . .] My mom's worried about Lena because she doesn't have a paraffin stove and then they go and buy her a paraffin stove [. . .] I think we are a warm culture and we [. . .] Our moms are sentimental [. . .] Perhaps that's how black people see us [. . .] What I have also surmised from black colleagues is that they appreciate that we are straightforward. What you see is what you get. It is not 'we make terrific little chats with you, but behind your back we gossip about you'. If we don't like you [. . .] we will definitely show it.

Firstly this interview text attests to the continuing social removal of black and white people in postapartheid South Africa, a condition that facilitates white talk (Steyn 2003), including the mobilisation of imagined black subjects to exonerate white selves. The narrative is replete with vaunted racial equality, confusing social proximity with political equality: 'grew up together'; 'did things together'. However, the centre remains white, with blackness as the necessary co-constructive appendage. In this case, the co-construction is wielded for rehabilitative ends, to indicate the 'non-racism' of 'the white'. Whiteness is the prime mover to such an extent in this narrative that it mobilises blackness to exonerate itself. Contradictions in the text reveal its rehabilitative function: the white family 'loves' the black domestic worker; the respondent reports instructing the worker to teach her children Zulu, but the family uses her 'Christian', rather than her vernacular name. The othering phrase 'them' is persistently utilised in denoting black people. The object status of 'the black' extends to the use of the indefinite article 'a', as in 'a Maria' and reinforces objectification and a sense of white ownership of the black other. Throughout, the use of black women's bodies as labour surrogates for white women is invisibilised. Another silence is the co-constructive relation with hegemonic whiteness: a collective of 'straightforward, good' Afrikaners is constructed in opposition to an elided 'English' identity that therefore implicitly cannot be trusted. Momentary curiosity about how the black other might perceive the white Afrikaans self is answered with the black other being commandeered to verify Afrikaner goodness. The emphasis on 'warmth' and generosity towards others stands in contrast to individualism and is about communalism, which in this case is extended to the black other, not as racist paternalism, but because of Afrikaner goodness. The reference to food makes it about the home, the hearth, where women reproduce the 'us'. Sandra's intervention facilitates an outright recuperation of Afrikaner whiteness by applying *ordentlikheid*. A similar discursive manoeuvre occurs in the following text.

Good white/Good black IV: 'There is a thing of decency'

> Sandra (43): And I think one should make the effort to understand their tradition if you at all want to get somewhere with them or want to be part of or want respect from them. I, for example, went to a sangoma [traditional healer] induction. It was terrible, I almost died because goats are slaughtered and everything [. . .] Old Liesbet [. . .] she who had worked for me already ten years [. . .] you know I arrived [wearing] jeans and they just put a cloth around me and I [. . .] love cultures terribly [. . .] Many people don't want to know [for example] 'she does not look me in the eye' [. . .] they rather look down. It is a form of respect [as opposed to] we that look you in the eye that talk to you [. . .] 'Respect me, look me in the eye' [. . .] Her sangoma induction for me [. . .] my eyes opened [. . .] the sangomas of course have to lie on the ground [. . .] you can't be higher than your older sangomas [. . .] I was in this little room [. . .] I had to cut cabbage for at least an hour. My arm was [. . .] almost exhausted.
>
> Nita (62): Be glad it wasn't onions.

Sandra: With the young women [. . . I] cut the cabbage in big black pots [. . .] but that's not actually what I wanted to say. My whole point is is is [. . .] be polite. You can see it at this table too and it's a big part of our Afrikanerdom. There is a thing of decency that was bred into us, what she [Willemien] also said: you speak English because her husband is English [. . .] just take into consideration [. . .] especially our generation, we can really make a difference if we know what we are busy with.

Sandra's narrative is replete with repetitive admissions of uncertainty, contradictions and confusions, further indicated by incomplete and incoherent sentences and self-professed distraction towards the end of the above excerpt. Could it, perhaps paradoxically, gesture towards transformation in the self/other relation, partly aided by its texture of intimacy and positive affect? The narrative contains a plea for recognition of the other, not least based on an experience of the subject taking her body out of its white comfort zone into a space where she was other. The narrative suggests ambivalence, which could work to 'interrupt the subordinating charge' of racialised discourses (Rattansi 1994: 68). Afrikaans writer Antjie Krog advances that a complete metamorphosis is necessary: 'of tongue, of voice, of being, of identity' (West 2009: 71). Sandra's narrative suggests some movement towards such radical change, but the possibilities are interrupted by essentialising, fetishising and spectacularising discursive features. The narrative invokes favourite recitations of apartheid tropes of South Africa as ethnic patchwork. Blackness is conjured as 'terrible' spectacle, articulated with elements relying on colonial associations of blackness with primitiveness or as being close to nature: 'ground', 'goats', 'big black pots', 'tiny room', 'slaughter' and 'cloth' (instead of civilising clothes); and as 'culture' and 'tradition' with opaque habits, opposed to a whiteness that is Western (wearing 'jeans') and rational ('understand'). 'Them' is exoticised in relation to the thoughtful, considerate, decent 'me'. The narrative places the white self centrally but, unusually, distinguishes between different whitenesses, with specific reference to the focus group ('at this table too') as part of whites who 'want to know' the exotic black other, opposed to those who 'don't want to know'. Those 'who want to know' do so for divergent reasons, ranging from instrumentality ('if you want to get somewhere with them') to belonging ('want to be part of') and acknowledgement ('want respect from them'). Such seeking of knowledge of the other involves time and making the body available for labour. It could be lethal ('I almost died'), but could also enable an induction into difference (from the all-seeing white eye to 'my eyes opened'), with a rewarding embrace ('they just put a cloth around me'). The reference to the other focus group members suggests that the narrative is a response to image management pressures felt in the focus group space, based on a reading of the other participants – to show that Sandra shares in the 'thing of decency that was bred into us', that she is one of the decent 'us'.

While these mobilisations entail hard identity work, the sublime object – *Blank Suid-Afrika* (White South Africa) – can be no more. At best, moral slights can be delivered to the democratic project of postapartheid South Africa, with the hope that these will reinstate the myth of white goodness and make subjects *ordentlik* again. Another strategy is concession to Anglo cultural elements. This move holds not only the promise of white elevation, thus finally shaking off the compromised whiteness of Afrikanerhood, but also the possibility of disappearing into global hegemonic or Anglo whiteness, as discussed in the next section.

DISAPPEARING INTO HEGEMONIC WHITENESS OR WHITENESS INCOGNITO

Ann Stoler (2002b: 377) criticises the recurrence in historiography of the conjecture that 'racist excess' is typical of lesser whiteness, as opposed to 'civil and educated' white men. It is a fiction that serves to obscure racism in the rest of society. Indeed, a prevalent attribution of apartheid as an exclusively Afrikaner project (for example, Charton 1975) – despite the majority of WESSA voters shifting to the National Party by the 1960s (Van der Westhuizen 2007) – deflects accountability from the WESSA subject position. The exemption from apartheid stigma afforded to English whiteness partly explains a push by white Afrikaans subjects to disappear into the hegemonic order of globalised Anglo whiteness, the privilege that the WESSA positionality already enjoys. This privilege of unmarked whiteness is here also called 'whiteness incognito', as it affords the opportunity to white Afrikaans-speakers of passing unnoticed.

The historical wound: 'We now have to prove that we have arrived'

In her book *Country of My Skull*, Krog reminds us that 'the story of the brutalities inflicted on Boers by the British lies at the heart of the sense of embittered entitlement which characterised central elements of Afrikaner culture and identity before and during apartheid', forming a 'core cultural truth' (Coullie 2014: 16). The next excerpt shows that even after apartheid the historical wound of the South African War remains close to justify the quest after the spoils of whiteness. The historical underpinnings of the aspirational relationship of Afrikaners to WESSA identity are self-reflectively uncovered, with the initial view through the prism of class:

> Elsebeth (48): Durbanville is not the normal South Africa [. . .] We're not average; we are privileged. We have good schools, there's little violence, there's not really criminal activity [. . .] It is an unnatural fairy world that we live in. I can't express an opinion about other people in South Africa because I don't know how they live. We are behind the boerewors curtain.[16]

A follow-up interview question about the prevalent consumerism in these communities elicits the following response:

> Elsebeth: It's about [. . .] grandpa and grandma always being desperately poor and grandpa always remembers how the English did them in, and the concentration camps [. . .] He says it in a joke, but still. He bought policies at Sanlam and so on and they have paid out, so he's a bit better off and his children could go and study and they got bursaries because they're white.[17] So they are leading even better lives and we now have to prove that we have arrived.
> Lida (42): But it's basic human nature, not so?
> Elsebeth: Yes, it's the same in the black market.
> Lida: That South African War [. . .] all those things [. . .] all those apartheid laws, you know, were the Afrikaner trying to build himself up [. . .]
> Anke (46): At the expense of others [. . .]
> Lida: A beautiful ideal, unfortunately at the expense of a whole lot of other people in the country [. . .] In other words, what was done to the Afrikaner in the Second War of Liberation, he then went and did to other people.

Elsebeth exposes 'the English' as constitutive outside to 'the Afrikaner'. She historically situates this construction as commencing during the South African War, continuing through Afrikaner nationalist mobilisation and capture of state power and Afrikaners' attainment of white middle-classness. It persists in postapartheid consumerism, as class-based 'Afrikaner' reiteration of accomplishment qua 'Afrikaners' of equivalence with hegemonic whiteness ('the English'). This uncovering is resisted by invoking 'the black market' as being 'the same'. The use of 'black market' seems curious unless it is unpicked as per the earlier analysis: it refers to black consumers, but with the connotation of criminality that this phrase carries in everyday parlance. A narrative rehooking of elements foregrounds Afrikaner-as-victim. Disparate elements come together, drawn from postapartheid discourses (the inclusive term 'South African War' to stress the war's effects on all South Africans) and from Afrikaner nationalist *verkrampte* (reactionary) discourses ('Second War of Liberation' stressing 'Afrikaner' resistance against imperialist Britain). This contradictory discursive moment could be as a result of the intervention that 'the Afrikaner' building 'himself' up was at the expense of others, disrupting the normalisation attempted with the phrase 'basic human nature'. The Afrikaner nationalist notion of apartheid as an ethical ideal is presented alongside the implicit truism of victims as historical agents repeating the crimes committed against them. Neither the 'original' crimes nor 'the Afrikaner' crimes are stated. The perpetrators of the original crimes during the 'Second War of Liberation' – the 'English' – remain unnamed, as the normative white identity, but also the outside in reaction to which 'the Afrikaner' is generated.

Conceding to Anglo culture as white elevation: Proudly Afrikaans English-speakers

Afrikaner identity is premised on the Afrikaans language, reworked by Afrikaner nationalism to be 'the key cultural expression of a great *volk*' (Vincent 1999: 60), but still containing traces of its historical 'association of being the language of the underprivileged'. Hovering between these two poles, Afrikaner identity is produced through its claim to speaking Afrikaans and the routine relinquishing of social space to English. In the interview extract below, the social displacement of Afrikaans triggers resistances that are constitutive of Afrikaner identity even as, paradoxically, social space is ceded to the hegemonic WESSA identity. 'That makes me angry, yes,' Sandra says. Out of the slight, the injury of denial, the Afrikaner is conjured in a complex interplay of appropriation and repudiation. Ceding social space allows appropriation of an element constitutive of English whiteness:

politeness (Njovane 2015). The temporary abandonment of Afrikaans as the linguistic bedrock for identity is covered over with an articulation of Afrikaans identity as 'politeness' and 'accommodation', resonant of 'manners' as a key element in nationalist discourses on 'Britishness' (Thomas 2006: 466–7). This appropriation extends to a conflation of 'politeness' with the trope of how 'Calvinist' Afrikaners are. In yielding to Anglo culture as a sign of 'manners', politeness becomes *ordentlikheid*. This manoeuvre produces Afrikaner identity by affirming its positionality as a secondary and aspirational whiteness in attempted fulfilment of normative whiteness ('I struggle with my English, but it gives me a kind of "I can" feeling' / 'I'd feel too bad switching to Afrikaans because I'm afraid they'll think they speak bad English'). This is noted across generations.

Leah (49): When I look at Johannesburg where we live [an affluent, multiracial, centrally located suburb], 70 per cent of the people speak Afrikaans, but we all speak English [. . .]
Sandra (43): That makes me angry, yes.
Pieta (35): Isn't it just the lingua franca?
Nerina (32): If you go into a shop in Johannesburg you automatically speak English.
Willemien (33): It is [. . .] the effort we make with other people, not so?
Nita (62): The accommodation [. . .]
Willemien: Yes, we are now going to speak English to you because you are English.
Pieta: Because it is polite [English word used] to do that.
Leah: The Calvinism shines through, it is the politeness [use of the English word here].
Willemien: You will get one English person and five Afrikaans people [. . .]
Nita: But [. . .] it gives me a kind of 'I can' [feeling]. If you can't, I can. [. . .] I struggle with my English, but I can.
Sandra (43): From my side it is just polite [. . .] Johannesburg is essentially an English settlement, poor whites, rich English in the 1920s [. . .] I just get angry when people knowingly in a group [speak English when most are Afrikaans].
Pieta: I will speak to someone on the telephone and they will start in English and at some stage I'll hear the person is Afrikaans [. . .] and

then I'd feel too bad switching to Afrikaans because I'm afraid they'll
think they speak bad English [. . .]
Nerina: That happens to me on a daily basis.

As can be seen, subjects also resist concession of space, feeling 'anger'
when English is spoken in majority Afrikaans contexts. The source of the
resistance is revealed as not a problematisation of WESSA identity, but as
a competitive relationship with white English-speakers. Subjects are upset
about the displacement of Afrikaans by English identity, a stubborn affective
remnant that can be drawn back to the historical displacement of one settler
class by another at the southernmost point of colonial Africa.

In conclusion, the concept of *ordentlikheid* allows for the discernment
of the productive interactions between various social markers of difference
– particularly class, race, ethnicity, gender, sexuality and age. Historicising
ordentlikheid shows its development over time, drawing on 'salt of the
earth' notions cultivated by outsiders and insiders before the advent of
the twentieth century. Questions over Boer or Afrikaner whiteness are
addressed head-on by Afrikaner nationalist reworkings of earlier tropes to set
this settler group apart from the British/WESSAs, while still being entitled
to the privileges of whiteness, a process that culminates in apartheid. The
stigma of Dutch/Boer/Afrikaner backwardness in relation to European
modernity, exemplified by poor whiteism, is resolved by interventions
by successive colonial and apartheid governments. But when apartheid
eventually provokes opprobrium from Western white metropolitan centres,
Afrikaners have a new stigma to contend with: that of oppressor.

In Afrikaans white subjects' efforts to restabilise the discursive field
after apartheid and make themselves *ordentlik* again, strategies of change
to reinfuse their identity with moral worth are detected at two frontiers of
identification: the black other and the WESSA other. At both frontiers, class
and race are intimately imbricated, to the extent that class serves as vehicle
for race. The race-class deployment particularly reasserts blackness as inferior
to stem the disturbance of race as validation of unequal social and material
relations after the advent of democracy. The frontier effects with the black
other reveal the deployment of labour divisions to position white/black as
a service relation and to naturalise a 'lesser' status for people racialised as
black. Black moral repositioning is a result of the international opprobrium
that apartheid provoked and the confirmation of its defectiveness as moral

order in its collapse. In reaction, moral equivalences are fabricated between the apartheid and the democratic dispensations to paint black people with a colonial brush as inherently morally corrupt while rescuing apartheid's creator, 'the Afrikaner', from ignominy. Various strategic reversals are mobilised to rescue much-vaunted 'white goodness'. Some of these reversals are paradoxical, as whiteness seeks to draw on the newly acquired moral capital of blackness to re-upholster itself, even as it casts moral suspicion over blackness. These manoeuvres are also evident in the next chapter on *Sarie* magazine: the discursive strategy called 'whitewashing the blackout' entails deploying 'good blacks' to shield *Sarie's* white subjects from accountability for the privations that institutionalised racism brought upon black people.

The WESSA frontier stands in stark contrast to the frontier with the black other. The relationship is aspirational, with *ordentlikheid* deployed to install white Afrikaans subjects as equal to the historically ascendant WESSA identity. Still smarting from the historical wound of the South African War, the drive continues to share the spoils of whiteness and to iteratively demonstrate that 'we have arrived'. The subaltern status of Afrikaner whiteness is evident in the pronouncements of shame and anger, the yielding to superior Anglo whiteness and the sense of elevation that subjects derive from this yielding. Being accepted by hegemonic global whiteness after the democratic break of 1994 opens the possibility of unmarking, of erasing the mark of an ethnic whiteness, by disappearing into invisibilised Anglo whiteness or whiteness incognito. It presents the possibility of overcoming the twofold stigma: Afrikanerhood as lesser whiteness in relation to the WESSA identity and Afrikanerhood as morally stained as a result of its intimate implication with apartheid and resultant culpability.

This finding is taken further in the next chapter on *Sarie* magazine as a discursive instrument in the modernisation of Afrikaner whiteness, driven by an aspiration to achieve equal status with the hegemonic and globalised Anglo (bourgeois, heteromasculine) whiteness of the more successful settler class, 'the English'. This aspiration manifests in rising to unmarked status, whiteness incognito, or, as discussed in the second last chapter of this book, withdrawing into neo-nationalist enclaves studiously policed in accordance with the models of *ordentlikheid* and the *volksmoeder*.

2

Be Good to Yourself to Be Good to (White) Others

Sarie Magazine's Technologies of Heterofemininity

Anchoring *ordentlikheid* is the *volksmoeder*, Afrikaner nationalism's version of the 'mother of the nation'. The *volksmoeder* designates 'Afrikaner' women as the physical and moral reproducers of the *volk* and its boundaries, as discussed in depth in the next chapter. Hence, Afrikaner women are the keepers of *ordentlikheid*. To explore the recuperation of *ordentlikheid* with the aid of the *volksmoeder*, I turn to sanctioned cultural discourses as presented in *Sarie* women's magazine.

On 6 July 1949, the year after the National Party (NP) came to power, the first issue of *Sarie* appeared. The front cover depicts a woman in 1940s' fashions. Positioned next to the image is a faint outline of the same woman in *volksmoeder* attire – that is, a nineteenth-century bonnet and long dress associated with '*Voortrekker* women' (Brink 2008: 7) (see picture below). The yoking of these two images makes up the discourse of *Sarie*, here called 'Sarielese', which inducts adherents into a particularist femininity, attaches them to modernising white Western femininity, but simultaneously stringently regulates and polices them in accordance with the *volksmoeder* model. The display of the *volksmoeder* image signalled the magazine's continuation of the legacy of *Die Boerevrouw*, an Afrikaner nationalist magazine that was published between 1919 and 1931: *Die Boerevrouw*'s iconic cover always featured the *volksmoeder*, as portrayed in a sculpture by Anton van Wouw (see Chapter 3).

During Afrikaner nationalist rule, *Sarie* worked as a cog in the 'apparatus of domination' (Foucault 2004: 45). Its owner, the company Nasionale Pers (translates as National Press and publicly known by its shortened moniker Naspers), was founded in 1916 as the media arm of the Afrikaner nationalist *volksbeweging* (people's movement). The company benefited from state contracts during the twentieth century, catapulting it to its current position as the largest media company in Africa and the second largest in the southern hemisphere. A company-sponsored hagiography titled *Oor grense heen* (Across borders) (Beukes 1992) admits that Naspers saw its role as purposively steering Afrikaner consumers in accordance with NP policies. In Althusserian terms, therefore, it interpellated subjects on behalf of Afrikaner nationalism, a process facilitated by the company's dominance in the Afrikaans-language media market, which developed into a monopoly from the 1990s onwards. *Sarie*'s advent in the crucial year after the NP's rise to power advanced Afrikaner nationalist hegemonisation by aiming specifically to interpellate subjects into a particularist version of 'woman': the *volksmoeder*, modernised to add shine and glamour – not unlike a hair product – to its ethnoracial heteronormativity.

WOMEN'S MAGAZINES, INDIVIDUALISM AND CONSUMERISM

Individualism has been a staple, albeit variable, discourse of Western women's magazines. Marjorie Ferguson, in her content analysis (1983) of British women's magazines, finds a switch between the themes of 'getting and keeping your man' and 'self-help' (as manifested in 'free choice' and 'perfect self-presentation') (52). From the 1940s to the 1980s, 'getting and keeping your man' drops in prevalence from 59 to 12 per cent while 'self-help' grows from 13 to 47 per cent (50–3, 96–100). In her critical textual analysis of women's magazines in the United States in the 1980s, Ellen McCracken (1993) finds a 'commodity base' as an 'essential characteristic of feminine desire', alongside 'consumerist competitiveness and reified individualism' (299). These studies describe the formation of a postfeminist and neo-liberal discourse.[1]

Natalie Fuehrer Taylor (2010), analysing women's magazines in the United States in the 1990s and 2000s, argues that instead of second wave feminism's rejection of popular culture as reproducing gender inequalities, third wave feminism posits that women access feminist principles through popular culture, rather than through political activism (218–22).[2] Women's

Consuming the *volkseie*, or '*volk*'s own': a page from the July 2009 anniversary edition of *Sarie*, with the heading '*Het jy geweet?*' (Did you know?), interpellating readers with Sarielese's heady mix of Afrikaner nationalism and capitalist consumerism during apartheid.

magazines 'inspire women to forge their own unique selves' and 'create the lives they want' (230). This might mean embracing idealisations of marriage, motherhood and beauty that contradict feminism. For Taylor, these are not contradictions, however. She contends that women's magazines advance third wave feminism's concern with independence and equality and create a sense of a common political position as women, but without prescribing how women should act (226, 230). Such incongruities are exposed as untenable in Shelley Budgeon's (2011) critical analysis of third wave feminism, discussed further below.

In South Africa during the 1970s, former *Sarie* assistant editor Alba Bouwer (in Maritz 2012) remarked that 'judging by our newspapers and magazines', 'little women' (*vroutjies*) were concerned only with appearance, of both body and home.[3] Prosperity had led to an 'ominous, self-indulgent love of comfort':

> Excessive emphasis on external appearance – 'the well-groomed image and the right outfit', as the women's pages often describe it – with a girl in the end seeing herself as a delicate twining plant that has to find her support wall at all costs and does not have to concern herself with the country's affairs because that is after all a man's world.[4]

In her analysis of a *Sarie* article of May 1992 on the Convention for a Democratic South Africa (CODESA) negotiations in the early 1990s, Loraine Maritz (2012) finds an iteration of a femininity that was ignorant, disinterested and flippant about politics. Maritz concludes that this construction of *Sarie*'s resonated with the politically disconnected Afrikaner femininity generated during the period of Afrikaner nationalist state control and also reflected the apathy and confusion resulting from the sense of loss of Afrikaner identity after the collapse of state power. *Sarie*'s CODESA article is here read as interpellating subjects with an incantation of a femininity that was hegemonic during at least the 1970s and 1980s. Maritz finds another three *Sarie* articles in the period 1992–6 tracking political efforts at the institutionalisation of women's human rights in South Africa during the transition to democracy. A special current affairs section was even created in the magazine. This political engagement suggests that *Sarie* was incorporated by the discourse of constitutionalism during the 1990s, with its allocation of human rights to women. Nevertheless, *Sarie*'s 'feminist phase' was a brief hiatus before it followed Western women's magazines' descent into postfeminism.

In step with the wider rethinking of consumption, South African cultural studies questions the privileging of (masculine) production (previously posited as 'real') in relation to (feminine) consumption (previously posited as 'impulsive and trivial'), with the argument that consumption and commodities can offer liberating meanings (Nava 1999: 51). Miranda Joseph (1998: 27) suggests understanding consumption as constitutive of subjectivity and Sarah Nuttall (2006: 272) argues that 'the market' is a 'vector' for generating postapartheid identity, particularly in remaking race. Consumption enables culturally encoded identity productions forged by 'actively negotiated consent' (Narunsky-Laden 2008: 129). Commercial media, as a mode of consumption, manufacture, verify or refuse identities (Hadland et al. 2008). Consumer magazines can serve as 'cultural tools', making available identificatory repertoires of norms through goods and lifestyles, particularly in relation to group solidarity (Narunsky-Laden 2008: 131).

Deborah Posel (2010: 164) shows how selfhood-producing consumption was linked during apartheid to the 'acquisition of symbolically loaded goods' as a sign of respectability: 'Workings of race became inseparable from the symbolic logics of material acquisition and deprivation [and] social advancement.' While she writes with particular reference to black people, it is posited here that selfhood, consumption, race and respectability became similarly entwined for Afrikaners as 'marked whites'. Stuart Hall (1997b) reminds us to explore how capitalism drives Westocentric global mass culture to 'invade' and 'weave' particularist forms into its expansion (29). Naspers, as a company producing and adhering to the particularist discourse of Afrikaner nationalism, segments its target market in accordance with apartheid boundaries (Du Plessis 2012). Thus, Thomas Blaser and Christi van der Westhuizen (2012: 387) ask: 'Could we speak of an ethnicised group of individual consumer-citizens, constructed through the twin operations of defensive ethnicity and neo-liberalism with their shared utility of facilitating retreat from public spaces?' This chapter explores how consumption is intertwined with ethnicity and neo-liberalism in *Sarie*'s virtual white space to accomplish a revised version of the *volksmoeder*'s Afrikaner womanhood, tailor-made to be *ordentlik* again.

THE CULT OF HETEROFEMININITY

Sarie's commercial success has persisted after the end of formal apartheid. At the time of this analysis, it was the second-largest women's magazine in South Africa, with a circulation of 132 646 units and a total readership of 904 000. *Sarie* maintained its prominence, even though it was aimed at a comparatively small section of the population – Afrikaans-speaking, middle-class women – and despite its origins as one of the cogs in the *volksbeweging*.

The popularity of *Sarie* makes it a foremost example of culturally sanctioned knowledge aimed at individuals who occupy the subject position under review in this book. It is a technology of normativity, conveying 'preferred meanings': taken-for-granted 'everyday knowledge of social structures, of "how things work for all practical purposes in this culture", the rank order of power and interest and the structure of legitimations, limits and sanctions' (Hall 2006: 513).

Sarie has the features of a typical, mainstream, Western women's magazine, as described above. Each edition starts with several double-page advertisements for hair products, perfume, cosmetics and other consumer items. The magazine is voluminous at between 178 and 210 pages per edition and features full-page advertisements on every second page and sometimes even more frequently. The twelve editions of *Sarie* for the year 2009 formed the focus of my analysis as the magazine's 60th anniversary year, occasioning commemorative content on its Afrikaner nationalist history, which was of specific interest in my research.

The data is gleaned from four categories of text: the front cover, the cover article, the editor's letter and readers' letters. Where relevant to the analysis, other articles were included, specifically those pertaining to constitutive outsides, or outsider figures that constitute the white female subject in question. The choice of the front cover was based on its status as 'interpretive frame' of what is to follow (McCracken 1993: 32). The front cover also displays the normative 'role model' femininity in an embodiment of *Sarie* discourses, which features in the cover article. The editor's letter was selected as the primary site for the 'official' version of *Sarie* discourses. Editors of women's magazines function as 'high priestesses to the cult of femininity', gatekeepers of the feminine agenda (Ferguson 1983: 188). The readers' letters were selected as messages mediated and standardised to fix *Sarie* discourses, as part of the 'complex structure of dominance' of the mass media communication process that determines messaging from all sources (Hall 2006: 508).

The rest of this chapter unravels the textual tapestry of *Sarie* magazine, with its interwoven narratives aiming to refix a dislocated white femininity. *Sarie* purveys a changing ensemble of elements to make a subject position intelligible, articulating a particularist whiteness, middle-classness and heterofemininity.

As discussed, democratisation wrought a crisis in the space of representation (Laclau 2004: 319). Within this dislocation of the social, I find that *Sarie* discourses draw on sedimented residues of historical antecedents, rearticulating these discursive elements to:

- renovate the *volksmoeder* nodal point through suture with domesticated, previously abjected outsiders and a revamped father-husband masculinity;
- re-secure beleaguered Afrikaner whiteness through denialism-erasure and the re-inscription of nostalgia.

Women's magazines tell women 'what to buy': they are a form of popular culture dependent on women still mostly being assigned the task of reproduction (McCracken 1993: 2–5). This chapter shows neo-liberalism as a new surface for the re-inscription of *volksmoeder* femininity. Neo-liberalism prescribes consumerism as a mode for self-actualisation. It is a technique that *Sarie* subjects apply in their continuous aspiration to accomplish a certain version of white heterofemininity. Consumerism assists with the reinstatement of normative *volksmoeder* femininity through the commodification of culture, demarcated by a masculinity that keeps this femininity white and in check.

SARIE'S SUBJECT

Sarie deploys narratives of 'celebrity lives' as achievements of the ideal. The cover articles on celebrities represent them as venerated subject positions; therefore, celebrities serve as surfaces displaying normative directives or performatives. Performatives produce what they name and therefore have subjectivating effects (Butler 1993: 106–7). These celebrity texts detail iterative pursuits of the promise of cancelling the shortfall between subjecthood and *Sarie*'s normative ideal. The subject is analysed as 'in pursuit' because it is invested in achieving completion. However, fulfilment is a 'phantasmatic promise' (220). Paradoxically, incompletion works as a constitutive process (Laclau 1996: 79) because the subject remains in a repetitive quest for wholeness – Jacques Lacan's *jouissance* (A.M. Smith 1998: 81). This wholeness is pursued through identification with hegemonic projects, but repeatedly subverted by plural meanings overflowing the social. This overflowing, or overdetermination, prevents the subject from finding closure through suture with a signifier of its own. In this case, heterofemininity is the floating signifier overdetermined with meanings. As a technology dispensing discourses for the interpellation of subjects, *Sarie* wields a revised *volksmoeder* nodal point to stay the flow of meaning. Celebrities serve up the performatives to gather subjects around *Sarie*'s revamped *volksmoeder*.

Sarie's tales of 'celebrity lives' pursue a narrative pattern of individualism, a feminine version of the 'hero's journey': trials and tribulations, followed by ponderings on how to surmount individualised obstacles, culminating in the inevitable confirmation that the heroine/celebrity will forge ahead.[5] The trials collectively form a particular version of 'doing woman': losing weight; finding a man (whether the celebrity wants to or not, *Sarie* wants her to); staying pretty; fighting old age and fat or a combination of all of these. Articles are sojourns into a variety of disasters that subjects are compelled to ward off to achieve beauty and other goals of *Sarie*'s heterofemininity and thus verification from men pursuing its co-constitutive masculinity. Sarielese foregrounds those elements that fit *Sarie*'s hegemonic cookie-cutter mode of heterofemininity while de-emphasising or abjectifying outliers that do not.

In the rest of this chapter, I distinguish eight discursive strategies that together form Sarielese:

- modernising the *volksmoeder* – whiteness incognito;
- consuming self – the compulsory choice of heterofeminine embodiment;
- it's all in the *Sarie* family: accessing an 'I' through a patriarchal 'we';
- whitewashing the blackout;
- (sm)othering centre;
- compulsory heterosexuality – try and try again;
- panoptical masculinity surveying the *volksmoeder*'s limits;
- *Sarie* as white space.

DISCURSIVE STRATEGY I: MODERNISING THE *VOLKSMOEDER* – WHITENESS INCOGNITO

White, Western, middle-class heterofemininity looms large in the accomplishment of *Sarie*'s ideal womanhood, with women interpellated to embody Afrikaner nationalist modernisation through Western cultural accoutrements. Nevertheless, their ethnic identification remains equally valid, with the combination of 'modern' and 'ethnic' femininities serving as a blueprint for this particularist femininity.

Sarie is read here as technology in the service of *ordentlikheid* (see Chapter 1). Therefore, *Sarie* is an instrument disseminating the Afrikaner nationalist discourse of the modernisation of a subaltern whiteness aspiring to equal status with the hegemonic and globalised Anglo (bourgeois, heteromasculine) whiteness of the more successful settler class in South Africa – the English. Sarielese hitches signifiers of consumerism and individualism with, paradoxically, the 'Afrikaner' collective. This is done in the following ways.

The editor's letters of July and August 2009 mark the 60th anniversary of *Sarie* with a parable positing an equivalence between the Estée Lauder company and the Naspers magazine, putting their starting dates 'a year apart [1948 and 1949], indeed continents and an ocean apart but both with one goal: to make women feel good about themselves and their world in the language of their heart. Lauder's language was beauty; our language was Afrikaans' (Editor's Letter, July 2009). With the articulation of 'Lauder', the editor deftly reinvents *Sarie*: from Afrikaner nationalist vector to a neutral contributor to the universal history of beauty. This voids not only *Sarie*'s politics, but also that of hegemonic *volksmoeder* femininity, while invoking elements such as the Afrikaans language and feminine beauty necessary for the continued reproduction of consumers of the magazine. The reification of an unchanged 'Afrikaner' femininity dehistoricises it in the same breath as affirming that 'everything has a history' that possesses 'value and truth', as the editor's letter asserts, borrowing the latter phrase from Estée Lauder executive Aerin Lauder in an interview with the *Sarie* editor-as-globetrotter 'in New York'. Implicitly, Afrikaner nationalist historical machinations – indeed, apartheid! – are confirmed as 'valuable' and 'true'.

Sarie serves as an ethnic gateway/gatekeeper to Western heterofemininity: the editor describes the founding of *Sarie* as aiming to 'unlock a whole new world to women in Afrikaans. A world of Audrey Blignaut and

Alba Bouwer, Chanel and Dior.'[6] This confluence of Afrikaner nationalist female role models, Afrikaans writer-journalists Blignaut and Bouwer, with Dior and Chanel as symbols of Western heterofemininity signifies Afrikaner women's accomplishment of the normative ideal of Western white heterofemininity.

Sarie's story in the July 2009 editor's letter contains two explosive dates: 1948 and June 1976. The editor presents a parallel history, which elides the political origins of the magazine's discourse. The trite as truth displaces the political. The editor cites June 1976, but not as the date burnt into history as the start of the black youth revolts that precipitated the conclusion of formal apartheid. In a manoeuvre of erasure and transplantation, the editor cites June 1976 as the publication of a departing editor's inanity of finding it 'a pleasure' to work at *Sarie*. Strikingly, the editor gives 1948 as the founding year of Estée Lauder, instead of 1946, the correct date. Despite meticulous whitewashing, *Sarie* is haunted: even if attributed to the magnificent history of international beauty, 1948 slips in as the year in which the NP's reign commenced, inadvertently conjuring the spectre of apartheid.

A neo-liberal-inflected trope of 'from small-town girl to globetrotter' is repeatedly administered as a format for subject formation, playing on the ostensible rural character of Afrikaner identity that underpins the construction of *ordentlikheid*. The *volksmoeder* is rearticulated with neo-liberal discourse: the promise of self-actualisation is about achieving equivalence with hegemonic bourgeois heterofeminine whiteness, while retaining ethnic particularity. These processes of actualisation are carefully sanitised of the political to render these subjects without accountability.

In the February 2009 edition, co-constitutive relationalities are conjured among three personas:

- 'our golden girl' Anneline Kriel, Miss South Africa in 1970;
- the 'forgotten' Pearl Janssen, who was Miss Africa South of the same year; and
- South Africa's first Miss World, 'Penny Coelen from Durban'.

The discourse is *Sarie*'s version of white Afrikaans identity as aspirational. The ambition for equivalence with white, English-speaking South Africans (WESSAs), as found in Chapter 1 on *ordentlikheid*, also reverberates through *Sarie* discourses. *Sarie* seeks to prove that Afrikaans white women 'have arrived' and delivers the elevation promised by acceding to global Anglo whiteness in the form of Western women's magazines. 'Annie' and 'Pearl' both aspire to achieve Anglo femininity as signified by the white, English-speaking Coelen, but only 'Annie' becomes Miss World.[7] Neo-liberal rationality's depoliticising effects are wielded to erase 'Annie's' victory as the result of the spoils of whiteness. The text is thoroughly sanitised to avoid confrontation with the apartheid advancement of white people at the expense of black people. 'Pearl' aspires to white femininity: her long, black hair was 'smooth' and worn in a 'Farah Fawcett-style' (reference to a white American film actress); 'I looked up to Penny Coelen [Miss South Africa and Miss World in 1958]. I wanted to be like her.' But she fails. While Janssen disappears from the public eye, 'Annie' has South Africa 'burst[ing] out of its seams'. The 'South Africa' signified here is in fact *Blank Suid-Afrika* (White South Africa) as represented in NP discourse. The signifier 'our girl' in the article renders the *volk* equivalent to the country, as per the phantasm of the Afrikaner nation state.

In contrast to Janssen, 'Annie' accomplishes normative white Western femininity: she was 'the nearest we ever got to our own [British Princess of Wales] Diana'. 'Annie' confirms Afrikaner whiteness as counterpart to normative WESSA whiteness in the construction of White South Africa. The *volksmoeder* nodal point is therefore renewed, with a chain of equivalence yoking the signifier 'Annie' with 'Diana' as the pinnacle of white Western heterofemininity. Thus the *volksmoeder* is modernised. However, there are limits to this modernisation. *Sarie* declares 'Annie's' multiple marriages unacceptable, thereby disciplining her, but more specifically the consumers of the discourse. Still, her status as mother and her current marital monogamy retain her as a valid feminine model for the reassertion of the *volksmoeder* in the guise of international beauty queen.

The article headlines effect the universalisation of rearticulated *volksmoeder* femininity, in contrast with the marked marginalisation of black femininity: 'Always Annie', 'who lives in the sky', as opposed to 'Pearl of the Flats', pointedly terrestrial. 'Annie' as embedded past convention is 'invested with the political power to signify the future' (Butler 1993: 80). The editor's letter explains the privileged signifier 'Annie' as: 'all of us, Afrikaans, English, rich, poor, from places big and important to small and far-flung, have an equal chance in the big world out there'. A particularism is projected as universal but, notably, race is again subject to elision, as is further explored in the analysis of the discourse of 'whitewashing the blackout' later in this chapter. Apart from whitewashing 'Annie' as *volksmoeder* to remove both the apartheid stain and black people from her world, the neo-liberal notion of assuming responsibility for one's life opportunities, or lack thereof, is further used to revamp the *volksmoeder*.

DISCURSIVE STRATEGY II: CONSUMING SELF – THE COMPULSORY CHOICE OF HETEROFEMININE EMBODIMENT

Sarie's marketing in the contemporary era is framed by the idea of 'me', spelt out with the following four phrases on the spine of the magazine: My *Styl*, My *Inspirasie*, My *Lewe*, Myself (My Style, My Inspiration, My Life, Myself). 'Myself' is an anglicisation.[8] Appropriating an English concept to articulate 'self' in the signifying chains of Sarielese works in two mutually entangled ways: it designates Afrikaans feminine identity's aspiration to accomplish hegemonic (white, Anglo/Western, hetero-) femininity and fortifies it with postfeminism and neo-liberal subjecthood.

Sarie's editorial strategy crystallises the four elements of 'me', stated by the editor as follows:

- 'We are an intimate part [. . .] and a true extension of her lifestyle and life philosophy. [. . .] We tell typical South African stories that keep her feeling good about herself and her world. This is who she turns to for [. . .] life's key solutions [. . . and] her special inspiration.
- My Style: Glamorous content that inspires. Local and relevant global trends.
- My Life: [. . .] Fashion for a personal style. Beauty to look and be your best.
- My Inspiration: Good food and wine [. . .] Decor and DIY [. . .] Travel ideas and destinations.
- Myself: Reflective and motivational content that focuses on self-realisation and self-awareness' (*Sarie* 2011 advertising rate card).

These four elements stitch together *Sarie*'s version of the stock-in-trade of Anglo-American women's magazines:

- commodified desire and consumerism;
- technologies of femininity, such as beauty, fashion and domesticity;
- intimacy with readers; and
- self-help (Taylor 2010; McCracken 1993; Bartky 1990; Ferguson 1983).

These elements are articulated with neo-liberal individualism ('me'), postfeminism ('feeling good about herself and her world') and what Nikolas Rose (1990) calls a 'therapeutic culture of the self' involving self-realisation and self-awareness:

> We always have a choice. We can decide what to do with every circumstance and event [. . .] We feel frequently we have no control [. . .] that life throws us about mercilessly [. . .] But human nature is full of vitality [. . .] [There is] always hope [to discover] inner strength (Editor's Letter, October 2009).

> You have to change things within yourself, and suddenly you feel free. You always have to exercise choice in life (Michelle McLean cover article, November 2009).

Activated in these texts is the neo-liberal mode of governmentality that 'convenes a "free" subject who rationally deliberates alternative courses of action, makes choices and bears responsibility for the consequences of these choices' (Brown 2005: 43). *Sarie's* ideal subject position is articulated with a psychological discourse on self-improvement and obligatory choice (Lazar 2011; Rose 1990). This subject is gendered, in that 'freedom' requires successful management of the body, particularly exercising the discipline of feminine beauty, with accoutrements to curb the excesses of femaleness. Neo-liberalism and postfeminism both impose 'the obligation to shape a life through choices in a world of self-referenced objects and images' (Rose 1990: 257). These objects can be found in, among other things, the mass media's transmission of 'lifestyle'. 'Lifestyle' culture induces the individual to be 'the kind of subject who can make the right choices' (McRobbie 2007: 36). 'Every aspect of life, like every commodity [. . .] is a mark of our individuality, each is a message to ourselves and others as to the sort of person we are [. . .] illuminating the self of he or she who consumes' (Rose 1990: 227). This involves the patriarchal mode shifting from objectification (women reduced to objects, either as bodies or body parts [McCracken 1993: 122–5]) to subjectification (the ways power operates in the constitution of subjectivities [Gill 2009: 100–1]) through the consumption of commodified femininity.

At play in actualising the *Sarie* self are repetitions of rituals of induction and grooming into white heterofemininity through consumerism. By consuming commodities, a subject renders white heterofemininity. The cover article on Michelle McLean (November 2009) features a photo of McLean in a designer dress, surrounded by mounds of shoes with the caption: 'This Errol Arendz dress with its ethnic feel symbolises our love for Africa and the dozens of pairs of shoes reflect Michelle's passionate personality.' The editor's letter of August 2009 declares that the perfume Chanel No. 5 has a 'strong hold on our emotions'; it 'still holds the promise of glamour and freedom, as Mademoiselle Coco Chanel promised women from the beginning'.

Rather than the editor's proffering of 'freedom', Michel Foucault's conceptualisation of 'docile bodies' (1991: 181–2) is more apt here to describe a 'perpetual and exhaustive [. . .] regulation of the body's size and contours, its appetite, posture, gestures and general comportment in space and the appearance of each of its visible parts' (Bartky 1990: 80). Inscribing white, Western heterofemininity on the body requires abiding by prescriptions for hair distribution, body fat and accessories that affect bodily movement (Orbach 2009). Women's magazines not only commercialise the bodily marking of 'woman' as feminine other, but also serve as inculcators of technologies of femininity (Blackman 2008: 25–6).

Every front cover interview in *Sarie* features a 'celebrity' produced by teams of technicians, whose names and duties are listed, as well as the products and prices. The Anneline Kriel cover article (February 2009) shows five decades of her life over an expansive eleven pages. It reiterates a subject position articulating self-policing of feminine embodiment and technologies of femininity, overseen by experts in the 'science of femininity', with injunctions of consumption as a mode to achieve the prescribed identity. Journalistic ethics are overridden as advertising and editorial contents are conflated: embedded in editorial text are life-size photos of beauty products alongside detailed titles of each product – for example, 'green tea and cucumber in Dermalogica Soothing Protection Spray (R440) protects your skin against attacks from the environment'. A photo of Kriel barefoot at 'barely 20' 'in London' is accompanied by: 'Early ageing already starts in your young days – it is just not yet visible', followed by a quotation from a dermatologist, Dr Suritha Kruger. The article also quotes skincare expert Stephanie Hugo from Johannesburg: 'Before 25 you can get away with just an eye gel'. Make-up artist Algria Ferreira-Watling 'believes' that in 'your 20s', 'you can be just who you want to be!'

These significations are repeated in readers' letters, articulated with the masculine/feminine dualisms of active/passive, public/domestic and brawn/beauty:

> I miss Saturdays – my dad and brother at a rugby game, my mom and I on the bed. We feast on chocolate and [. . .] *Sarie*. When I was 11 years old I started to join conversations about beauty and recipes. I had a cut-out with beauty tips for every day [. . .] Bathing oil and foam bath [. . .] skin oil and body powder! In my teen years I started experimenting with *Sarie*'s beauty ideas – homemade facials and lemon juice for shiny hair. A cut-out from the 60s says [. . .]: 'some girls are blessed with a beautiful skin and a pretty figure [but] even you with your freckled face, pug nose and chubby little body can be attractive if you are spanking clean from your shiny brushed hair to your toenails. My daughters also know that' (Theresa Smith, Rondebosch, August 2009).

The focus on the body in magazines such as *Sarie* intensified with postfeminism's insertion of 'the body' in the space that 'the home' occupied in the 1950s (Gill 2009). The body is 'a signifying practice within a cultural field of gender hierarchy and compulsory heterosexuality', 'an object of systems of social coercion, legal inscription, and sexual and economic exchange' (Butler 1990: 189). Postfeminism figures femininity as a 'bodily property' (Gill and Scharff 2011: 4). 'A sleek, controlled figure is essential for portraying success, and each part of the body must be suitably toned, conditioned, waxed, moisturised, scented and attired' (Gill 2009: 99).

What do these new prescriptions mean for those women whose bodies are used to fence the *volk*? In a cover article on Cindy Nell, she looks 'rested' and 'perfectly made up' behind her fashionable 'large sunglasses'. She is dressed in a 'tight turquoise top that compliments her brown skin, courtesy of her own tanning lotion, Caribbean Tan, that she developed. It's the second best seller in the country' (January 2009). Bodily distinctions are classed, as they produce bourgeois taste as normative and 'as expressing the quality of superior distinctiveness' (Blackman 2008: 62). Neo-liberal governmentality produces the middle-class, white, female body in opposition to the working-class body that is 'beyond governance' (Skeggs 2005: 965, 968). Differentiation within whiteness determines access to choice. While the working class has a 'lack of access to the techniques for perform[ing] the good self', 'the middleclass has no choice but to choose' (974), as expressed in the following excerpt:

> 'I have the right knowledge now to keep my weight stable.' [Her decision to] chuck her 'overweight clothes' [. . .] is the psychological proof that she is on the right path to keep the weight devil bridled forever [. . .] 'I want to be a healthy mother [to my daughter]' (Bertha le Roux cover article, April 2009).

> 'Of course I, typical woman, sometimes see someone who is fat [when I look in the mirror]. But I also see a wiser woman who [. . .] wants to make the right decisions [. . .] (McLean cover article, November 2009).

The postmodern turn has left the dichotomous feminine norm of 'fat=bad' (even 'evil') as opposed to 'thin=good' intact, but with the change that 'looking after oneself' is 'a moral value' (Orbach 2009: 4, 141-2). Thus responsibility must be assumed for displaying the 'correct' body as a sign of an ethical self. This ethical self involves being a 'healthy mother', with the implication that overweightness is a malady that derogates motherhood. Photographs accompanying the McLean article show her as underweight and without musculature, being the same body size as her ten-year-old son, who is photographed with her. This femininity's class and race status is corporeally inscribed, in that 'fat' is equivalent to lack of responsibility and morality (Skeggs 2005: 966-8, 974).

The reader is interpellated into a construction of 'self-confidence' predicated on a body 'under control'. *Sarie* verifies this subjectivity, as with the heading and blurb of the Le Roux article that read: 'Prettier, thinner Bertha. Look at me now!'; 'She shines with self-confidence [. . .] and shows her body proudly in tight-fitting clothing.' *Sarie* similarly authorises Suzette van der Merwe: 'She is still thin, spontaneous and well-groomed' (cover article, September 2009).[9] At times *Sarie* allows the 'celebrity' to talk back, but only within the discipline of feminine body management: 'I do not want to follow strict diets [. . .] I do not have to prove myself' (Nell article, January 2009).

A July 2009 reader's letter confirms the subjectifying effects of *Sarie*'s prescription of self-management, edited by the magazine to emphasise selfhood born from the 'right' corporeal choices:

> *Sarie* changed my life. Thanks for the article about Bertha le Roux, who's lost so much weight. I immediately [. . .] started with the diet. [. . .] When I feel like the wrong kinds of food I also read the article over and over for inspiration [. . .] (Michelle du Toit, Highveld).

Consumption, also of the magazine itself, is articulated with the intergenerational transfer of disciplines of femininity, which includes curtailing the unruly excess of the female body (Grosz 1994):

> [*Sarie* was] there when my eldest daughter was baby. She made herself up from head to toes with Vaseline. She saw how pretty you are and just wanted to do it like you [. . .] (Liz Botha, Georgia, USA, September 2009).

> 'My one constant message to [my seven-year-old daughter] is: Skye, you've got to be a lady' (Van der Merwe article, September 2009).

> 'I don't want [my daughter] Kiana to grow up with body issues that she learnt from me as mom' (Le Roux article, April 2009).

The mother's disciplining of her daughter installs a hierarchy that contrasts with the intergenerational construction of masculinity. With masculinity, the hierarchy is inverted: the son is infused with the power to serve as (masculine) verifier of his mother (as feminine) (McLean article, November 2009).

Sarie interviews with 'celebrities' are cast in confessional mode. Foucault (1998: 58–70) traces the genealogy of Christian procedures of confession reconstituted in the scientific terms of psychology. Thus the sexual was recast into sexuality as regulatory regime. Rose (1990: 217, 245) argues that the operation of psychotherapeutics has expanded beyond sexuality and pathology to manufacture an autonomous self for 'the analyses of social ills and cures, as the object of expert knowledge'. In the *Sarie* interviews, litanies of emotions are dissected in a psychologised discourse and the failures and triumphs in the accomplishment of hegemonic feminine embodiment are minutely and iteratively detailed. Foucault (1991: 183) calls these painstaking techniques a 'new microphysics' of power; Rose (1990: 239) regards them as a perpetual self-surveillance of the performance of self in its minutiae:

> The fear that she will pick up weight again will always gnaw at Bertha. [. . .] 'Anything can happen [. . .] When [. . .] I am frustrated, I want to eat. I don't know where it comes from . . . I have to sort [it] out (Le Roux article, April 2009).

> 'Pants or a top focus your attention on your body and about that you are forever critical.' She thought her legs were too thick even though people told her they were her best asset. (Her feet are also a source of embarrassment. She takes her Tods off and shows slender feet without nail polish, with a skew toe that bothers her) (Kriel article, February 2009).

Sarie's prescriptions combine the acknowledgement of 'life's challenges' with resolution through technologies of femininity and consumerism. A September 2009 reader's letter (by Elsabé Olivier, Brooklyn) describes her relief when she consumed *Sarie* after radiation and a hysterectomy. This fits with an observation about the great, life-enhancing import of pretty things for women, as made by the last male editor of *Sarie* (Izak de Villiers, 1983–91) to one of his successors, the second female editor (Michélle van Breda, 2001 to the present) in the magazine's 60-plus years of existence. De Villiers was a former Dutch Reformed church minister who served as the magazine's patriarch to the mostly female staff, even after stepping down. Van Breda duly relayed his 'frequent plea' 'to make pretty' in her editor's letter (November 2009) as follows: 'Women like pretty things. Life is challenging. Make *Sarie* the one thing that spoils her [the reader]. She deserves it.' Both the hardships and their resolutions are tinged with racialisation because, while white, Afrikaans, middle-class women as a group are more affluent, with greater social opportunities than ever before, and enjoy formal human rights for the first time in the country's history, they are addressed as subjects who suffer. The sources of these trials and tribulations are not explored through critical contextualisation. Indeed, as I discuss later, Sarielese studiously avoids contextualisation. Instead, the resolutions for the challenges include accessing a sense of belonging through consumption of technologies of femininity, as presented in *Sarie*. *Sarie* projects itself as a refuge, an Afrikaans white space. Through (its) consumption, the reader accesses femininity *and* community (see Chapter 5 for more on this).

DISCURSIVE STRATEGY III: IT'S ALL IN THE *SARIE* FAMILY: ACCESSING AN 'I' THROUGH A PATRIARCHAL 'WE'

McCracken (1993: 299) observes that women's magazines 'assimilate an idealised individual consciousness to a similarly idealised group consciousness as one of their primary narrative strategies'. Women's magazines' subjectivating discourses of normative femininity, consumerism and individualism are reproduced through a sense of community – interpellating readers 'as if we were all girlfriends' (Taylor 2010: 226). Women's magazines therefore serve as an interface between group and individual as part of their interpellation of subjects. Postfeminism in the West claims that a shift has occurred away from 'others' to the 'self' for women and that they can participate in a 'culture of the self that endorses self-invention, autonomy and personal responsibility' (Budgeon 2011: 284). The proviso is that women have to proclaim that gender equality has been attained, thereby losing gender as tool for analysis and politics, even as gender difference is reified. The result is a tension between embracing individualised agency and performing women's normalised subordination within gender relationality (285). The conflict between individualism and social relationality is resolved in *Sarie* by converging the neo-liberal dictum of a decontextualised responsibility for self with the *volksmoeder* dictum of women assuming responsibility for others, while also being solely responsible for their own failings. This is firstly done with the articulation of '*Sarie*-as-family' with 'inspiration', incessantly iterated to promote the magazine in its own pages. Both notions advance the commercial interests of the magazine, as '*Sarie*-as-family' builds brand loyalty and the 'inspiration' on offer is to be found in consumerism and materialism, ideological drives on which the magazine depends for sales.

Sarie–My Inspirasie [*Sarie*–My Inspiration], the branding motto of the magazine, was inaugurated in 2001. The contents page (*Sarie*, January–December 2009) is divided in accordance with this theme and spells out its four categories that are also, unusually, reflected on the spine of the magazine: *My Styl, My Inspirasie, My Lewe, Myself* (My Style, My Inspiration, My Life, Myself). Thus the magazine seems purposively styled in correspondence with the neo-liberal and postfeminist dictum of individualised self-investment.

Individualised 'inspiration' and collective 'family' stand in tension with each other. *Sarie*-as-family is encapsulated in the recurring subtitle of the editor's letter: 'We, You and I'. The use of 'we' to promote articles on the front cover contributes to the sense of a collective, which is strengthened by the conflation of readers with *Sarie* and the representation of *Sarie* as an anthropomorphic 'she', as in 'she is pretty' or '*Sarie* stood by me'. According to the editor's letter in the 60th commemoration edition, each time *Sarie* tells an 'endearing South African story', '*Sarie*'s story' and 'readers' stories' 'interweave', creating an 'emotional tie'. Furthermore, 'about *Sarie* one feels, as Alba Bouwer said years ago, like a family member or someone who lives close to you'. *Sarie* in the postapartheid context of 2009 was therefore still invoking the imagined community of the *volk* – but reconjured within the *Sarie* space. The contemporary resonance of this myth is confirmed with the inclusion of the following letter, which speaks of the continued embeddedness of *Sarie* in a neo-nationalist imaginary. The manufacturing of the '*Sarie* family' resonates with the nationalist conception of the nation as the family writ large (McClintock 1993). *Sarie*'s 60th anniversary presented an occasion for nostalgia for white days gone by. Displayed in a pink block on the letters page of the July 2009 edition, a letter starts:

Still My Inspiration
1949. 60 years ago. I am 14 years old and in high school. The Voortrekker monument is unveiled and two teachers grow their beards for the occasion. Both rust brown. And my grandma buys me my first *Sarie Marais* [. . .] (Magda Frick, Gordons Bay).

Afrikaner nationalist images are conjured as old familiars that need no explanation: the Voortrekker Monument, Voortrekker male performativity and reproductions of previous editions of the magazine, with its original title *Sarie Marais*, to complete this reliving of white days. The 'I' is accessible through this 'we'. This is the family that demarcates the extent to which individualist 'inspiration' may be acted upon.

The purported 'inspiration' of neo-liberal and postfeminist self-actualisation possesses an ethnic twist, courtesy of the *volksmoeder*: the ideal self can be accomplished through consumption that enables care of others. In an editor's letter (December 2012) that reduces agency to 'keeping on dreaming' and 'waiting for surprises', the editor writes: 'Reach for the stars' is 'a kind of confirmation' that 'we can': 'a little voice says: I *am* more. To be *more* and to offer more is how we have been put together.' This directive is also highlighted in a 'pull quote' underneath the photo. Similarly, the editor's motto is 'Give of yourself', inserted in two columns during the course of 2009. 'Giving of yourself' is hitched with *Sarie*'s branding motto 'inspiration'. Again, another version in the May 2009 edition is: 'You can never ever make yourself feel better if you don't make someone else feel better.' These are read as productive iterations functioning as performatives. *Sarie* discourses recalibrate the Western rhetoric of neo-liberal individualism and rational choice to realign this femininity to one that constantly derives its sustenance from other people. This trope of selfless service is a primary sedimented trace of the *volksmoeder*. Rearticulated with the neo-liberal notion of the consumer-citizen devoted to self-improvement, it now says: 'Make yourself the best you can so as to serve others.'

A heading for a reader's letter (March 2009) iterates 'Give of Yourself'. Another is headlined, 'To Think of Others'. Sarielese consists of attempts at confirming selfhood over and again, drawing on a construction in which woman-as-wife/mother hinges on the self as 'being for others'. These attempts fail and cause intense existential anguish, editorially utilised as affective displays that are elevated to letters of the month:

Lord [. . .] despite my own admonitions [. . .] I have again failed. I have collapsed into a routine of getting up, going on, planning weeks ahead [. . .] Did I build sand castles with my grandson [. . .]? Did I really hear when my children told me something? I am guilty [. . .] (Letter of the Month, Annien Teubes, Moorreesburg, January 2009).

I have my own business, a permanent post and do extra work [. . .] It is not enough. I realise I am emotionally absent from my husband and children because I focus on the wrong things. [. . .] Let go of the thoughts about losing our home [. . .] (Letter of the Month, Alta van Spreeuwenberg, Pretoria, March 2009).

It is a renewal of self-sacrifice, a *volksmoeder* element reinvented with postfeminist and neo-liberal elements.

The central *Sarie* tropes of 'give of yourself', conjoined with 'inspiration', have the subject in question consuming for others. The readers' letters page exemplifies this. Through its title, '*My Sê Tel*' (My Say Counts), *Sarie* suggests that the voice of the reader/'ordinary woman' 'counts'. Instead, the letters page is overrun with promotions in a recurring blurring of the media's ethical distinction between editorial content and advertising content. Product placement is achieved on every page, in several editorial features – with prices – and even in a cover article (February 2009). Letters are mediated to the extent that uniformity in tenor and style is achieved, placing a question mark over whether letters are indeed from different 'readers'. All letters bar one in the year 2009 are uncritical of, or promote, the *Sarie* discourse. The one (faintly) critical letter still capitulates to *Sarie*'s conflation of consumerism and pleasure:

> I like to read Sarie and see the prettiest shiny things, most beautiful people and places where I will never go. You know, I also desire these things [. . .] The Bible says you may not desire [. . .] what now? [. . .] It comes and lies here in my heart to be cherished [. . .] Thanks, Sarie, that I at least can see everything (Jennie Agenbach, Okahandja, August 2009).

A more apt heading for the readers' letters page, instead of 'Your Say Counts', would be 'Say after *Sarie*'. Who gets to 'say' or, as Foucault (1998: 11) puts it, 'who does the speaking' and what are the 'positions and viewpoints from which they speak'? 'My Say Counts' is in dialogue with '*Laaste Sê*' (Last Say), a column written by the former *Sarie* editor and ex-church minister, De Villiers,the *Sarie* family's paterfamilias. The *Sarie* family has a father who literally gets the last word on the last page of the magazine, exemplifying the paternal guidance of Afrikaner women by Afrikaner men. The paterfamilias represents the constitutive heteromasculine outside to *Sarie*'s heterofemininity. The editor attributes her idea of 'giving of herself' to the former church minister and editor, whom she acknowledges repeatedly as her mentor. Having a say that counts means submitting to consumerism and to delimitation by an ethnic family presided over by a patriarch. This point is further developed later in this chapter and in Chapter 4.

DISCURSIVE STRATEGY IV: WHITEWASHING THE BLACKOUT

Only four readers' letters in 2009 refer directly to black people, of whom all are nameless and in relations of service to the letters' authors, with the exception of one passing reference to Anglican Archbishop Emeritus Desmond Tutu. Another four letters refer indirectly to black people, encoded as 'criminals'; 'incompetent'; 'domestic servants' and the 'younger generation', with whom middle-aged Afrikaner men cannot 'compete'. In Sarielese, black people only surface from this generalised elision if they fit meritocratic ideas that make them 'deserving' (for example, in the editor's letters of June and October 2009). Black subjects are also authorised when they take individual responsibility for lost 'opportunities', which are, in fact, the result of apartheid oppression. Apartheid as systematised oppression is otherwise erased in Sarielese.

Wendy Brown (2005: 42–3) analyses how neo-liberalism employs the modes of depoliticisation, decontextualisation and desocialisation of subjects to deny structural contingencies and to maintain unequal power relations. She notes neo-liberalism's fiction of a rational agent, who is fully accountable, whatever the structural constraints. Failure to achieve prosperity is depoliticised as a 'mismanaged life'. Neo-liberalism 'figures individuals as rational, calculating creatures whose moral autonomy is calculated by their capacity for "self-care" – the ability to provide for their own needs and service their own ambitions'. Postfeminism similarly demands denial of the 'classed and raced constitution of the "successful" feminine subject', in return for a coherent narrative of choice and autonomy (Budgeon 2011: 285). Whiteness, bolstered with these neo-liberal and postfeminist erasures, is at work in *Sarie*'s treatment of Pearl Janssen, who received the 'black' beauty title of Miss Africa South in 1970, as mentioned earlier in this chapter. Next to the blurb for an article on former Miss World, Anneline Kriel, who received the 'white' Miss South Africa title in 1974, the promotional line 'Our Forgotten Miss SA' on the February 2009 cover page suggests the excavation of Janssen. It promises her reinstatement in the 'history of beauty', the overturning of forgetting in favour of remembering and the 'coming to speech' of 'those reduced to silence' (Eribon 2004: 9) – it promises the opposite of the expunging work of whiteness.

But *Sarie* excavates Janssen not to confront the oppressive practices of apartheid or to rectify elisions in historical accounts. Instead, *Sarie* recasts her exclusion in the rhetoric of 'the market', where subjects find, or miss, opportunities. Apartheid discrimination against black women is reinvented as 'life not always being fair, and that we aren't always granted equal chances and the acknowledgement that we deserve', as the editor's letter explains Janssen's lost life opportunities (February 2009). This strategy is bolstered with an exoticisation of Janssen in articulations such as 'opulent', 'sensual' and fertility. Ross Chambers (1997: 194) points out that exoticising effects a disconnection between subject and object that facilitates forgetting and denial of historical contexts. In Sarielese, exoticisation is yoked with neoliberal elements. Janssen's is a case of 'playing the dice as it rolls for us' (Editor's Letter, February 2009) – a depoliticisation hinting at the neoliberal form of what has been called 'casino capitalism' (Strange 1986). Implicitly, 'Pearl' did not play the dice 'well', based on 'the assumption that a person's economic fortunes derive from qualities of the person' (West and Fenstermaker 1996: 376).

'Pearl's' ostensible 'message of hope for us all' and that 'it's time to fly!' (Editor's Letter, February 2009) earns her *Sarie*'s verification of her worthiness as subject. The editor's letter thus erases Janssen's actual life conditions of poverty as a result of structural racist discrimination and reinscribes them with individualising self-help clichés. These deployments allow this version of white femininity to hide the real-life devastation caused by the subjugation and marginalisation of black women. It also removes from view the Afrikaners who were instrumental in the creation and maintenance of apartheid that robbed Janssen of the material and other possibilities that could have come with employment in the international beauty industry.

'Pearl' as 'good black' (see the discussion below on the 'good homosexual') is allowed entry into Sarielese to shield whiteness from accountability for the privations that institutionalised racism brings upon black people:

- *Sarie*'s version of 'Pearl' acquits white people, and Afrikaners in particular, by apportioning blame not to apartheid or racism, but to the 'beauty industry': 'I had nothing. I was so disillusioned and then I realised: the beauty industry destroyed my life.'

- 'When I see a Miss SA nowadays, I am not sad or bitter [. . .] it is not their fault that I was born at the wrong time.'
- 'Now we should all just have hope and look ahead because it does not help to ruminate over the past.'

Notable is the elision of race and apartheid as productive of Janssen's subject position, rewritten as, at best, an agentless 'wrong time' or, at worst, 'Pearl's' own error of being born at that time. Another instance is the recoding of apartheid as the euphemistic 'years of difficulty' (Editor's Letter, May 2009). *Sarie*'s version of 'Pearl' also lends credence to a prevalent white discourse of the need to 'move on' and 'leave the past behind' (Van der Westhuizen 2017). This fits with the discourse 'Good white/Good black: Black verifier of *ordentlikheid*', as analysed in Chapter 1.

In a reader's letter, titled 'Like Her Own', similar tactics to the Janssen article are employed. It emerges that a 'good black' adheres to the revered sacrificial femininity of the *volksmoeder* while also serving as the workhorse standing in for the white woman's reproductive duties (see Chapter 3). She risks her life by remaining loyal to whiteness and facing down the 'bad black':

'Why do you love this white child? What about apartheid?' the robbers wanted to know. 'Where was he during apartheid?' defended she. 'His mom knows nothing about apartheid' (January 2009).

The 'good black' acquits not only the white child of culpability for apartheid, but even its white mother. The letter elides the identity of both the 'good black' and the author, as the letter writer is merely identified as 'Kian's mom' while the 'good black' remains nameless. Therefore a double erasure is effected of both the white woman and the black woman, as the white man (or boy) is the centre, in relation to which they both stand as constitutive outsides. This is an iteration of normative masculinity's primacy, here advanced through the signifier of a sacrificial motherhood, which the white boy receives in a double dose – from a black mom and a white mom.

Apart from the 'good black' exonerating Afrikaans whites, *Sarie* otherwise tightly circumscribes the possible relations between black and white women. The March 2009 cover article renders unintelligible an interaction between a black woman and a white woman that is not based on service by the former to the latter. The article's focus is on a 'day in the life' of a white actress, Amalia Uys, on an Afrikaans, predominantly white television show. A noticeable number of photos show Uys in intimate conversation with, and physically embracing, black actress Vuyelwa Booi. While the photos display affection and at the very least friendship, their relationship is not reflected in the text. Instead, despite a lack of evidence in the photographs provided, the captions render Uys 'star-struck' with white Afrikaans male actors on the set. The erasure is expanded with captions overwriting the visual messaging of the photos with insertions of white figures *not* in the photos. 'Vuyelwa' as racialised other is allowed in the text only when Sarielese invokes her ostensible difficulty with Afrikaans words and thus her failure of the *Sarie* criterion of speaking Afrikaans, thereby foregrounding her otherness beyond the visual marker of skin colour. While Uys and Booi's intimacy in the photos troubles *Sarie*'s version of race, the suppression and reinterpretation of the visual images in the text encumbers the potential problematisation of Sarielese that these images pose.

The erasure of race and the normalisation of racial marginalisation and oppression centres the marked whiteness of Afrikanerhood as normative whiteness in the *Sarie* symbolic field. This feat is mostly impossible outside of the pages of *Sarie*. These discursive manoeuvres legitimise a hegemonic position for Afrikaans white femininity vis-à-vis racialised femininity.

DISCURSIVE STRATEGY V: (SM)OTHERING CENTRE

The signifier 'compulsory heterosexuality' is articulated with the *volksmoeder* nodal point through the application of discursive strategies of erasure, stigmatisation and entertainment to achieve homophobic othering. In the rare case (Caster Semenya in the editor's letter, October 2009) where female masculinity (Halberstam 1998) features, it is not named as such and is incorporated into the normal. Lesbianism is shrouded in silence in cover articles, readers' and editor's letters and on front covers. According to Foucault (1998: 27) this silence, 'the things one declines to say, or is forbidden to name', 'functions alongside the things said, with them and in relation to them' as part of the strategies permeating discourses. *Sarie*'s silence about lesbianism could be read as a strategy of exclusion of 'contestatory possibilities' to instead implement the heterosexual norm and enable the assumption of (hetero)-sexed positions (Butler 1993: 109). Such a strategy conceals the extent to which its closed spaces are dependent on oppositions with outsider figures for their constitution (Smith 1994: 24). Abjection renders heterosexuality viable at the expense of homosexuality *not* through refusal, but through identification with abject homosexuality, which must be concealed (Butler 1993: 112). This 'identification with abject homosexuality' refers to the constitutive split at the origin of each identity (Laclau and Zac 1994), the productive exclusions at the root of every identity. Not confessing to the constitutive outside also facilitates the obfuscation of the coercion and political struggles producing the exclusions. By repressing the other, the malleability of social structures can be obscured and social coherence (normative heterofemininity) achieved, albeit only temporarily (Laclau 1990: 173).

In comparison, male homosexuality avoids blanket negation. Male homosexuality is signified as a 'problem' to be 'solved', an emergency (see the article, 'Dilemma: My Son is Gay', *Sarie*, October 2009). 'Being gay' is yoked with 'never a "typical" son'; artiness; interior decorating and a 'molly-coddling' mother. Despite gay men's engagement in these 'feminine arts', effeminacy is repudiated. Only straight-acting men are allowed. In accordance with the problem-solving logic, the 'Dilemma' article features three opinions of 'experts'. The psychotherapeutics on offer in the article speaks out against homophobia and disavows the need for the 'gays' in question to 'change'. But gayness is essentialised as an immutable condition. 'Mothers' are instructed to extend their womanly duty of support to their homosexual sons and to their husbands struggling with their sons' homosexuality.

However, this leniency towards sexually non-conforming men is counteracted in another article in the same edition of the magazine. A popular Afrikaans singer (Nicholis Louw) stands accused of violating 'the heterosexual presumption of the symbolic domain' (Butler 1993: 110). He is interrogated about 'gossip' that he might be gay. The stigma of child sexual assault is attached to the identity, alongside non-conformist utterances. In the article, 'Nicholis' deploys iterative defences of heteronormative compliance: the marriage imperative; the male sexual prerogative; the masculine pursuit of cars. These 'productive iterations' have subjectivating effects, in that 'Nicholis' seeks to be a 'culturally viable sexual subject'. 'Nicholis' confesses in life-and-death terms to the obliterating effects of homosexuality – how he, along with his parents, would be destroyed if the accusations of homosexuality should continue, without naming it as such. This could be read as an example of 'the imaginary misrecognition of "the ego" as it "recognises" itself in the ideological formations which constitute it' (Althusser 2008: 171). This exemplifies how the *Sarie* discourse constitutes 'sexed subjects along the heterosexual divide to the extent that the threat of punishment effectively instils fear, where the object of fear is figured by homosexualised abjection' (Butler 1993:110).

But *Sarie*'s treatment of male homosexuality also resonates with Judith Butler's (1993: 111) notion that the assertion of heterosexuality does not always require full renouncement of homosexuality: homosexuality can be 'entertained'. However, entertaining it only lasts insofar as it remains 'entertainment', either as a figure of incomplete sexual subjectification or as powerless to rearticulate the law of heteronormativity. This 'entertainment' is confirmed in the instalment of the male feminine in the signifying chain of the *Sarie* discourse. Nataniël, one of *Sarie*'s four male columnists in 2009, is a popular, gay Afrikaans singer-comedian. He is male-bodied, but wears material accoutrements that do not conform to normative masculinity. In his irreverent column for *Sarie*, called '*Kaalkop*' (Bald Head, an untranslatable wordplay on his hairless cranium and an Afrikaans expression for being forthright), Nataniël plays the role of jester, traditionally 'a eunuch, or a "female male", castrated and thus sexually neutered and safe' – similar to lesbian columnist Marianne Thamm in *Sarie*'s English-language counterpart *Fair Lady* (West 2009: 108). The jester is simultaneously the 'Wise Fool' and an outsider, a favourite figure of Afrikaans cultural narratives employed to speak the 'truth' about the Afrikaans condition. Nataniël's other, complementary subject position within the *Sarie* discourse is the 'gay man as best friend', the confidant and trusted adviser of the straight woman, who knows not only about style, but also understands emotions and speaks the 'truth' about what it means to be a woman. The caveat for this instalment is the desexualisation of the male feminine, which Nataniël personifies with his childlike voice on stage and the general submergence of his sexuality. In this innovation, harnessing the male feminine links what is new in the postapartheid moment (the greater social visibility of gay men) with consumerist agency and the myths of the *volksmoeder*. Apart from his column, *Sarie* front cover articles on Nataniël reiterate *Sarie* subjectivity: diets, etiquette and Christmas 'togetherness'. A *Sarie*-branded notebook included with the May 2009 edition contains a maxim 'from Nataniël': 'You can never ever let yourself feel better if you don't let someone else feel better.' Thus the *Sarie* discourse 'entertains' male feminine difference by counteracting its possible subversive postapartheid effects and using it to re-upholster *volksmoeder* elements. Despite the margin having been folded back on the centre, no space is created in the sexual order for a counter-discourse and resubjectification (Eribon 2004: 7, 145, 313). Nataniël is *Sarie*'s safe homosexual, or 'good homosexual', as per Anna Marie Smith's (1994: 242) formulation: 'Contemporary homophobia constructs the mythical figure of the "good homosexual" and promises to include her within the normal in return for her denunciation of her fellow queers.' Male femininity is subjected to domestication in the *Sarie* discourse.

DISCURSIVE STRATEGY VI: COMPULSORY HETEROSEXUALITY – TRY AND TRY AGAIN

In the marking of 'woman', subjects utilise technologies of gender to materially imprint a certain standard of femininity upon their bodies. This imprinting awaits masculine verification in order to commence reproduction. Reproduction affirms accomplishment of *volksmoeder* heterofemininity, projected as 'wholeness'. This persistently iterated myth is yoked in Sarielese with the above-described recalibration of the neo-liberal focus on the self. Sarielese aims to steer this particularist subject towards a self-production that is intent on 'heterosexual union', including by employing performatives of everyday heteronormativity – for example 'through thick and thin' and 'forever'. A woman not tied to a man is figured as 'lacking' in femininity and subjecthood, more broadly, with hetero-union proffered as remedy:

> Businesswoman, TV presenter, motivational speaker – but now, for the first time, Cindy Nell feels like she does not have to prove herself anymore. And the crown on her happiness is her *trouman* [literally, marry-man] (Nell cover article, January 2009).

> She knows the right man will come at the right time (Elma Postma cover article, June 2009).

> We will rather stay in an unhappy relationship and convince ourselves it is not that bad. There are always hundreds of reasons to stay and so few to end it (Nell cover article, January 2009).

As Foucault (1998: 102) reminds us, discourses deploy contradictions, which should not detract the researcher from examining a discourse's power effects and the power relations sustained by such deployment. *Sarie* rebuts everyday failures in women's accomplishment of the heteronorm with a two-pronged strategy:

1. projecting the collapse of the fantasy of heterosexual union as devastating to women and iteratively invoking such failures to highlight contrasting moments of a 'model' femininity that is nevertheless geared at overcoming the failures;

2. seemingly refusing the criterion of masculine verification, only to overturn the refusal with naturalisations of the trope that the maintenance of relationships is a woman's responsibility, while hiding the oppressive dimensions of heteronormativity.

The loss of hetero-union causes devastation for a pleading, immobile woman, 'left behind' by an active man, as in this reader's letter, reproduced with its original heading:

Please Come Back
My life falls apart piece by piece. [. . .] My unconditional love was not big and good enough for my husband. [. . .] How do you break off a piece of heart? We are, after all, one. I pray you realise we belong together [. . .] I thank God for keeping me upright [. . .] (New Hope, Pretoria North, April 2009).

Departure from the heteronorm can only be tolerated in extreme circumstances. It requires a paradoxical lesson in femininity, which is to continue abiding by heterosexuality. Subjects reach for neo-liberal psychotherapeutics in seeming denials of masculine verification:

Her divorce taught her [. . .] you can't just throw it away. You have to [. . .] learn from it. 'Everything is dark and black [. . .] As a woman you tend to think that if you change, your relationship will be better. But [. . .] if you try and be someone that you are not, it won't fit' (Anna-Mart van der Merwe cover article, August 2009).

Even a perfectly beautiful former Miss Universe sometimes doubts herself. There was a divorce that made her feel like a huge failure; after that, a broken engagement. She started to wonder if she completely lacks the ability to make the right choices in love. [. . .] Michelle realises now that one can't expect of someone else to complete you. You first have to be happy and love yourself (McLean cover article, November 2009).

Sarielese revamps feminine service with neo-liberal self-responsibility and self-actualisation, irrespective of gendered power relations:

Amor and Joost van der Westhuizen, perfect couple, fairytale life [. . .] the shock came like a punch to the stomach: Joost and a stripper in a sex video [. . .] Amor was making food when Joost told her [. . .] 'Questions milled in my head. Am I not good enough? What did I do wrong? [. . .] My aim in life is to serve in a way that makes me happy . . . I am his wife. I have his children. What kind of woman would I be if I did not stand by my husband? I promised to be there for him in good and bad times' (Amor Vittone interview, December 2009).

The 'give of yourself' performative receives a postfeminist boost in which 'woman's duty to serve man' is refurbished as a way that 'makes me happy'. It articulates women taking responsibility by being useful wives and mothers. Male infidelity and betrayal is attributed to the female subject's own shortcomings that require self-correction.

Self-production in service to others permits *Sarie* to diverge from postfeminism by adopting a stance of relative lack of sexualisation. The most prevalent iteration featured on the front covers of *Sarie* during the period 2009 was heterosexual relationships with men (n=40), outnumbering maternal relationships with children (n=16), 'body' (n=26) and 'home' (n=3). *Sarie* cover articles wield celebrities to highlight heterosexual relations as the predominant theme in all 2009 editions, except March. The front cover promotional 'plugs' for the articles yoke 'relationships with men' with 'romance'. Yoking with 'sex' is notably infrequent (n=7). Indeed, sex is comparatively scarce in Sarielese, in contrast to a contemporary context of

Western women's magazines suffused with postfeminist hyper-sexualisation (Walter 2011; Attwood 2009).

Maternity is built into *Sarie*'s feminine sexuality, rendering it subservient to keeping the family intact. The husband can be ejected from the family if caught out in infidelity, but male straining at the harness of monogamous marriage is naturalised as 'manly'. This womanhood struggles to pin down its relational manhood amid the prevailing dichotomies masculine/feminine, active/passive and public/domestic. A wife should still seek the cause of her husband's infidelity within herself, as part of her (maternal) responsibility for his (boys will be boys) sexuality.

It is a sexuality that depends on masculine activation and therefore professes a lack of knowledge. Boundless masculine sexuality is celebrated, in contrast with a femininity anxious for the 'perfect wedding night'. Sexual innocence/ignorance is feminine and sexual desire/knowledge is masculine, with marriage as the site for this complementary completion. A distinctly childlike disposition is inscribed on the surface of this feminine sexuality through rhetorical repetitions, such as 'fairytale wedding/life'; 'princess' and 'knight on a white horse'. These idealisations hide the political implications of heterosexual identifications and the reality of violence.

As can be seen from the princess metaphors, an infantilised femininity is verified by a paternal masculinity. The cover text of November 2009 reads: 'Michelle McLean and her No. 1' – 'No. 1' referring to her son. A 'pull quote' in the interview reads:

> When I am with [my son] Luke, I learn a lot about myself. He has to know that I [. . .] support him [. . .] I would lose my temper [. . .] and [. . .] say, 'Mom is a brat' (McLean cover interview, November 2009).

McLean as adult woman renders herself a 'brat' in Sarielese in relation to her son, elevating him to a knowing father figure to her toddler. Paradoxically, her infantilised figure still fulfils the role of supportive mother/daughter to her father/son. *Sarie*'s version of Amor Vittone also infantilises herself with diminutions:

> [The children] ask: 'Mommy, why is your *hartjie* [little heart] sore?' [. . .] I also tell them: 'Dada made Mommy's little heart sore' (Vittone interview, December 2009).

Repetitions in identifications are never identical and contain violations of the rules of discourses (A.M. Smith 1998: 79). Momentary potential for self-creation occurs in the different decisions taken in the constituting of subjectivity (Laclau 1990: 44, 173). Celebrities' occasional resistances spill over into Sarielese, but are domesticated, such as the following normalisation of gender violence:

> 'He did not take no for an answer when he phoned me [for a date].' [. . .] Before the wedding she already experienced Bowen as jealous and controlling and she realised it would not get better. But she became pregnant on the honeymoon . . . Because she did not work, she was dependent on Bowen for everything. 'I gave up my power as woman [. . .] I did not believe I was good enough. The marriage was emotionally destructive [. . .] But [. . .] marriage is forever, through thick and thin [. . .] I decided that I had made my choices and that I should [. . .] try my best to be a good wife and mom' (Suzette van der Merwe interview, September 2009).

Stalking, abusive behaviour, intimidation and possible violence by a man become a woman's responsibility to manage, by subsuming her self with the mantra, 'I should try my best to be a good wife and mom.' To reinforce this containment of women's agency, *Sarie* inserts the article headline, 'I Have Never Been in Love'. It pointedly contradicts Van der Merwe's notion that the sacrifice of her independence was the sacrifice of her 'power as a woman'. The headline invokes legitimisation by the masculine other, which in this case is still out of reach. The word 'already' in the introductory blurb to the article alerts the reader to a non-normative element that is presented as problematic: 'Suzette van der Merwe has already been married twice but she has never really loved [. . .] Going forward she wants to trust her heart, rather than her head.' The words 'Suzette' and 'heart' are accentuated with large pink font. Thus Van der Merwe's unhappy marriages signify failure to achieve feminine completion as a result of her inappropriate adoption of a masculine attribute, rationality (trusting her head). Lack of independence and male coercion and violence, as hinted at, are both normalised.

Other closure-failures similarly invoke accusations of unfemininity: an unstable home life made businesswoman and former beauty queen Cindy Nell 'hard as a rock' (January 2009). This is followed by a *Sarie* editorial interjection as correction: 'Then it is good to hear you are pretty and nice.' The article depicts Nell as incomplete, despite career success and own wealth. A *trouman* (marry-man) is needed to make her whole, a condition clinched when 'the sun catches her engagement ring'. To be 'more than a beauty queen' cannot be accomplished in the 'hard' (masculine) activities (such as business) she is engaged in, but by entering a union with a man and thus becoming 'soft'. That this attempt at wholeness is in fact an 'imperfect repetition' (A.M. Smith 1998: 79) is confirmed by her having been married previously. In contrast, the husband-to-be's status as a businessman and property-owner is deemed sufficient, with no hint of his being incomplete.

Sarielese disciplines celebrities as protagonists of its heady heteronormative tales. Female independence is articulated with failure. Actress Elma Postma (June 2009) travelled 65 000 kilometres for an Afrikaans pay-TV programme. Despite the programme's title *Boer soek 'n vrou* (Farmer/Afrikaner seeks a wife), Postma as presenter is not the *boer* seeking a wife, but is rather represented as 'sexy' interlocutor that finds wives for *boere*. An Afrikaner woman criss-crossing the country articulates elements such as public sphere, career, mobility and detachment from men. While the programme's content is heteronormative, Postma represents a subject position too unfettered, risking the multiplication of possibilities and the threat of unruliness for Afrikaans women. *Sarie* intervenes to domesticate the freewheeling woman:

> She wonders sometimes if she is not too independent for a relationship. 'I take big decisions about finances and property on my own. [. . .] I do not have to ask anybody's permission [. . .] But I want to be soft again and I want to hand over [. . .] It would be nice if [a man] could look after me a bit.'

> 'Life is not about money and what you achieve. It is about love [. . .] about relationships. If you are 80 and you are lucky enough to have a man in your life, it is wonderful. Without that you are a has-been actress with a few photos on the wall' (Postma article, June 2009).

In *Sarie*'s manufacturing, Postma's independence is yoked with the threat of becoming unfeminine. The stigma of 'the woman on the shelf' is conjured for 30-year-old Postma. Femininity means submitting to 'love' and handing over power to a man, as (masculine) career accomplishment is not the correct mode of actualisation for a subject seeking verification as 'Afrikaner woman'.

DISCURSIVE STRATEGY VII: PANOPTICAL MASCULINITY SURVEYING THE *VOLKSMOEDER'S* LIMITS

Sarie's technologies and constructions of femininity occur under supervision. Rose (1990: 239) speaks of a 'reflexive self-objectifying gaze' targeting the self; Ferguson (1983: 65–8; 112–13) genders it as an 'invisible man' operative in women's magazines; McCracken (1993: 14, 112–16, 306) finds an 'implicit male surveyor' of normative femininity and Sandra Bartky (1990: 72, 80) describes the relentless internalised gaze of the 'panoptical male',[10] an invisibilised centre from which emanates patriarchal power.[11]

In a departure from Western women's magazines, Sarielese does not consistently hide the operations of its panoptical male, but rather parades a hegemonic Afrikaner masculinity iteratively delimiting femininity. This masculinity double-marks the *Sarie* subject position: as feminine and as Afrikaans. It acts as a normalised and constant standard legitimating the *Sarie* version of Afrikaner femininity and inscribing and policing its limits and thus the borders of the *volksmoeder*. Examining these positionalities in relational form reveals a femininity yoked into a chain of meanings with dependence, weakness, suffering, emotionality, immaturity, self-sacrifice and selflessness. Its superior co-construction is a masculinity hooked into a signifying chain with father, protector, God, adviser, leader and knower.

The regulatory prevalence of this masculinity was epitomised by the patriarchal succession of male-only editors at *Sarie* between 1949 and 1991, of which the above-mentioned church minister, Izak de Villiers, was the last. It is dispersed throughout the magazine. At the time of the analysis, men wrote four of the six monthly columns, including '*Laaste Sê*' (Last Say), a column written by De Villiers after he stepped down as editor. Subsequent to his death in 2009, tributes (December 2009) positioned him as the grand patriarch of the '*Sarie* family' of readers and staff. Jointly with André le Roux, another columnist self-positioned as 'brother' (Letter, November 2009) in relation to De Villiers's paterfamilias, he counteracts the 'self-empowerment' that the neo-liberal discourse may effect by setting the limits of '*Sarie's* inspiration' that women may garner from the magazine's pages. This regulatory operation is in the service of a masculinism drawing on

Afrikaner nationalism. In a tribute to De Villiers in a letter from another of the many former male editors, he is 'saluted' as a 'blueblood Afrikaner'. Afrikaner nationalist icons and poetry are invoked in an erasure of women and a confirmation of the Afrikaner nationalist project as quintessentially about men and their status:

> About him I can repeat the words of the poet Jan F.E. Cilliers about General Christiaan de Wet: 'Be still, brothers, a man passes' (Fritz Joubert, November 2009).

While a brother editor laments 'the passing of a man', a former female editor is rendered child in a quotation where De Villiers approvingly authorises her accession as editor: 'Remember, my child [. . .] when I wanted you to succeed me [. . .]? Yes, Reverend Izak. But, Reverend Izak [. . .]. No, my child, no [. . .].' Thus slippage occurs in Sarielese between man and father, also exemplified in the following letters from women, directed at their husbands:

> In difficult times you carry me [. . .] you hold me tightly and sometimes I even see the pride in your eyes (Unfinished Diamond, Centurion, June 2009).

> I miss our days of cherishing and protection, when I would be cradled in your arms, safe (Wife of a Stranger, Klerksdorp, February 2009).

The distinctions between 'man as husband', 'man as father' and 'God the Father' blur as signifiers attached to these categories coincide. Sarielese invokes Christian nationalist notions of the patriarch as the family's interlocutor with 'Our Heavenly Father'. The interchangeability of terrestrial and heavenly masculinities resonates with Christina Landman's findings in *The Piety of Afrikaans Women* (1994), constructions that have shown longevity into postapartheid South Africa (Landman 2005):

- A reader declares to her husband: 'You who see angel wings in the clouds, you are the one with the biggest wings' (Letter of the Month, Marguerite Dippenaar, Norwood, February 2009).
- Letters about De Villiers hint at the divine: 'Good old spirit' and 'Bread and sardines' (insinuation of Jesus Christ) (November and December 2009).

De Villiers as approachable patriarch ('like a dad') is a knower of women 'because he had so much respect for them' (Editor's Letter, November 2009). It is a masculinity that determines which women may speak: while an anecdote relays De Villiers's mother's defence of his right to speak, he 'inspires' a reader to put 'a guard in front of' her mouth (Letter, Crizelle Dempers, Bothasig, December 2009). This masculinity may or may not explain itself, in contrast to a femininity that seeks its recognition:

> It is part of being a woman to want to know [. . .] A man's attitude is: this is what happened, let's move on (Vittone interview, December 2009).

> Communication problems easily slip into a marriage, so I wrote to him: [. . .] 'Thanks that you sometimes say nothing when words can be redundant' (Unfinished Diamond, Centurion, June 2009).

Sarielese also naturalises 'husband-father gone wrong'. *Sarie*'s editorial decision to elevate the phrase 'sometimes you are familiar' to a heading for the following letter contradicts the despair and the suggestion of violence by emphasising the potential for continued 'normalcy':

Sometimes You Are Familiar
In your place is a man that hurts me, scares me, a man that revolts me (Wife of a Stranger, Klerksdorp, February 2009).

In emphasising the reference to the familiar, rather than the threat, Sarielese normalises male violence. Similarly, in the following letter, a reader tells the story of a friend, 'the life of the party', who confessed to 'the secret' of being a child victim of intra-familial sexual assault and who as a result wears a 'mask':

Dad's Princess
Thank you to my dad because he treated me like a little girl when I was one. When he came into my room it was to rub cream into my legs suffering from growing pains [. . .] how lucky I am not to have my childhood murdered like the Annas. To all the dads that protect and love their children – you made us princesses (Princess from Murrayfield, Pretoria, January 2009).

'Annas' here refers to the bestselling Afrikaans book *Dis ek, Anna* (Lötter 2004), later translated into English (*It's Me, Anna*, 2005), an autobiographical tale about child sexual assault within an Afrikaans family. In the letter's text those damaged by a coded violence are othered as 'masked' 'Annas', their innocence 'murdered' because of their 'secret'. The men who 'murder' are elided from the text; rather, the reader thanks an idealised father – the king to her princess – for not assaulting her. The threat of masculine sexual violence is always already present (Peterson 2000); therefore, she is grateful for the exemption. However, the example of exemption is sexually loaded ('coming into' her room and 'rubbing' her legs), thereby confirming the king's right to, at the very least, access her body, with implicit male sexual licence. Gratefulness from women is in order should men magnanimously not exercise these rights. The power that is granted to men determines whether a woman will be a 'murdered' 'Anna' or a 'loved' 'princess'.

Men as surveyors of women, an 'everyday panopticism' (Foucault 1991: 212), are naturalised in Sarielese:

> I gather my courage and ask how he found me in the packed café. He says: 'Easy, [X] said you'd wear red and smell of roses.' [. . .] The description could have been so different. [He] could have said I am roundish with brown hair, or that my front teeth are skew (Veralda Schmidt, Kyalami, January 2009).

> I page through my wife's *Sarie* and enjoy the beautiful photos of the women. There are few things as pretty as a woman. I believe it is God's 'cherry' on His creation (Lukie Carelsen, Waterkloof Ridge, September 2009).

Masculine surveillance in *Sarie* is further analysed in the next two chapters, examining the hierarchical gender binary of this ethnic particularity, in the form of the *volksmoeder*/the patriarchal overseer and the concomitant gendered circumscription of white Afrikaans women.

DISCURSIVE STRATEGY VIII: *SARIE* AS WHITE SPACE

The final strategy in the formation of Sarielese is the positioning of *Sarie* as white refuge, a re-creation of a lost white world. As South Africa moved from apartheid to democracy, Afrikaner neo-nationalist elements effected a reverse manoeuvre. Afrikaner nationalism's *volk* – a particularist family constellation writ large before and during apartheid – is flipped around and projected into privatised white spaces. Class-based consumerist choice is the tool for the demarcation of these spaces. *Sarie* serves as one such (virtual) white space away from democratic troubling, a stand-in for a lost Afrikaner nation-state. As described above, black others are only allowed in Sarielese to exonerate white selves and remove apartheid's moral pollution. Fully absolved, the resuscitated *volk* in miniature holds sway in white spaces where the terms are set for the allowed heterofemininity. This strategy is explicated further in Chapter 5 on the spatial permutations of Afrikaans whiteness.

In conclusion, *Sarie* is an instrument in the modernisation of a subaltern whiteness aspiring to equal status with the hegemonic and globalised Anglo (bourgeois, heteromasculine) whiteness of 'the English'. This aspiration is about ethical viability – the establishment of *ordentlikheid* – which is again pressing, as subjects work to rinse the stain of apartheid from 'the Afrikaner'. Afrikaner whiteness's ambition of equality with hegemonic Anglo whiteness, and of re-establishing *ordentlikheid*, is figured in 'woman' as the carrier of racial and sexual respectability. The *Sarie* discourse, Sarielese, consists of performatives for a mode of 'doing woman' at a gender-sexuality-race-class juncture that melds local particularity and Western 'universality'. *Sarie* resolves the prevalent tension in Western women's magazines between an assertion of agency versus a submission to oppressive gender relations by articulating two complementary injunctions:

- the neo-liberal and postfeminist call to self-responsibility and self-improvement; and
- the *volksmoeder* dictum of selfless assumption of responsibility for others while also assuming sole culpability for any failure in the accomplishment of heteronormative prescriptions.

This self-for-others woman-as-wife/mother is the 'I' accessed through the 'we'. This is the postapartheid *volksmoeder* form of ethnoracial heterofemininity that *Sarie* advances to rehabilitate 'the Afrikaner' and to reinstate *ordentlikheid*.

To constitute the 'we', Sarielese subjects black people to a blackout by excluding them from *Sarie*'s white world. Black others that are permitted to escape blackout in Sarielese are domesticated to exonerate *Sarie* subjects from apartheid culpability and to assume personal responsibility for apartheid privations, which are dehistoricised and decontextualised. As with black others, so with lesbian others: Sarielese thwarts potential for sexual and gender counter-discourses through an abjecting lockdown on lesbians. In contrast to black others, lesbian others are completely exiled. The *Sarie* world is therefore not only white, but also heteronormative. In contrast, gay male others are permitted, but primarily in the capacity of male feminine vassals channelling the prescripts of the *volksmoeder*, such as the maxim 'from Nataniël' quoted earlier in this chapter: 'You can never ever let yourself feel better if you don't let someone else feel better.'

Subjects access both community and femininity through the consumption of *Sarie*. These machinations are overseen by a hegemonic masculinity, a conflation of God-father-husband-man. This panoptical masculinity is not always implicit, internalised or invisible, as in Western women's magazines, but foregrounded. It actively delimits the *Sarie* subject position, double-marking it as feminine and Afrikaans. In *Sarie*'s version of postfeminism, the concomitant sexuality remains childlike until activated by masculine verification, after which it also turns maternal to assume responsibility when men step outside of conjugal monogamy, as compelled by an ingrained 'manliness'. An always-present threat of male sexual assault regulates gender relations. The patriarchal overseer counteracts whatever inadvertent feminist effects *Sarie*'s neo-liberal espousal of self-actualisation might have. The culturally sanctioned, re-upholstered postapartheid version of the *volksmoeder*, as found in Sarielese, is approached from a different vantage point in the next chapter: that of subjects either abiding by or resisting its interpellation.

3

Silence, Service and White Sex
The Lives of the *Volksmoeder*

THE DEATH REPORTS ARE PREMATURE
In the quest to recoup *ordentlikheid*, dominant discourses such as those of
Sarie magazine draw on the mainstay of the *volksmoeder*, or mother of the
nation, as we have seen. To resist the egalitarian and liberating possibilities
that the democratic subversion of race and gender brings, *Sarie* gives the
volksmoeder a facelift, so to speak, with the aid of neo-liberal and postfeminist
interventions.

    Sarie's turn to the *volksmoeder* to rebut postapartheid potentialities serves
as a reminder of its workings as a privileged signifier. It is the nodal point
where meanings of class, race, ethnicity, gender and sexuality converge
and are adapted to effect social hierarchy, regulation, exclusions and
inclusions among white Afrikaans-speakers and their others. From the late
nineteenth century onwards, the *volksmoeder* discursively morphed from the
kragdadigheid (forcefulness) and *veglustigheid* (combativeness) characteristic of
its deployment in the South African War of 1899–1902 to actively recruiting
subjects for Afrikaner nationalism in the 'feminine' spheres of whites-only
welfare *and* in politics as the twentieth century progressed. By the 1930s, after
white women's campaign for the franchise succeeded, the *volksmoeder* was
used to reorient Afrikaans white women towards self-sacrifice and domestic
cloistering for God, *volk* (people or nation) and fatherland. This group's
domestic containment reached its zenith during Afrikaner nationalism's
control of the state in the form of apartheid. Seen in this historical context,
Sarie's version of the *volksmoeder* in the postapartheid era merely adds self-
improvement and self-responsibility to woman-as-wife/mother. Therefore,

true Afrikaner womanhood means to still be in the service of others – a self-for-others.

The *volksmoeder* therefore forms the pivot of the Afrikaner identity's sex-gender system, as Gayle Rubin (1975) calls the arrangements that turn biological facts into social relations and produce heteronormativity. Conducting an analysis that problematises this system and makes it strange allows for an understanding of heterosexuality as institutionalised and therefore an understanding of 'the ideological and organisational regulation of relations between men and women' (Ingraham 2002: 83). If gender and sex are analysed as institutionally and historically bound to heterosexuality, it allows for the 'unmasking' of heterosexuality's 'meaning-making processes' in relation to 'larger historical and material conditions'.

This chapter explores the actualisation of Sarielese, *Sarie*'s set of discourses, in women's lives. I first sketch the ideological and historical context of the *volksmoeder*, before bringing the concept into the contemporary moment through research with Afrikaans-speaking white women in postapartheid South Africa. This is an investigation into whether the Afrikaner nationalist nodal point of the *volksmoeder* has retained its purchase and, if so, how the subject positions under review are absorbed in and absorbing of postapartheid discourses of democracy and human rights. I argue that reports of the death of the *volksmoeder* are premature since this mode finds new leases on life in reworkings of silence, service and sexuality purposed for white reproduction. Similar to the unexpected findings on *Sarie*, I discover that postfeminism and neo-liberalism provide succour to these three well-worn precepts of the *volksmoeder*. Also, the women interviewed draw on and elaborate *Sarie*'s sanctioned discourse.

WHAT IS A NATIONAL FAMILY WITHOUT A MOTHER?

Benedict Anderson's evocative concept of nations as 'imagined communities' (1991), in which in the mind of each member 'lives the image of their communion' (5), put paid to the idea that nations are 'organic, natural givens, flowering spontaneously into history as the teleological unfolding of a national spirit' (McClintock 1990: 199). Anne McClintock stresses that Anderson inflects his concept differently to Ernest Gellner's (1964) influential assertion that nationalism invents nations where none exist. Instead of nationalism as masquerade, which suggests that 'true' communities could exist, Anderson's relevant contribution here is: 'Communities are to be distinguished, not by their falsity/genuineness, but by the style in which they are imagined' because 'nations are [not] allegorical phantasmagoria of the mind, but [. . .] intricate social fabrications invented through daily contest – in newspapers, schools, churches, presses and popular culture' (McClintock 1990: 199), as is also shown in the previous chapter. The approach adopted here is therefore that, drawing on Aletta Norval (1990: 140), Afrikaner nationalism, as an ideology, is not false consciousness or merely the belief system of a specific class. Rather, it is a 'will to totality'. It works as 'a discourse which attempts to constitute the social as closed, to construct meanings and to mute the effects of the infinite play of differences'.[1] By the 1990s it was understood that Afrikaner nationalism could no longer be ascribed to the pursuit of a 'primordial ethnic agenda' or 'an unchanging, timeless tradition', as both liberal-pluralist and Afrikaner nationalist scholarship had done before (Dubow 1992: 209). Neither was there an 'organic "Afrikaner identity" rumbl[ing] though South African history and mysteriously unit[ing] all Afrikaners into a monolithic *volk*' (Hofmeyr 1987: 95).

Instead, modernity involves a 'narrative of the nation' that conceals disparities such as gender, class and race and 'stitches up' such 'deep internal divisions and differences' (Hall 1992: 297-9; see also 1996) into a family of the nation (McClintock 1993: 64). This narrative, through prescribed continuity and a performative strategy, iteratively seeks to domesticate the disruptive potentials of the cultures of the everyday into a 'community', argues Ali Rattansi (1994: 41). The family resemblance between collective identities, such as nations and ethnicities, is due to a shared 'cultural politics of representation' (74).

Stuart Hall's 'stitching up' resonates with Ernesto Laclau and Chantal Mouffe's (1985: 127-44) concept of 'chains of equivalence', in which different identities or particularities are strung together to construct a hegemonic formation, such as the nation (Chipkin 2007: 195-6). In this book, it is the *volk*. Nationality subsumes or expels differences to present itself as uniform (Hall 1997a: 22). It furnishes the subject with an identity, as it produces a self exclusive of other identities (Eisenstein 2000: 37) through 'frequently violent and always gendered social contests' (McClintock 1993: 61). This is done through the 'invention and performance' of social difference within the 'national family of man' (64). The family legitimises social hierarchy – woman to man, child to adult – 'within a putative organic unity of interests' and therefore sanctions exclusions and hierarchies in the nation (61, 64).

Zillah Eisenstein (2000: 42), in criticising Anderson (1991) for not gendering or racing his 'imagined community', describes the nation as a fraternity for which women, silenced, furnish the borders. The Afrikaner nationalist *volk* had an actual fraternity, or brotherhood, in the form of the Broederbond (League of Brothers), which was heavily invested in not only racial but also gender differences (McClintock 1993: 71). The Broederbond was founded in 1918 as a secret male society that became the hub of a network of Afrikaner nationalist organisations in the *volksbeweging* (people's movement), which extended into the state (Wilkins and Strydom 2012). Central to weaving differences out of sight to constitute the family of the Afrikaner nation is the paradoxical trope of the *volksmoeder* – 'invisibly visible as a symbolic fantasy' conjured in an attempt to neutralise the problem that 'real, actual women' pose for the patriarchal nation (Eisenstein 2000: 43). Nationalism yokes 'woman' into a chain of equivalence with motherhood, nurturance and caregiving, displacing the actual variance among women (41).

Flora Anthias and Nira Yuval-Davis (1989: 7–10) discern the following primary modes of women's engagement in ethnic and national processes: biological reproduction; symbolic figuration of differences and boundaries; reproduction of the national culture; and participation as supporters and nurturers of men. Afrikaner nationalism mostly articulated motherhood with a circumscribed bourgeois prescription of passivity and domesticity, figured in the *volksmoeder* (Walker 1995: 422).

A SHORT HISTORY OF MEANINGS OF THE *VOLKSMOEDER*

The *volksmoeder* signifier served as a nodal point for the production of an 'Afrikaner femininity' from the rise of successive waves of Afrikaner nationalisms after the South African War and throughout apartheid rule (1948–94), reinforced by idealised constructions of middle-class respectability and 'racial purity' (Keegan 2011; Hyslop 1995; Brink 1990). Earlier productions of Dutch/Afrikaans settler women before the war were as 'pioneer woman', 'Voortrekker woman', 'Afrikaner woman' and 'Boer woman' (Du Plessis 2010: 170). A significant 're-gendering' of Afrikanerdom happened during the war, according to Helen Bradford (2000): Boer men were reluctant warriors at the beginning of the war and only eventually forged into a '*volk* of *broeders*' (a nation of brothers) partly as a result of pressure from the women to fight. As Boer fortunes shifted during the war, the women continued to agitate for independence, in contrast to the Boer leadership who became convinced of the need to surrender. In response, the Boer leaders reassigned women from 'heroines' to 'vulnerable victims in need of protection', while promising men the reinstatement of male authority. The rearticulation positioned the defeated *volk* as feminised and the men as having to reassume patriarchal authority, while the women and the feminised language (the 'mother tongue') became symbols for the fledgling *volk*. Patriarchal power replaced fraternity and the 'thousands of Joans of Arc' were rendered mothers of the nation (214, 219–20).

The predominant notions of Boer women in the first few decades after the end of the South African War were as tough, self-sufficient survivors in a harsh environment, where they continued to preserve racial 'purity' in the face of black 'barbarism', instigators who pressurised their men folk to remain at war with the British and as 'religious, freedom-loving, honourable, selfless and incorruptible' (Vincent 2000: 64). The 'orthodox version' of the *volksmoeder* prescribed Afrikaner women's 'highest calling and greatest fulfilment [as] to be found in [their] own home where [they] would physically and morally reproduce the nation'. Contestation of women's suffrage meant that the Afrikaanse Christelike Vrouevereniging (ACVV – Afrikaans Christian Women's Association) in 1907 expressed its opposition to the vote, as 'a feminine woman does not vote', while cultural entrepreneur M.E. Rothmann emphasised maternity before citizenship for women in the 1920s, even as she supported women's suffrage (Du Toit 2003: 166–7, 174). The Nederduits Gereformeerde Kerk (NGK – Dutch Reformed Church), a primary member of the Afrikaner nationalist *volksbeweging*, opposed women's franchise in 1920 by arguing that the vote belongs to 'man as head of the family' and not to 'woman as helpmate' (Gaitskell and Unterhalter 1989: 64).

Revisionist feminist studies have challenged the notion of 'Afrikaner women' as passive receptacles of Afrikaner nationalist discourse (Du Toit 2003; Bradford 2000; Vincent 2000, 1999; Kruger 1991). Marijke du Toit (2003: 155, 176) questions contradictions with regard to the agency of Afrikaner nationalist women in some studies (for example, Brink 1990 and Gaitskell and Unterhalter 1989). She takes issue with Bradford's (2000) description of the 'hegemonic gender identity of "the Afrikaner nationalist"

[as] male', arguing that male dominance does not deny subjectivity to women. She exposes the political effects of *vrouesake* (women's affairs) on Afrikaner nationalist mobilisation, for example, how the ACVV actively participated in the production of Afrikaner nationalist discourse through manufacturing racialised others. In the beginning decades after the South African War, 'a political charge' was added to the earlier productions of the *volksmoeder* (Du Plessis 2010: 170). Afrikaner nationalist women expanded the *volksmoeder* discourse in the 1920s to argue successfully that they were concerned with the well-being of both family and state (Vincent 1999: 69). Louise Vincent finds that middle-class and working-class women both wielded the *volksmoeder* discourse to remain in the Afrikaner nationalist fold while allowing them activism in the public sphere through the Nasionale Vrouepartye (NVPs – National Women's Parties) and the Klerewerkersunie (Garment Workers' Union) (Vincent 2000, 1999). Middle-class Afrikaner nationalist women were heavily involved in racialised welfare activities uplifting poor white people. These activities were carried out by the ACVV and the NVPs, women-only provincial entities separate to the male National Party (NP). Upliftment was intrinsically part of Afrikaner nationalism's political programme (Vincent 1999) for the gendered interpellation of subjects as 'Afrikaners'. But ACVV women raised the hackles of men by speaking in public, a novelty eventually made acceptable by emphasising speakers' maternal and familial characteristics (Du Toit 2003: 167). Granting the franchise to white women in 1930 had a racial purpose for premier J.B.M. Hertzog's NP: to shore up the white vote, which showed women's political rights hinged on utility to *volk* and whiteness (Gaitskell and Unterhalter 1989: 75). The scene was set for Afrikaner women's circumscribed membership of the *volk*: a woman's citizenship was mediated through her maternal function to the *volk*, which hinged on her matrimonial relationship with a man (McClintock 1993: 65). After white women won the franchise, the NP insisted on the absorption of the NVPs, a move resisted but eventually succumbed to. A few women leaders who had risen through the ranks of the NVPs went on to occupy political office. After the NVPs' demise, however, Afrikaner women mostly disappeared from public leadership positions (Vincent 1999: 64). The *volksmoeder* discourse that permitted political engagement had been adapted to redirect white Afrikaans-speaking women to the domestic sphere and away from politics and the labour market after white women gained the vote and the NVPs merged with the male NP (68–9).

As the Afrikaner nationalist state increasingly took charge of welfare functions, such avenues for women's political participation were closed down, resulting in the virtual disappearance of Afrikaner women from the public realm. In return for succumbing to interpellation by 'an exclusive ideology of motherhood and the isolation within the home that it implied' (Gaitskell and Unterhalter 1989: 64), 'Afrikaner women' gained access to whiteness with its concomitant privileges and powers.

After the Second World War, as happened in the West with the promotion of the 'cult of domesticity' aimed at getting women out of the workplace and back into the home (Katz 2000: 144), the daughters of Afrikaans white female factory workers entered the labour market in smaller numbers than their mothers. Victorian domestic ideology held traction neither for the necessarily self-sufficient Boer frontier women of the nineteenth century nor for the Afrikaner nationalist first-wave upliftment feminists (Willoughby-Herard 2010) who reworked the *volksmoeder* as both public and private mother after the war. But an adjusted version made itself felt, corralling Afrikaans-speaking white women back into the home from the 1930s onwards, while facilitating the regendering and re-creation of 'ideal' womanhood (Brink 1990: 274). The basic unit of Victorian bourgeois society was the 'patriarchal autocracy' of the family, based on a male formulation of female helplessness and dependence and reinforced by a bourgeois wife's performance as a 'lady', that is, someone who does not work (Hobsbawm 2003). The performance was of a 'pretty, ignorant and idiotic slave' whose only possibility for demonstrating superiority was through her mastery over servants (279–81).[2] This condition was akin to what Afrikaner women collapsed into after white women gained the vote in 1930, but it was not devoid of politics, as is argued later.

Some white middle-class women formerly active in charity work were able to, through apartheid welfare for whites, use their skills to access remunerative work (Brink 2008: 12). Ambitious middle-class Afrikaner women were still limited, however, to 'feminine' jobs – nursing and teaching – because of their 'nurturing skills'. The 'creation and defence of the Afrikaner home' was Afrikaner women's primary service into the 1960s' (Gaitskell and Unterhalter 1989: 64). A shift is seen in the 1960s: the home was displaced as 'key Afrikaner nationalist base' for defensive nation-building to become 'a focus for the display of newfound prosperity' (65). At that time, the *volksmoeder* was 'moulded in a different, more worldly form'

(Brink 2008: 12), as was seen in the previous chapter on *Sarie* magazine. 'Modern' Western white femininity was imported through translations of books for female adolescents from the United States. However, Western sexual interpellation was intercepted with Afrikaner nationalist tracts aimed at girls, condemning lesbianism and exhorting readers 'not to break out of the rock from which you are carved'. An embrace of Afrikaner nationalist cultural and religious values was the proviso for 'social acceptance' (13).

By the 1980s, woman, home, Western femininity and consumerism served as reflectors of Afrikaner masculine glory, as poet and author Antjie Krog describes:

> The Afrikaner woman, in my view, is a privileged species, unique on Earth. We enjoy the limitless freedom [of] time granted us by cheap, intelligent, black domestic help. So we can select the titbits and specialise in entertaining, or designing clothes, or studying, or gardening, becoming a connoisseur in silver, and making our own pots or poetry for Christmas [. . .] I blame the men for it. They like it that way. The more idle their wives, the more successful they obviously must be. Most have remained totally unliberated, living the way their ancestors did – complaining about the government, hunting up north, or telling racist jokes in clouds of *braaivleis* [barbecue] smoke (in Cloete 1992: 53).

THE WEAPON IN THE HOME

A demonstration of the *volksmoeder*'s double-edged meaning during the early decades of Afrikaner nationalist contestation, and its potential as a symbol for the pacification of women in the public sphere, can be found in the contradictory words and activities surrounding the Jan F.E. Celliers poem *'By die vrouebetoging'* (At the women's protest). In 1915, Afrikaner nationalist poet Celliers contrived a model for the *volksmoeder* in this poem. Subsequently, it was frequently used to call upon and rally white Afrikaans women with a discourse that was eventually turned against their public participation in politics. In that year the poet witnessed the demonstration of 4 000 Afrikaner women agitating for the release of Christiaan de Wet, previously a Boer general in the South African War. His poem replaced the reality of the 'active, women-led demonstration against the state' (Swart 2007: 50) with a passive, patriarchally disposed femininity:

I see her wait, patient, without word
As she has waited for a hundred years, and suffered
I see her win, through suffering just like Him
I see her win for husband and son and brother
because her name is *Vrou* [Woman/Wife] and Mother (Van Rensburg
2012: n.p.; translation from Afrikaans).

This womanhood is verified in heterofamilial relation to manhood. Some 25 years later, in 1940, Afrikaner women again marched to the Union Buildings – 7 000 participated – and confirmed an enduring identification with Celliers's vision of Afrikaner womanhood by quoting his poem in the petition they handed over (Swart 2007: 54). This longevity must have been bolstered by the 1938 commemoration of the Great Trek, with wagons retracing the northward Dutch settler journeys undertaken from the Cape Colony a century before. McClintock (1993: 69) analyses the myth of the Great Trek as showpiece of Afrikaner nationalist historiography, with each trek 'figured as a family presided over by a single epic male patriarch'.[3] These meanings were conjured during the commemoration where each wagon bore the name of a great Great Trek male leader – except one. The exception was a wagon bearing the legacy '*Vrou en Moeder*' (Woman/Wife and Mother), symbolising woman's 'national identity [as] lying in her unpaid services and sacrifices, through husband and family, to the *volk*'. As with other nationalisms, the Afrikaner variety represented men as the 'political and economic agency of the *volk*', while women were the keepers of tradition and the moral and spiritual mission, a gendered division of labour signified by the *volksmoeder* (71).

This conflation of woman/wife as mother received 'intellectual grounding' from Afrikaner nationalists such as sociologist Geoffrey Cronjé (1945; Cronjé and Venter 1958) for the greater part of the twentieth century. Its longevity was assured through its adaptation to changing gender relations, which included the emergence of a limited number of white Afrikaans-speaking women in sectors outside the household. For example, by the 1970s, one of the few white Afrikaans-speaking woman sociologists, Dina Wessels (1972: 383, 397), provided 'scientific' backing for the *volksmoeder* prescription, without naming it as such: a woman's 'highest calling' remained the reproduction of children within the home and only when she was 'partially freed from her family duties' (to be *completely* free could not even be contemplated) may she enter the labour market and then only for part-time work. This intervention should be read against the backdrop of second wave feminism among white Western women, who represent a femininity aspired to by Afrikaner women. Hence, Afrikaner nationalist women who held some status occupying a position outside the home had to keep Afrikaner women 'safe' from the undesirable, feminist part of Western white femininity emerging at the time.

The literal domestication of Afrikaner women through their relegation to the 'private' sphere of the household and their concomitant invisibilisation, particularly from the 1930s onwards, does not divest the identity of political content. Indeed, it paradoxically demonstrates the feminist notion of the private being political. The public/private division serves to obfuscate the identity construction and related group production that happens in the 'private sphere' (Peterson 2000: 58). Studying European women, Dreama Moon (1999) describes the home as a space of enculturation, which reproduces discourses about gender, race, sexuality and class into which women (and men) are inducted.

In Afrikaner nationalism 'women's work' was politicised in the home as a space for the induction of children into Afrikaner nationalist culture and apartheid race relations with domestic workers (Du Plessis 2010: 163-7, 188). The apartheid Afrikaner family was the site of production of racialised, classed and sexualised femininities and masculinities in service of the *volk*. As engaged but marginalised producers of Afrikaner identity, Afrikaner women 'were complicit in deploying the power of motherhood in the exercise and legitimation of white domination' (McClintock 1993: 72). The 'Afrikaner woman' was the weapon in the home. This troubles attempted insulation of the feminine domestic from the masculine political domain and subverts Afrikaner women's denial of political culpability. A rare glimpse of Afrikaner women's political motherhood outside the home was gained in 1986 when it was deployed in the NP's search for pliant black collaborators at the height of anti-apartheid resistance. One of the handful of female NP members of parliament, Rina Venter, led her party's outreach programme, which targeted black women, on the basis of women's 'common interests as mothers and creators of life [. . .] The version of motherhood here is crucial: mothers are still seen in a very domestically limited role, united in a concern for their children' (Gaitskell and Unterhalter 1989: 67). This gender demarcation persists among subjects, who belonged to

Afrikaner nationalist organisations during the apartheid era, as this excerpt from my research shows:

> Ansie (57): [It's] the stereotypical view of womanhood [. . . white and black women] are after all carers [. . .] It is a cultural thing [. . .] In every country it would be different, but [womanhood] is the softer side of humanity [. . . I would want] transparency to talk [to black women] about normal things as with girl friends [. . .] How are your children? You? Your husband?

The suggested topics of conversation between essentialised women, 'black' and 'white', resonate with the *Sarie* instruction of a womanhood that exists for others. The conversational items and their sequence (How are your children; you; your husband) devise a femininity immersed in compulsory hetero-motherhood.

Afrikaans-speaking white women's domestic banishment only ended during the transition to democracy in the 1990s when they emerged from the home to re-enter the public domain in significant numbers. Given this significant change, Ria van der Merwe (2011) and Elsie Cloete (1992) both believe that the *volksmoeder* is no more. Cloete contends that material advances have rendered the *volksmoeder* 'inappropriate' and 'redundant'. Replacing white Afrikaans-speaking women's 'first confinement' as *volksmoeders* (48), their second 'confinement faces [. . .] especially first-world women [. . .] The visual images in the mass media of beautiful women and how to become more beautiful, and therefore more acceptable (to men), place women under even greater patriarchal control than in the past' (54). Van der Merwe (2011) also concludes that the *volksmoeder* is superfluous, interpreting its sexualisation from the 1970s onwards as an indication of 'the Afrikaner woman' being 'downgraded' from 'active' fundraiser and organiser in NP election victories to 'pin-up girls'. Both these authors confuse postfeminist gendering and sexualisation with an end to the *volksmoeder*, but, as I show in this book, postfeminism has in fact provided a new lease on life for the *volksmoeder*.

Elsabé Brink's contention that the apartheid triumph of Afrikaner nationalism emptied the *volksmoeder* of her 'emotional carrying capacity' (2008: 13) is also not borne out by my findings. Closer to the mark is Brink's own comment that 'the generally human values that characterise the *volksmoeder* will [. . .] survive in a different form in the 21st century' (14). I argue that these 'generally human values' and 'characteristics' are more usefully understood as normative injunctions – directives and rules – which manufacture, regulate and discipline subjects at intersections of race, sexuality, gender and class to produce the 'Afrikaner woman'. These 'human values' and characteristics operate as prescriptions directed at individuals to compel them to pursue a particularist ethnoracial model of femininity. Constitutive *volksmoeder* 'values' retain their identitary charge in the democratic context. The 'values' or, more accurately, iteratives that continue to reinscribe subjectivities with the hegemonic Afrikaans white femininity of the *volksmoeder* are: service, silence and sexual accessibility purposed for white reproduction – modes that all draw on ideologies of compulsory heterosexuality and compulsory motherhood.

VOLKSMOEDER INCOGNITO

The transition to democracy decentred the apartheid imaginary and dislocated the 'Afrikaner' identity. The *volksmoeder* became a floating signifier in the postapartheid field, flexible and filled with divergent and clashing contents. Perhaps this is the reason for the impression that this symbol is no more. It is difficult to pin down, as my research finds: the *volksmoeder* evades, is contradictory – a sign of both oppression and liberation. Or perhaps it is more a case of the *volksmoeder* mutating into multiple *volksmoeders*. Its meanings shifted throughout the twentieth century, a fluidity that continues even as its pivot remains woman/wife-as-mother. The conflation of the words 'wife' and 'woman' in the Afrikaans language hardly assists subjects in finding a way out. *Vrou* denotes both these things, an inadvertent admission of the interchangeability of woman and wife, with these concepts merging to form a heterosexual injunction.

My study elicited a discourse in focus groups that mostly indicates a lack of direct identification or associations with the *volksmoeder* among subjects. They ridicule the term. An age difference is notable, as subjects able to recall the *volksmoeder* are mostly between 59 and 65 years old. Nina (65) traces it back to the girls-only, 'formerly' Afrikaner nationalist elite school, Afrikaanse Hoër Meisieskool (Afrikaans Girls' High School) that she attended. The school's use of the symbol of the *volksmoeder* stems from the inclusion of words from the Celliers poem on the cover of the magazine *Die Boerevrouw* (The Boer Woman) in one of the earliest iterations of the trope woman/wife-as-mother. The magazine, launched in 1919 by the Afrikaner nationalist cultural entrepreneur Mabel Malherbe (Stanley and Dampier 2007; Dick 2004), featured the poem's conclusion: '*Ik sien haar win, want haar naam is Vrouw en Moeder*' (I see her win because her name is Woman/ Wife and Mother) alongside a photo of a 1907 sculpture by artist Anton van Wouw (Van Rensburg 2012). The sculpture, called *Die Noitje van die onderveld, Transvaal, Rustenburg sijn distrikt* (Young lass from the back-country, Transvaal, Rustenburg district), depicts a young woman in long dress and bonnet, hands folded in front of her body and head tilted forward, communicating passivity, but also solemn contemplation and possibly mourning. Founded in 1920, the first Afrikaans school in the capital city of Pretoria was divided into what became two elite Afrikaner nationalist schools in 1930: Afrikaanse Hoër Meisieskool (Afrikaans Girls' High School) and Afrikaanse Hoër Seunskool (Afrikaans Boys' High School). The girls' school took the *noitje* image and the line from the Celliers poem, '*Ek sien haar wen*' as its school badge and motto, which are still in use today. However, since 2016, the *noitje* looks up, a change made by the school that provoked outrage from some parents and alumni and was only gradually accepted. Nina describes how she 'resented' the display of the sculpture at the school. Her recitation of the conclusion of the poem met with exclamations of disbelief by the 30-, 32- and 46-year-old respondents in the group.

Respondents' ignorance about the *volksmoeder* can be read as the result of the sedimentation of the political sources of 'femininity-as-motherhood'. For Laclau (1994: 3–4), society presents itself as 'a *sedimented* ensemble of social practices' that are accepted as such and whose founding acts are not questioned, concealing their political character. But the social always overflows the institutionalised frameworks of society, with social antagonisms revealing the contingency of those frameworks. The more the foundation of the social is challenged, the less sedimented social practices can ensure social reproduction and the more new acts of political intervention and identification are required. Democracy has a revelatory function, as it shows us that behind the sedimented forms of social organisation lies the political moment of its originating institutions (Laclau 1990: 173). This book finds that democratic currents of feminist egalitarianism fracture the sedimentation to reveal the politics of the *volksmoeder*. After the official end of apartheid, *volksmoeder* femininity has been challenged in co-constitutive antagonisms by resistant or dissident femininities. Thus, this book finds a multiplication of *volksmoeders*. Playwright Yael Farber evokes *volksmoeder* femininity as follows in her 2012 play *Mies Julie*: The '*boeretannies*' (farmer aunties) who had 'their hair and nails done on Fridays like they were going to battle' (Als 2012). Postapartheid democratic discourses have female-bodied subjects spilling out of this armoured *volksmoeder* container.

Thus, the exact poem and depiction that Nina (65) and other respondents found oppressive, Nerina (32) recovers with her rearticulation of the *volksmoeder* with democratic discourses, particularly feminist empowerment. Describing incidents in the late 1990s after the country's first democratic election, Nerina reworks elements to find her 'feminist roots' at the same school found oppressive by Nina:

> Nerina (32): Affies [Afrikaans Girls' High School] was very, very traditional, but I found my feminist roots there [of] women that move away from boys. We rebel, you're a woman, you do your own thing, you don't wait for men to encourage you [. . .] I was there between 1993 and 1998 so it was exactly in the [democratic] transition period. If I weren't in Affies, I would perhaps not have my strong feminist [. . .], to stand up as a woman. I read [. . .] that from the 1900s to 1914 the Afrikaner woman was actually very strong with the [1915] march they did. Then the National Party came and put the Afrikaner woman back in the kitchen. They were still these strong women, but you were told, 'No, you just have to raise children and there's not really a big role for you.' Only after 1994 did it come out that you as a woman can fully have a career. Only in the 1980s did you thaw and get away [. . .] look at the history of the National Party, there were women ministers only in the 1980s [. . .] Affies drilled it into us: the women who walked to the Union Buildings [in 1915] and there was a [Celliers] poem.

This narrative echoes the socialist Garment Workers' Union's rethreading of Afrikaner nationalist tropes about nineteenth-century resistance to British imperialism to bolster their working-class agenda (Brink 1990: 288), as in the words of garment worker Anna Jacobs: 'We, workers of our state and for all the women in our country, shall take the lead and climb the Drakensberg again' (Walker 1995: 433). They sent their own Kappiekommando (Bonnet Commando) to the centenary celebrations of the Great Trek in 1938, in a 'radically different interpretation of the event to the meaning given to it by its Broederbond organisers' (O'Meara 1997: 5).

Nerina goes further in yoking feminism with *ordentlikheid* to produce an incongruous feminist 'lady' rebutting hegemonic Afrikaner masculinity:

> Nerina: My feminist side was strongly activated. I met the bullies from the [twin male school Afrikaans Boys' High School]. They were chauvinist and they looked down on the women and in counter-reaction my friends and I felt. 'We are strong women and we will resist them' [. . .] The [female] teachers encouraged us to be strong women, to study. A lady always has respect, you stand up when someone enters a class. Those refined things. People respect you because you have good manners and you can express yourself. It was never in my frame that I need a man to make me a successful woman one day. Everything for myself, my dreams, I just have to work hard, study hard. A strong Calvinist work ethic, a lot of pressure on us to excel, there were many opportunities at school. There were no boys, men, to intimidate you.

Nerina's historicisation of the *volksmoeder* enables the recovery of repressed elements of what was a nascent first wave feminism, albeit racist, among Afrikaner nationalist women (Willoughby-Herard 2010): *volksmoeders* as 'strong women' who were political agitators and had 'a strong Calvinist work ethic'; *ordentlikheid*'s lady with good manners, who 'has respect'. It enables remembering how these Afrikaner nationalist feminists' political ambitions were thwarted by their domestication ('put back in the kitchen'; 'No, you just have to raise children and there's not really a big role for you'), despite their being 'strong women'. The recovered elements are brought into articulation with South Africa's post-1994 constitutional democracy's feminism of equal human rights and women's empowerment. A feminist *volksmoeder* is created. The *volksmoeder*'s gender script is radically rewritten in the claiming of voice and self: 'You can express yourself. It was never in my frame that I need a man to make me a successful woman one day. Everything for myself, my dreams.' It becomes performative, in that subjects embody the phrase by physically resisting hegemonic masculinity's 'bullies':

> Nerina: [Typical Afrikaner masculinity is] superior towards women. If you aren't a pretty little doll, then you don't really have a place. The [Afrikaans Boys' High School] boys erected a board [in the street between our schools] with a hippopotamus saying, 'Be careful'. They said we were fat. Their name for the girls was Putco buses. Nobody was

fat. It is an easy way for men to make girls feel insecure. There were a few eating disorders. It was these chauvinist strong men, 'main men' [telling] those typical toilet humour jokes about women. My one friend, because she challenged them, they hit her with a [cricket] bat. One guy was [temporarily] suspended.

The *volksmoeder*'s rearticulation in a dissident subject position shows that, while the 'Afrikaner' exterior of this particular whiteness might suggest its contents were homogeneous, it is predicated upon repetitive internal differentiation and hierarchisation, as seen in the above text. These internal differences were constructed with reference to its constitutive black outside, drawing on colonial divisions. In the report above about those who challenged the status quo, a discourse is exposed in which the feminine other is rendered equivalent to the black other *and* to the animal other. In this complicated dynamic, the internal Afrikaner feminine is reminded of its otherness by being equated with the expelled black other as punishment for failing to submit to normative heterofeminine embodiment, as policed by hegemonic masculinity. The otherness of blackness is amplified by an objectification that invokes colonial constructions of the voluminousness, 'too-much-ness' of the black female other. This is done with the signifier 'Putco buses', which refers to a bus company associated with daily dispatches of buses filled to capacity with black people transported from the townships to work in white South Africa's cities. The close resonance and mutuality of class and race is discernible here, as these were specifically workers from the labour reserves of the dormitory townships surrounding white South Africa's cities. The equation of the Afrikaans girls as 'fat as hippopotamuses' invokes an almost palpable embodiment. Violence punctuates hegemonic masculinity's power to name and discipline, whether through direct assault (using a cricket bat) or through violence 'turned within': feminine subjectivation through eating disorders. The interview excerpt reveals the interconnected racialisation, gendering, classing and sexualisation of the *volksmoeder* disciplinary schema in its marking of bodies and delineation of subject positions. Notably, the regulation draws directly on the colonial schema in which the 'female' is equated with 'animal', 'body', 'blackness', 'object'. Nerina's lack of reflection on the racialisation implicit in the marker 'Putco buses' suggests that this dissident subject position resists the racial script of the *volksmoeder* less than the gender script.

Subjects that fail to acknowledge the *volksmoeder* revert to racialisation. Re-obscuring the *volksmoeder* leads to a misrecognition in which nationalist motherhood equates with black femininity, in a symbolic conflation of black women's bodies with fertility. Thus, in a strange twist, the *volksmoeder* comes to signal the black other. Respondents refer to 'Zuma' as a catch-all name for the wives of South African president Jacob Zuma and to African National Congress Women's League leader Winnie Madikizela-Mandela, who are all designated as *volksmoeders*.[4] Notable about this racialising association is the erasure of the political aims of the term, in that individuals such as the very respondents of this study were the targets of the *volksmoeder* discourse. While some respondents, by their location of the term within the currently dominant African nationalism, detect the similarity in function when compared to Afrikaner nationalism, the lack of recognition of its Afrikaner nationalist location hides the foundational *volksmoeder* directive, which is that of reproduction. This happens despite this directive being currently formative of their own (white) subjectivities, as can be seen below. Whiteness is an (invisibilised) perk substantially alleviating white women's burden of reproductive labour through black female labour. Middle-class whiteness liberates certain female-bodied subjects from the otherwise compulsory feminine duties of reproduction. Therefore, these subjects can afford to reiterate the conflation of motherhood and womanhood as the full extent of reproduction is not demanded of them. Black women serve as their reproductive stand-ins.

A dissident voice challenges other respondents' equation of the *volksmoeder* with black womanhood and redirects the discourse back at 'white' Afrikaans women:

Lida (42): Winnie Mandela. There are *volksmoeders* in all cultures.

Corlia (59): *Volksmoeders* today are the woman in the township [South African term for predominantly black urban areas dating from apartheid] today raising her kids on her own [. . .] and working at ten homes.

Anke (46): That is fundamentally where I depart [. . .] Why does a *volksmoeder* have to be the mama in the township? She's a *volksmoeder* [pointing at respondent Elsebeth who earlier spoke about her 'brown' child].

Corlia: So we are all still *volksmoeders*.

Elsebeth (48): I perhaps teach my children different things [. . .] My mom never took me and my brown friend, who I didn't have, to drop her at her home, so that her children can see there are children staying in [informal housing . . .] My children are exposed to such things and we can't pull up our noses because we live in a luxury house. Look at that child's heart, that's what is important.

Laclau's point is substantiated: challenges to the foundation of the social encourage political innovations to sustain the status quo – in this case, the *volksmoeder* is reworked to become black, which allows the reactivation of the colonial trope of black female fecundity ('raising her kids') while obscuring the political directives that white women are subject to.[5] The dissident intervention in the last excerpt trips up the white talk and reasserts that compulsory motherhood applies interracially.

Compulsory motherhood is co-implicated with female heterosexuality. As Judith Butler (1990: 126) would have it: 'The maternal body is an effect or consequence of a system of sexuality in which the female body is required to assume maternity as the essence of its self and the law of its desire.' The following sections shed light on this co-implication by unpacking how the ethnosexual system built around the *volksmoeder* makes maternal bodies.

MISRECOGNITION OR NOT, THIS IS COMPULSORY WOMAN-AS-WIFE-AS-MOTHER-HOOD

As discussed above, this book finds the political sources of the directive of woman/wife-as-mother sedimented. Subjects therefore delink presumptions of heterofemininity and its attendant naturalisation of 'woman as nurturer/caregiver' from the Afrikaner nationalist project, which predicated womanhood on motherhood in the form of the *volksmoeder*. Therefore, they mobilise woman/wife-as-mother without recognising the political propulsion behind it. The lack of discernment of this connection occurs despite intermittent refusals of the norm of woman/wife-as-mother. A dissident subject reflects on this phenomenon:

Katrien (42): It is culturally acceptable, the women frequently live through their children. I worked at a school [. . .] their whole being depends on it.

Dissident women identify motherhood as an ontological scaffolding: maternity as the mode of life and of being itself for women. Dissidents kick at the joints holding the scaffolding together:

> Katrien (42): I'm not married and I experience the pressure extremely strongly in [Cape Town's northern suburbs]. Specifically because I work with children. It is the parents' first need to know you are married and have children [. . .]
>
> Yvonne (47): And if you are married and you don't have children that becomes an issue [. . .]
>
> Katrien: That is the Afrikaans culture, very typical. If you don't go that way, there is something wrong with you. I'm at that point where I say, 'If only I was married and divorced' because it seems more acceptable [because] the next question is, 'Were you married?' and if you say, 'No', look, then there is something seriously wrong.
>
> Researcher: Why is it so important?
>
> Katrien: Is it not part of that culture, the place and position of a woman?

Thus the dissident position exposes the inner workings of 'Afrikaans culture'. This regulation operates through stigmatisation, in which the childless woman working with children is suspect. She is implictly dangerous and subjected to interrogation about her marital status and history. The line of enquiry suggests she can only be 'made safe' through marriage. A woman never married is a greater threat than a divorced woman, suggesting that any sign of having succumbed to male authority – even if it ended in divorce – is more acceptable than nothing at all. The spectre of 'the lesbian' floats about. The description of unmarried status as 'something wrong with you' evokes another female 'characteristic', of women not being in full command of their mental faculties. Not ever being married amounts to 'something *seriously* wrong'. Astutely, the dissident subject analyses these movements as disciplinary: corralling women into their correct 'place and position'. In the focus group context, the dissident disturbance provokes a normative intervention that exposes the props on which this version of compulsory hetero-motherhood rests:

> Antoinette (36): [laughing] My dad [. . .] supported us children tremendously. My dad said, 'You choose what you want to do, go

with it'. [. . .] I grew up in a very [happy] house. My [cousins], not one
of them is married and it buzzes in the family, the mouths are going:
'Why have they not married? What is wrong? Did marriage put them
off?' It's just strange to people, everybody has such high expectations
of people, that he should have a companion.

This confrontation is cloaked in laughter, but is nevertheless disciplinary: it
is not *whether* something is 'wrong', but that something *is* 'wrong' if someone
remains unmarried. The normative subject's commitment to woman/
wife-as-mother is explicable if the production of gender is understood as
indistinguishable from the production of human beings (Butler 1997: 44).
Gendering hinges on the social regulation of the family as a site for the
reproduction of heterosexual persons 'fit for entry into the family as social
form' (40). The heterosexual family manufactures 'naturalised sexes [. . .] to
secure the heterosexual dyad as the holy structure of sexuality, they continue
to underwrite kinship, legal and economic entitlement, and those practices
that delimit what will be a socially recognisable person' (44). The iterative
'wrong' in the text is the denial of social recognition through the employment
of stigmatisation. Being unmarried is 'strange' because it is the opposite of
acceding to the holy dyad: fulfilling the 'high expectations' that every 'he'
should be linked to a 'companion'. Lacking in this regard evokes policing
('mouths are going'; 'buzzing'). Conformism ensures a 'happy home', the
'prize' of heteronormativity (Steyn and Van Zyl 2009) for the 'neutral' male
everybody, presided over by 'Dad', whose stamp of approval is indicated at
the start of the intervention. The norm of compulsory heterosexuality is
thus reasserted to correct the dissident utterances. Notable is the insertion
of 'choice', which is the primary trope of the overlapping rationalities of neo-
liberalism and postfeminism. The addition of choice gives Dad's directive
a palatable update, but the unfolding tale soon shows that marriage is only
a choice as long as you comply. Another notable feature is that both the
dissident and normative subjects confirm that the latter directly intervenes
to rebut discourses of non-conformism. This is an aggressive pursuit of
subjects that is here read as a specific ethnic variation on the heteronorm,
as compulsory heterosexuality assumes primary importance in establishing
claims on subjects as 'Afrikaners'.

Butler (1993: 107) cautions that resistance predicated merely on failure
to accomplish an identity prescription – in this case of hetero-motherhood

– is politically inadequate. The reason: it does not rework the injunction that produces the failure in the first place. This is exemplified by the subject position expressed as follows:

> Yvonne (47): People always say to me, 'But one has to have children.' My reaction is, 'The only thing you have to do is to breathe, otherwise you die.' They will never ask, 'Why don't you have children?' Many people just assume I don't have children [. . .] because I took this selfish decision because of my work. It is absolutely not true [. . .] It is because we had problems and decided that's it.

Yvonne exonerates her supposed lack as the result of biological reasons and not 'selfishness', suggesting that pursuing her own career would amount to selfishness. This justification contradicts her own problematisation of the prescription of reproduction, a prevarication that undermines the potential for resistance.

This is not to say that failure of womanhood-as-conjugal-heteromaternity can never dislocate the *volksmoeder* order. Instances when this possibility arises are when a lack of accomplishment opens a door to equivalences among differences. For example, a subject creating an equivalence between 'othering due to failure of the heteronorm', on the one hand, and 'othering due to failure of whiteness', on the other. If one stitch of *volksmoeder* prescription comes undone, the whole pattern can start to fray, as in the following moment in which an equivalence is drawn between everyday heteronormative and racist interrogations:

> Tani (32): The next question when you are married is [. . .], 'Why don't you have children? [. . .] You've been married [many] years. What is wrong with you?' [. . .] But one does not have the skills to deal with that because it is not taught at home [. . .] How do you handle people who aren't like you? How do you handle racist people? [. . .] These are those uncomfortable things that you rather [. . .] that is why you won't tell people to stop being racist because it is so uncomfortable. You rather sit there and you [. . .] okay, I try not to think about it and whatever and you try to get out of that moment, but actually Afrikaans people never sit and talk about [. . .] real issues. It is always superficial, dirty jokes around the braai [barbecue]. [. . .] The things that are

important just never get discussed. [. . .] It is also one's right not to have children.

Emma (46): You have to be able to say, 'You know what? I hate children.'

Questioning becomes possible: 'How do you handle people who aren't like you?' The momentary exit route of refusal opens up: 'It is also one's right not to have children.' For the dissident subject position, it even allows the ultimate repudiation of the *volksmoeder* dictum: a woman who exclaims, 'I hate children.'

THE 'SMALL POWER' OF 'THE AFRIKANER WOMAN': SILENCE, SERVICE AND WHITE SEX

Nascent Afrikaner nationalist feminists were 'jealously and brutally denied any formal political power', with 'small power' all that remained for Afrikaner women (McClintock 1993: 72). As a former woman leader, E.C. van der Lingen of the Cape NVP, asked five years after the NP captured state power: will the male nationalists allow 'woman' to help build a *volk* in 'her own independent way' or 'will it forever be her role to be only a shadow', banished to the household and behind-the-scenes party support (Van der Lingen 1953: 147)? Alas, as the second half of the twentieth century unfolded, the latter was her lot. Identities available to women in Western patriarchy are defined by locating them in hetero-relation to men: wife, mother, daughter, girlfriend (Jackson 1999: 130). Relegated to the home, this is the world that became entrenched for Afrikaner women. This section explores this particularist version of heterofemininity, as construed within the disciplines of silence, service and sexuality purposed for white reproduction that give effect to woman/wife-as-mother.

The trope of 'the silent Afrikaner woman' emerged strongly in the early years of Afrikaner nationalism after the South African War. The 1915 Celliers poem quoted above emphasises 'her' characteristics of speechless passivity: suffering; waiting patiently, wordlessly, eternally ('for a hundred years'). Celliers's vision for Afrikaner women retained traction, as demonstrated at the 1940 protest march when women quoted it in their petition. He contributed another poem to the Afrikaner nationalist canon, *Die Boere-vrouw* (The Boer Woman), again capitalising on the trauma of the South African War to link womanhood with silence, obedience and reproduction of the *volk*:

Seriousness is her being: she goes her way in silence
obedient on the long road of suffering
South Africa, your mother in her melancholy
that gives a nation to the world (Celliers 1908: 56; translation from
Afrikaans).

The imperative of silence extends well into the 1960s and 1970s, suggesting
a mostly successful insulation of Afrikaner women from the disruptions of
rising second wave feminism in the West. By the 1960s the 'can-do' aspect
of the *volksmoeder* had been replaced by the passivity of a middle-class 'lady'.
When the Afrikaner nationalist state took the war against the *Swart Gevaar*
(Black Peril) and the *Rooi Gevaar* (Red Peril) across 'the border' in the 1960s,
women were instructed by Afrikaner nationalist men to 'stand together' with
'their' men: this support would yet again be silent, as 'guardians of the inner
room that listen with an intuitive ear to the deepest stirrings of a *volk*' (Brink
2008: 13). During the increased militarisation of South African society in
the late 1970s, the NP yet again called upon Afrikaner women to be loyal,
'silent', 'spiritual' soldiers', 'a secret weapon' against the 'total onslaught' of
'Communist terrorism' (Gaitskell and Unterhalter 1989: 66). Therefore, by
the time of the militarist reform phase of apartheid, Afrikaner women could
still only listen and not speak, but were by then cloistered not just inside the
home, but in an 'inner' room. They were so deeply hidden as to be 'secret' –
the spiritual guardians, like their mothers and grandmothers, but now also
weaponised, as the military mood of the time demanded. Nevertheless, they
remained tucked away in the domestic sphere, the weapon in the home.

My study confirms the continued salience of silence across apartheid
and postapartheid situations:

Leah (49): You are seen at [the] table and never heard. We did not
grow up where you speak at the table [. . .] [It was] quite strict [. . .]
Dad speaks.

Katrien (42): [My brother (46)] is a typical Afrikaans man [. . .] When
he speaks, the woman stays quiet because he's speaking.

These two excerpts point to the longevity of the silencing of women in white
Afrikaans middle-class culture, which suggests that it remains a primary

prop for hegemonic gender relations. The following quotation is a reflection by a dissident subject on the intergenerational transfer of silence over time as the correct feminine mode:

> Andriette (56): I married into a [. . .] 1950s-type family where the man is the breadwinner [. . .] My mother-in-law was dependent her whole life, she simply fell in with everything [my father-in-law] said [. . .] That kind of position of power [. . .] I hoped to overcome it in my own marriage [. . .] But at times my husband sees it as I don't respect him if I differ from him [. . . as] the man makes the decisions. My father-in-law said, 'Don't worry, Mommy' and patted [my mother-in-law] like this.

This text suggests increased dependency as a result of increased domesticity. Pats on the arms of women relegated to small power. A pat to silence her. Demonstrating Michel Foucault's (1998) alert to the said running parallel to the unsaid, an Afrikaner nationalist tract from 1972 on prescribed Afrikaner womanhood, its all-encompassing myth-making ambitions clear from its title '*Die Vrou*' (Woman), reveals the things said in relation to those unsaid:

> Woman is unmissable for man's self-confidence [. . .] When he loses confidence in himself, in his work or in the world, it is his wife's admiration that keeps him going [. . .] Through the centuries woman has served as a mirror to provide a man with the enchanting image that he is twice his normal size. How on earth would poor man continue to make laws, write books and cast the world's biggest judgements if he could not at every meal see himself twice his normal format in the mirror that his wife holds up to him? ('Dr Goedhart' 1972: 368; translated from Afrikaans).

This directive, attributed to a male author bearing a pseudonym with the revered title 'Doctor', writes back to Virginia Woolf's (2005: 35) criticism almost half a century earlier, when she said: 'Women have served all these centuries as looking glasses possessing the magic and delicious power of reflecting the figure of man at twice its natural size.'

Woman-as-mirror is the collection of practices of heterosexual femininity required to project the enchanting image of 'man' at double his size. It rests on an 'ethic of service to men' (Jackson 1999: 167). Docile female bodies are produced as women police themselves and are policed to fulfil the heterosexual imperative of attracting and pleasing men, sexually and otherwise. These practices range from the micro-level ('how they sit and avoid eye contact'; being 'sexually attractive'), to supplying unpaid home-based labour, to withdrawing from public spaces (130). In an essay titled 'Husband-Right and Father-Right', Adrienne Rich (1979: 215) describes the patriarchal construction of the home as women's presumed sphere: it serves as the sphere of the emotional and the sexual from which men emerge to compete in the public sphere of power and to which they return 'for mothering, for access to female forms of intimacy, affection and solace unavailable in the realm of male struggle', as per the above prescriptions of 'Dr Goedhart'. The feminine ethic of service therefore encompasses the material, the affective and the sexual.

To enlarge husbands, women co-constitutively are required to 'dwindl[e] into a wife' in which the self is redefined and reshaped in response to 'the wishes or needs or demands of husbands' (Bernard 2002: 212) – that is, to serve men. For white Afrikaans women, this dwindling involves adopting a position of immaturity. This was also seen in the *Sarie* discourse in Chapter 2, in a reiteration of colonial binarist hierarchies of man/woman and adult/child, where the first term in each category holds greater status, including the privilege of humanisation. Infantilisation can be seen in the quote from Andriette above and in this one from Louise:

> Louise (43): Only after my dad's death did [my mom] say she always felt like one of four children.

In preparation for marriage, the diminution starts in girlhood, which inaugurates an adult/child hierarchy that exerts its power when the woman reaches adulthood – and beyond, even when she is much older:

> Andriette (56): There's probably a part of you that will always remain a child, where you carry these fears and respects within yourself [. . .] the *ooms* [uncles] [. . .] My husband is also an *oom*, but [. . .] I unconsciously fall back in this hole of, ' 'scuse me, I'm the little girl' [. . .], of, 'Listen to the uncle'. It is difficult for me to contradict them. I did not grow up like that where you just take them on and say, 'Oh really?'

Silencing ('listen to the uncle') works at the subjective level as a discipline of self-silencing imbricated with self-diminution, manifested in childlikeness.

Silencing further enables the ethic of women's service to men, a mainstay of the *volksmoeder* construction. The heterosexual union as a service relationship can be traced back to Afrikaner nationalist 'iconography of domestic service' (McClintock 1993: 72) of the first half of the twentieth century, which positions 'woman' as 'servant to the *volk*' (Cloete 1992: 51) and therefore to the family, as the cornerstone of the *volk*. As the focus of Afrikaner women's existence should be the home, this is where the labour starts, strictly delineated in terms of gender. Afrikaner nationalist sociologist Cronjé directed that a mother should be 'an examplar of understanding, love and subservience' (Cronjé and Venter 1958: 66). Subservience is to possess the qualities of a servant. The prescription shows remarkable longevity, as regimented hetero-duty continues in contemporary relations. The only respite is an adjustment that serves to domesticate women's shifting social position: women are allowed to work for a period, but then only in accordance with the prescribed gender division of extra-household labour. The brief public sojourn must end back in the home:

> Lindie (43): My dad [. . .] brought [us] up to be subservient [. . .] You had no aspiration to be a director. You will be a secretary and then a mom and a housewife.

Dissident positions highlight how, in the absence of women's concerted resistance, household labour remains outside the masculine purview of activities:

> Nita (65): [There were] a lot of small wars before [my husband and I] got where we are [. . .] It frequently came down to the care of the children [. . .] I said to him [that] if we wanted women to do more, then women would have had children on their own.

The gender labour division is inculcated during childhood and normalised and transferred intergenerationally, as was also found in research by Sinteché van der Merwe (2011). Pieta (35) describes her father as someone who 'never made food or washed dishes'. In her family, my sister's children, for example, now have men's jobs and women's jobs. Her little boy told his sisters he doesn't have to help with dishes because he helps with mowing the lawn.

Daughters may be expected to act as substitute servants to their fathers when their mothers are unavailable.

The last excerpt surfaces the performatives of a dialectic within which gender distinction determines male exemption from household labour, while household labour works as mode through which gender distinction is entrenched and masculine power further expanded. In another remarkable example of longevity, apartheid and postapartheid Afrikaans white men get to set the parameters of feminised service within the domestic domain, even determining what would be regarded in this order as 'woman's ambit': the exact terms of food consumed:

> Ansie (57): My dad wasn't an adventurous eater. Saturday evenings everything is *braaied* [barbecued . . .] Sundays my mom had to cook [. . .] very specific things [. . .] no alternative vegetable dishes, green beans, rice, potatoes, meat [. . .] Chicken is not big [. . .] It was quite [. . .] rigid.

> Nerina (32): Few vegetables, a lot of red meat, a lot of rice, chicken maybe, but never fish [. . .] Not too spicy or too many herbs [. . .] My mom can make tasty food, but he wants it bland.

In the older generation of women between 60 and 75 years old, the 'service of doing everything' could include daily regimens of women rising before their husbands to cook and serve them breakfast in bed. The labour gender division in the family underpins a social gender division:

> Nerina (32): I refuse to be that humble Afrikaner woman who is now suddenly helping in the kitchen and not sitting at the *braai* with the men. I know my mother-in-law thinks I am this terrible rebellious Johannesburg woman.

With service to men as the mark of femininity, its co-constitution is leisure as the preserve of men. Sometimes feminine service and masculine leisure combine through women's labour, in an expansion of gender-divided activity beyond the walls of the home:

> Nerina (32): [My dad] phones my mom [. . .] 'You have to do this and that' and my mom says yes [. . .] [like she is] his personal assistant [. . .] His hobby is cars, but he doesn't do anything, my mom does it all [. . .] Holidays, they go where he wants to go. He loves 4x4 driving, then they go for a week to the Kalahari and my mom says, 'Never again'. A month later, they're going again.

Sexual disruption may not translate into gender disruption, as the gender division of labour extends to otherwise abject lesbian relationships. Male-identified women in lesbian couples claim masculine privileges:

> Pieta (35): My mom thinks it's very funny because when X and Y [lesbian couple] visit my aunt [X's mother] and them, then X lies on the couch and Y helps in the kitchen.

But the prescriptions for feminine service are challenged, either through a conscious pursuit of different gender relations or in challenging the parental status quo, even in households in the *volksmoeder*'s sway:

> Pieta (35): I asked [my dad] if he knows how many sugars he takes because mom always puts his sugar in and she stirs it for him. Then he just laughs.

These resistances are further explored later in this chapter.

As mentioned above, the heterosexual union as a service relationship includes a division of affect, in which silence is again indispensible. In white Western femininity, women assume responsibility for 'making the relationship work' (Langford 2002: 231), dividing emotional from intellectual labour, the latter seen as a male preserve – a division that 'founding father' of sociology, Émile Durkheim, approved of (Jackson and Scott 2002: 5). Hegemonic masculinity includes the claim to emotional incapacity (Heaphy, Donovan and Weeks 2002: 253). *Volksmoeder* femininity manages affect as an element belonging to the family sphere on behalf of a masculine centre – whether wife in relation to husband or daughter in relation to father:

Andriette (56): It [is] the woman who keeps the family together, who makes the sacrifice, who says, 'For the sake of everybody [. . .] I will do myself a little short [. . .] so that everything doesn't fall apart.'

Elsebeth (48): My mom [was] definitely [. . .] not submissive, but the peacemaker. My dad was a difficult man. I understand why he had issues [. . .] he was the youngest [. . .] never good enough for grandma. When he arrived at home at 5 p.m. the food had to be on the table. He didn't like chicken [or fish], so we never had [that . . .] My mom kept him happy because she didn't want confrontation [. . .] but we were never brought up that girls are inferior.

Exits from matrimony occur, but remain fraught, signalling feminine failure across generations. Many women never leave:

Emma (46): My sister left her husband, to my mom's great shame because now two of her children are divorced. She has thus failed as a woman [. . .] My aunt said, 'If I could leave your uncle 40 years ago, I would have.' I wonder how many of that generation of women [would have done so if they could].

Elsebeth's affective labour as daughter to the 'difficult man' is clear from the excerpt above. Despite her insistence that this emotional economy of wife and daughters in relation to husband and father does not denote lesser status for women, the effect of the arrangement is compulsory matrimony for women, as can also be seen in the next text. The marriage must continue, in abidance with the performative "til death us do part':

Elsebeth (48): My mom couldn't take it anymore. She didn't commit suicide, she got cancer and died within three weeks and now she's free from that [. . .] She didn't have it in her to leave him [. . .] For better or for worse, you stick with the guy you married.

Silence is again indispensible, deployed in relation to sex to reinforce the matrimonial directive – another feature of this ethnosexual configuration that continues into the postapartheid era:

Tani (32): [. . .] I still think it takes a lot of guts to divorce, especially in Afrikaans circles.

Elsabé (41): There is a stigma-ish [. . .]

Tani: There is always somebody who says, 'But why? Have you seen the [church] minister?' [. . .] I think we are not prepared because we never talk about sex in the home and we never talk about relationships. Because things happen behind doors, you don't know what it is like to live with someone else. You are not at all prepared for what comes. I married straight out of home. I always thought we were terribly *verlig* [enlightened] and you know, but my mom never spoke to me about sex [. . .] My husband and I are are struggling to have children and it is very difficult because now [. . .] we have to talk about sex. Nobody ever spoke to us about sex and now the doctor is also talking to you about it. You want to die because you are not prepared for these conversations. I think it is the same with divorce.

Silence meets service meets sex in a gender division of knowledge/ignorance. In analysing this phenomenon, Nancy Tuana's (2002) conception of power/ knowledge-ignorance, to emphasise the politics of ignorance, is apposite. She asks: Who is advantaged and who disadvantaged? This composite stresses how ignorance is actively cultivated and that its cultivation is for political ends. The politics of ignorance links with the politics of sexuality. Sexuality is a public, everyday process of power relations (Bell and Valentine 1995: 146). Apartheid's everyday politics of sexuality involved 'unthinking' (that is, normalised) intergenerational transfer of sex as, in respondent Ansie's words, 'something that you use in order to have children the day you married': 'if I think back, it was a scandal to enjoy sex.' She finds 'Victorian' echoes (when 'you were buttoned up to under your chin') and, indeed, she is able to trace the directive back intergenerationally to the late Victorian epoch:

Ansie (57): It comes from my gran and then my mom. [They were] always told the day they arrived home pregnant, they could take their stuff and go. It was a terrible shame [. . .] My mom was a social worker, so she worked with all these unmarried mothers, so there was always a finger under my nose.

Read alongside silences, which are not merely repressive, but also generative of subjectivity (Foucault 2004: 29–30), discourses about sex are both disciplinary and productive. Said and unsaid are complementary: unapproved pregnancy is spoken and declared taboo; sex remains unspoken. Neither the possibilities of pleasure nor the realities of violence are allowed into this discourse. Later in this chapter, possibilities for the loosening of these strictures are discussed in relation to postfeminist and neo-liberal articulations. The silences about pleasure fit with the heteronormative directive that 'the primary purpose of human sex is reproduction' (Tuana 2004: 220). In the Afrikaner nationalist paradigm, a patriarchal 'familialism' based on the 'principle of reproduction' demanded from its subjects 'an unceasing aspiration to create a family', as apartheid sociologist Cronjé insisted (Cronjé and Venter 1958: 98, 101). As can be seen from the above excerpt, the family to be created fits into a strict framework. This sexuality is in service of the *volk*. Sexual activity outside the ethnonationalist fold is met with expulsion.

In answering Tuana's question about who benefits and who does not from a regime of (sexual) ignorance for women, the effect is to decline (sexual) agency to white Afrikaans heterosexual women and to produce a femininity that 'tiptoes around his chair' (focus group 1). My research finds the normalisation of the masculine sexual prerogative – with its implicit violence – across the apartheid and postapartheid eras. Ansie's mom always told her (note the use of the words 'man' and 'girl'):

> Ansie (57): The day a man marries he doesn't want someone [. . .] with experience. He's looking for a chaste *ordentlike* girl [. . .] I always believed my mom. There were strict rules [. . .] The stereotype is men can be looser [. . .] They are more accommodated because a man's needs are different. They are more physically oriented.

As described above, this ethnofemininity assumes an infantilised form. Feminine childlikeness includes being without 'experience', in oppositional co-construction with male knowing and concomitant sexual licence. Virginal display remains a prerequisite for this femininity into the twenty-first century. White Afrikaans femininity requires a demonstration of a lack of sexual agency and knowledge. Subjects recall officially sanctioned discourses, such as in *Sarie* women's magazine, as contrasting with the discourses of female sexual initiative emanating from English-language women's magazines, such as *Cosmopolitan*:

> Liesl (64): *Cosmo* says, 'This is how you can give him the best blowjob or how he can give you the best orgasm.'
> Anke (46): 'This is how to pick him up and how to identify the chancer who you don't want to go [home] with.'
> Researcher: Why doesn't *Sarie* address it?
> Liesl: It is not *ordentlik*.

Subjects identify 'sexual purity' and lack of sexual agency as elements that receive *Sarie*'s sanction:

> Nina (65): *Cosmo* says how you get a man in your bed and *Sarie* tells you how to keep him out of your bed.

This contemporary *Sarie* directive suggests a male hunter/female prey division persevering into postapartheid times. It echoes across decades in the norms propounded in the above-mentioned 1970s Afrikaner nationalist guidebook *Die Vrou*: 'Man cannot understand when woman alleges that she is unconscious of encouraging him. He also cannot understand why she looks over her shoulder when she runs away from him' ('Dr Goedhart' 1972: 369). Man/husband is the sexual agent and decion-maker and therefore the knower, in co-constructive opposition to the virginal-yet-coquettish-ignorance of woman/wife. This power/knowledge-ignorance regime hides the violence of the 'difficult man', the man who gets to silence and to speak.

> Emma (46): [My mom of 70-plus years old] says, 'But if your husband has to have sex, my child, then you have to [oblige].'
> Nina (65): Uh-uh – I almost fell off my chair.

> Andriette (56): The submission expected of women [. . .] sexual types of things [. . .] You had to kiss all the *omies* [uncles] and tolerate if they touched you. What standing did you have if you said this *omie* [uncle] is touching me? Many women were too scared to say anything.

Ansie (57): [The sexual part of my life is] amputated because of this collective consciousness that it isn't *ordentlik*. It's an Afrikaner thing. Other cultures are more open.

These excerpts show that violence includes compulsory male sexual access and female sexual submission, inside and outside of marriage, leaving an 'amputated' sense of self. To the division man/husband-woman/wife can be added father-uncle/girl. A dissident subject problematises the predication of 'woman's value' on 'man's happiness' – a predication that hinges on sexual compliance, as advanced by Afrikaans women's magazines such as *Sarie*.

AGENCY AND RESISTANCE: 'I DIDN'T KNOW WOMEN COULD OR MAY SOUND LIKE THAT'

Dissident women find divergent responses within families to the dominant form of femininity. Katrien's aunts were 'assertive', had 'opinions' and 'thoughts', liked 'debates' – they were 'strong women'. She didn't 'know women could or may sound like that', as, in contrast, her grandmother represented 'the conservative, more "little doll" side of "you have to dress, speak, look a certain way"', a position that is servile and bows before a masculine line of authority. The 'assertive feminine' side provides identitary openings: 'As little girl I always thought [. . .] I want to be [like my strong aunts].'

The dissident discourse acknowledges the 'unfeminine' possibility of women who are angry and 'hard' – and violent – in reaction to the reproductive service norm during apartheid, thus creating space for resistance to the normative *volksmoeder* discourse's thwarting of agency. This is a resistance against the invisibilisation of women's domestic work and against the normalisation of the masculine enclosure of women, disguised as 'safety':

Emma (46): My mom's eyes became rock hard [. . .] and flat from frustration from sitting at home with three tiny children [. . .] It must be soul-destroyingly boring however much you love your child [. . .] My dad said, all proud, 'No wife of mine will work.' Of course, I will work. You can see your mom is not happy [but] your mom wants you to do the same as her because to her it is a [. . .]

Nina (65): Confimation.

Emma: Not just a confirmation, but it is safe.

In the context of a research interview with guaranteed anonymity and with an interviewer who is also a white Afrikaans-speaking woman, an occasion for insider 'talk among women' arises: two respondents with fathers highly dependent on their wives remaining within *volksmoeder* strictures wished out loud that their fathers would die before their mothers as they (the interviewees) were not willing to look after their fathers (individual interviews 3 and 4). One added that her father would 'end up a bum' without her mother (individual interview 3). These narratives resonate with Elsebeth's story quoted above that her mother's only way out of the marriage with her father was to develop a fatal illness. Only death can part the *volksmoeder*'s male and female subjects – such is its normative weight for those clinging to it for meaning. In this case, the respondents were aged 32 and 35, confirming the family's centrality in the intergenerational transmission of the *volksmoeder* gender configuration and a postapartheid longevity of essential elements of this configuration. This contains a hint at the extent of resistance that is possible. A sense of containerisation – of being enclosed in an identification – seems to remove options for radical resistance from women in such heterosexual arrangements. However, the respondents' problematisation of their parents' relationships suggests some refusal of the transfer of these arrangements to the next generation.

The political possibilities outside the container are also curtailed by neo-liberalism and postfeminism, which obfuscate actual gendered, classed and raced contexts, causing women to individualise (that is, decontextualise and depoliticise) their failure to achieve normative femininity (Budgeon 2011: 285–90).

Neo-liberal and postfeminist erasure of the political context causes subjects to misunderstand power effects as their own, individual failings. Defensively, agency is claimed and victimhood denied. Agency becomes reinvented as an embrace of oppressive conditions while the actual destruction of human potential is vehemently refuted, as in this narrative quoted earlier in this chapter:

Elsebeth (48): My mom [was] definitely [. . .] not submissive, but the peacemaker. My dad was a difficult man [. . .] My mom kept him happy because she didn't want confrontation [. . .] but we were never brought up that girls are inferior.

Articulation with neo-liberalism and postfeminism gives sustenance to older discourses of gender essentialism and biological determinism, including ideas such as '1960s-style sexual liberation'. The following discursive elements are drawn on to resist, but ultimately reinforce the *volksmoeder*: 'ruler of the domestic roost'; 'the female neck to the male head'; 'a public prude and a private whore'; and 'the "choice" of compulsory motherhood'.

In discourses that hide the retrenchment of women's humanity, their relegation to the domestic sphere is recalibrated as making them powerful because a woman is the 'ruler of the domestic roost'. Strategic self-minimisation is revered as an exercise in power: if she is 'strong', she has to diminish herself to 'keep the crown on his head', even with 'lesser' masculinities, such as white men who are not Afrikaners. In what Katerina Deliovsky (2010) calls 'derived power', power is claimed in a formulation of 'woman-as-neck to man-as-head':

Pieta (35): My dad will definitely think he is is the head of the household, but my mom makes him think so [. . .] He is the head and my mom is the neck, she turns him where she wants him.

Volksmoeder femininity is a cumulative learning to keep masculinity intact, with women's self-actualisation read as 'damage' to men:

Pieta (35): Subtly, in her extremely feminine way, she gets her way without damaging her husband [. . .] The longer you are married, the more you understand how to go about achieving things [. . .] as though it is his plan.

The trope of 'womanly wiles' emerges, that is, of women's 'natural' disposition towards 'manipulation'. This can be understood as a reworking of power, as the subordinate ('Afrikaner' women) attempting to extend its agency by reformulating its navigation in a field hegemonised by an(other), that is, 'Afrikaner' men. The dissident subject position declines this schema, while paradoxically also summoning the stereotype of 'womanly wiles' as a mode for self-actualisation:

> Emma (46): My gran told me that [man-as-head to woman-as-neck] but no man is my head. I am my own head. Women [. . .] who say, 'You are the head' have ways to manipulate and there is guilt [. . .] My mom does it like this [emits a deep sigh], then my dad says, 'Jeez, okay.'

Notable is the longevity of 'the female neck to the male head' narrative, as 46-year-old Emma reports that her grandmother used it while 35-year-old Pieta reproduces it seamlessly. Its sedimented political origins could be the Afrikaner nationalist prescription of 'the Boer woman' as 'being second-in-command' and 'accepting her husband's supremacy over everything' (Cronjé and Venter 1958: 67).

'The female neck to the male head' is a heterosexual arrangement and turns on sex. Further to Foucault's (1998) discernment of a regulatory discourse of sexuality firmed up in the nineteenth century, Victorian conceptualisations in the nineteenth-century Cape colony posited men's sexuality as formed by 'uncontrollable passions and enticement by women' (Scully 1995: 345). The twenty-first-century version of these heterosexual performatives is notably similar, boosted by biologisation and 'nature':

> Elsebeth (48): All women are born with skills, all men are born with testosterone, so they use it. We use our feminine skills [. . .] if it is necessary to be a bit flirty. He uses his testosterone to manipulate me. It's fine, it's nature. It happens with animals.
>
> Anke (46): But it's unconscious [. . .] almost automatic.

The *volksmoeder*'s sexual dichotomy is normalised through the articulation of colonial remnants with postfeminist biological determinism: the male sexual prerogative (Herbert 2002; Potts 2002) as emanating from 'nature' and 'woman as wily manipulator' of 'men's sexual weakness' (Walter 2011; Attwood 2009; Kipnis 2006) reinterpreted as an 'automatic' skill. Part of the postfeminist innovation in this text is that both ascriptions are 'in-born'. The 'unstoppable male biological sexual urge' ('testosterone') is reinscribed as 'manipulation', in a contradiction that accidentally hints at its constructed nature and at the contestation over the terms of sexual access.

The discourses surfaced in this book do not reveal constructions of black male sexual peril that are comparable to discourses from the 1910s to the 1940s, a time when Afrikaner nationalist recruitment was at a sexual fever pitch, against a backdrop of generalised panic about white 'purity' across colonies (Keegan 2001; Hyslop 1995; Stoler 1989). Therefore, forgetting the origins of the *volksmoeder* identity includes amnesia about its relation to sexualised black bodies. The unequivocal colonial demand of marriage to secure white women's respectability (Scully 1995: 345) has been diluted with postfeminist sexualisation. Postfeminist individualisation assists with the relaxing of the postapartheid heteronorm for some Afrikaner women, as heterosexuality is reoriented to 'self-discovery' and 'attempting happiness' while 'not necessarily married'. While regulation of femininity is still focused on marital status, a 'mental shift' allows the acceptance of daughters' or own engagement in unmarried sex and maternity without marriage. Drawing on the '1960s sexual revolution' and its 'natural' suggestion that it is a 'normal need to have sexual intercourse with another person', combined with neo-liberal psychotherapeutics, marriage becomes less necessary to justify heterosexual intercourse for some subjects. However, this is a double standard, as male homosexuality can only be verified by the heterosexual other if 'monogamously uncelibate'.

Another adjustment is to the colonial prescription in terms of which working-class women and women of colour were denied respectability by virtue of their racial and class categorisation, while white women in co-productive contrast had to be chaste to be respectable (Scully 1995: 345). My research finds a narrative of 'sweet and naughty, with pearls' that attempts to negotiate persistent remnants of the colonial demand with the sexualisation demanded by postfeminism. Men want 'wholesome sweetness with a touch of naughtiness': women who are 'prudish in public but a whore in the bedroom' (focus group 2). The following narrative is with reference to the sanctioned discourse of *Sarie*:

> Anke (46): That thing of [. . .] I am going to put my pearls on [. . .] the reason why it works is because of perceptions that, for example, *Sarie* creates.
> Liesl (64): We want you to also be good in bed. But you must also be ladies [. . .] there is this *ordentlikheid* that has to go together [with being a woman]. You can't go walk in the street like a man.
> Anke: With a cigarette in your hand.

The English word 'lady' seems a residue from earlier editions of white English-speaking South African (WESSA) femininity and from Afrikaner nationalists' early twentieth-century manoeuvres in whitening Afrikaner subaltern whiteness with respectability, similar to male African nationalists' deployment of respectability in the disciplining of wayward black women (Thomas 2006: 466; Hyslop 1995: 60).

POSTFEMINIST TRIUMPH: CHOOSING MOTHERHOOD IS 'LIKE CHOOSING A CAR'

Especially productive is the postfeminist trope of free female agency as the ability to self-impose compulsory feminine regimes by 'choice'. In a narrative of 'woman's choice to be a natural nurturer', the neo-liberal and postfeminist trope of 'choice' is wielded to naturalise femininity-as-nurturance and to essentialise sex difference while denying concomitant subjection effects:

> Tani (32): It's natural for women [. . .]
> Elsabé (41): As nurturers [. . .]
> Tani: If it makes me who I am [. . .] that I make food [. . .] then I have a problem. I enjoy making food for my husband, he doesn't expect it [. . .] Women and men are different, after all.
> Elsabé: Ja, ja. And that's quite nice.

Articulations with 'choice' allow for iterative normalisations of the woman-mother equivalence underpinning the gendered division of labour of woman-as-primary-caregiver. In the narrative below, the dissident retort undermines the iteration with an insistence on men being co-responsible for reproduction:

> Andriette (56): My mom was a doctor and later a psychiatrist [. . .] First thing in the mornings, she [. . .] would put her face on [. . .] She said [. . .] 'Sorry, sick people are more important than you' [. . .] I chose to stay home. I almost died of boredom, but I didn't want to do that to my children [. . .]
> Tani (32): It's the balance.
> Nina (65): It's the balance, yes.
> Emma (46): But this is where the man comes in because it is [. . .] 'either my children or my work' [. . .] You have to be able to say, 'Hello, there are two of us.'

'Choice' is also explicitly welded with *volksmoeder* elements to 'freely' claim woman-as-natural-nurturer in a postfeminist juxtaposition with feminism's 'compulsory career woman':

> Pieta: Wasn't it expected in the 1980s [. . .] that a woman would work if [. . .] you wanted respect? I am [. . .] probably the offspring of a *volksmoeder* because I am like my mom. I want to be at home with my children. I chose my career so that I could do something at home when I have children [. . .] I love cooking [. . .] I am naturally a nurturer and free to do it. No one looks down on me.

Pieta places 'women's liberation' as interpellating Afrikaner women in the 1980s, rather than the 1960s. If any epoch in the second half of the twentieth century would be associated with Afrikaner women's re-entry into the public sphere, it would be the 1990s during the transition to democracy. This confusion between political moments could be attributed to the 1980s being regarded by many Afrikaners as the start of the end of white order, or more specifically, the white male order. It would be the decade when Afrikaner nationalism's grip on its female subjects started to slip – a grip that a subject abiding by normative *volksmoeder* prescriptions would wish to reassert, which Pieta does here with the help of postfeminist 'choice'.

A dissident reworking of 'choice' allows for unfeminine possibilities such as 'I hate it to be with my children', while acknowledging the middle-class contingencies producing this femininity, with consumerism among its generative modes:

> Elsebeth (48): [Sharing of household duties with husband] is my choice [. . .] Everything is about choice. It is my choice not to work [. . .] I choose to be with my children [. . .] I live in an unnatural world in Durbanville. It is not the normal South Africa [. . .] In Durbanville there are women who work because they enjoy it and then there are those [. . .] who are not willing to say, 'I hate it to be with my children', so she says, 'I work to drive the new blablabla Mini and my husband drives the new blablabla car and we have DSTV and go overseas.' I drive a fifteen-year-old car because it is my choice not to work.

Silence, service and sex culminate in women's silence as proviso for natural motherhood. The disciplinary effects of heteronormativity, as deployed by a defensive postapartheid Afrikaner masculinity, wear down resistant subjectivities as femininity is rehitched, including through violence, to *volksmoeder* dependence, self-silencing, ignorance, self-reduction and referred actualisation through (male) others. In this case, gender essentialism is revamped with neo-liberal and postfeminist 'choice'. Sense-making of capitulations to the heteronorm draws on postfeminist decontextualisation, which conceals political regulation. The naturalisation of motherhood, newly amplified by postfeminism, sees this subject turning against her own non-heteronormative accomplishment, which is a handyperson business:

> Katrien (42): The men are very insistent [. . .] that ultimately they make the decisions [. . .] They want prettier, more supportive women [. . .] who won't take them on on their opinions [. . .] He doesn't want to arrive at home in the evening and [. . .] be questioned [. . .] My friends would meet a nice guy and realise they're just too bright for him [. . .] but they compromise to reach their dream [of having children] They don't give their opinion [. . .] but it's okay because they've chosen that someone looks after them [. . .] It's like me wanting my own business [. . .]
> Researcher: Why don't men devote their lives to children?
> Katrien: It's about the sexes [. . .] Some women want to nurture naturally [. . .] It's like why do people want a certain car or overseas holiday? [. . .] I'm not willing to [. . .] make such compromises so it's probably a question of that not being my only dream.

Katrien relays a discourse that combines paradoxical elements: verification by the masculine, but also an advancement of a 'self-made' subjectification instead of normativity. Hers is the Foucauldian ethical self, articulated with Nikolas Rose's (1990) hyper-self-critical, psychologised governmentality, as discussed in Chapter 2. It is interspersed with postfeminist elements, which, despite claims of independence, sets up a femininity that hinges on verification from the masculine. Katrien's conundrum shows the fatal flaw in postfeminism's embrace of self-definition based on choice.

These findings also confirm research showing whiteness as firstly a masculine identification: white women may only access the privileges of whiteness through a gateway guarded by white men who determine access in terms of whether white women conform to the prescriptions of white heteronormativity (Deliovsky 2010). The capitulation can be read as white women conforming to a particularly restrictive ethno-heteronormativity in return for accessing the privileges of whiteness.

REPRODUCING BLACK: FATALLY FAILING THE *VOLKSMOEDER*

The machinations of *volksmoeder* heteronormativity, as discussed thus far, are directed by the nationalist imperative of reproducing the nation, its cultural norms and its boundaries. In the case of this identity, therefore, the aim is to reproduce the *volk*, which firstly is about physically bringing forth white offspring. The 200-year history of whiteness is suffused with notions of racial 'purity', with white women' bodies serving as the border discursively (re)installed and policed to ensure racially 'pure' reproduction (Painter 2010; Haste 2001). In particular, to be a 'good girl' in the white patriarchal bourgeois context is to be a good *white* girl, generating white children (Deliovsky 2010). This dictum works a double movement of control: it keeps 'her' in and it keeps 'them' out.

The postapartheid moment remains pregnant with continuities from its past, including a kind of pressure cooker effect in which subjects feel themselves compelled to breed white, a particularly stubborn remnant of the Afrikaner nationalist *volk* constellation. Put differently, reproduction of the black other constitutes a fatal failure of the *volksmoeder*. This regime works in two parts. The *volksmoeder* firstly is a repetitive citation of maternity as the accomplishment of 'woman'. This injunction comes with a proviso that steers subjects' responses racially. Without the apartheid state to promote white reproduction, it is now up to the institution of the family, the interface where racial disciplining of procreation happens through spoken and unspoken prescriptions:

> Leah (49): My husband's mom told me, 'You don't bring a *piccanin* [derogatory term for a black child] home, non-negotiable' [. . .] That was a selfish thing because I may want a child, no matter what colour [. . .] It's not going to work, not today, not in ten years' time [. . .] except if the child is white [. . .] We won't talk about it in the family [. . .] for the sake of peace and harmony.

This gender-sexual-racial regulation does not go unchallenged. But families eject those that deviate from the rule of white reproduction, even by adoption, as subjects in the Johannesburg focus groups indicated:

> Nerina (32): My husband's cousin adopted an AIDS orphan [read 'black child' . . .] and my family-in-law has cut them out totally [. . .] When they came to a [family] reunion, no one spoke to them.

The next excerpt exposes racialisation dynamics at play in a Cape Town focus group interview. The performatives are here read as generative of an everyday micropolitics of race and gender in which subjects manufacture positions in the here and now. Durbanville-based Elsebeth's decision to reproduce 'black' radically defies *volksmoeder* interpellation. This defiance springs from rearticulations of gender and race elements constituting her subject position, a disruption that in turn challenges the other subject positions in the focus group, with some scrambling to re-suture especially the resultant racial fissures. Violating the bedrock of the *volksmoeder* allows the decentring of whiteness, demonstrated both in Elsebeth's life and, upon her revelations, in the focus group itself.

Her decision to adopt a *bruin* ('brown', an Afrikaans postapartheid phrase for the apartheid categorisation 'coloured') baby provoked paternal expulsion:

> Elsebeth (48): The day I told my dad we're adopting a little boy [. . .] he said, 'Will it be a white child?' and I said, '99 point 9 per cent no.'

The focus group falls completely silent at this moment.

> Elsebeth: He said he won't be able to live with it.

Other respondents audibly sound their sympathy.

> Elsebeth: My dad has no contact with me [. . .] It's his choice.
> Corlia (59): Stoic Afrikaner [. . .]
> Elsebeth: Yes, because it will embarrass him. 'It doesn't fit in my little block.'
> Liesl (64): To be ashamed in public and also not-divorcing have to do with each other.

Elsebeth makes meaning of her father's response both psychologically and within the politics of the day. She regards Afrikaners as 'those Corné Mulder guys who won't even be associated with black people. My dad is an Afrikaner.'[6] Consequently, she disindentifies as 'Afrikaner' and instead identifies as 'a South African and an African'. Her use of the word 'embarrass' to explain paternal rejection confirms the affective dimension of fitting in 'the little block' of 'Afrikaner'. Another respondent equates Elsebeth's father's embarassment about his 'brown' grandchild to that about divorce, which exposes the co-implication of gender, sexual and racial regulation. But other subjects found the resultant disequilibrium caused by Elsebeth's narrative of her stand-off with her father too discomfiting and, in response, set out to discursively restore the family fabric:

> Anke (46): You may be a bit intolerant [. . .] I have sympathy [with him
> . . .] It's like telling a Muslim he must suddenly change his ways.
> Elsebeth (48): I understand why my dad does it [. . .] he was never
> good enough for gran [. . .] The eldest son was up there with [the
> biblical apostle] Peter [. . .] You do what you know [. . .] He's a terrible
> introvert [. . . who] pushes people away from him [. . .] I've stopped
> putting energy into that empty hole [. . .] It's bad for me.
> Lida (42): But it's ignorance and [. . .] fear.
> Elsebeth: It's still a choice.

Notably, other respondents, even dissident subjects such as Anke, contest Elsebeth's dislocatory narrative with exonerations of the father (proffering normalisation in the form of equivalence with 'other cultures' and 'ignorance'). But Elsebeth draws on discourses of ethical governmentality and psychotherapeutics to rebut these interpellations and to disrupt the law of the father (also see Chapter 2). Elsebeth also exposes the performativity delimiting whiteness: 'You do what you know.' Thus governmentality based on an ethics of self does not effect neo-liberal governmentality's decontextualisation and depoliticisation, but advances critical thinking about the political (gender and race) consequences of a decision.

Elsebeth's decision has also dislocated her own whiteness, as she admits to lapsing into racially marking her new child. The word 'klong', or 'klonkie' in the dimunitive', is a derogatory term for a black man, akin to the colonial English word 'boy', except that it is usually used for a young man while 'boy' is used for all age groups. Also, in contrast to its derogatory use, it is a term used in a non-discriminating mode in certain areas of the Western Cape to refer to a 'coloured' man or a white or 'coloured' boy or young man. White Afrikaans-speaking parents may refer to their son as '*klong*' as a term of endearment in echoes of the colonial equivalence of 'black people' with 'children' and of apartheid paternalism. Elsebeth's use of the term here is racially problematic, as she is white and her son is 'brown', suggesting a racial hierarchy imposed through the parent/child unequal division. At the same time, her narrative displays reflection that allows self-criticism as she grapples with coming to terms with difference that was stigmatised in the past:

> Elsebeth: Gramps is 80, Gran is 79 [her husband's father and mother]. They were [. . .] apprehensive about the brown *klonkie* we're bringing into the family [. . .] His hair [. . .] Let me tell you we all have racism in us. That first day when I held that brown *klong* I said to [my husband]: 'He smells different. Do you think it's his skin?' [Then] we realised because he's so fat he had a little wet spot where they didn't clean him properly.
> Researcher: In your head you first jumped to race as explanation.
> Elsebeth: Yes. And I have never seen myself as a racist, I have never blamed someone that parks badly because he's black. He parks badly because he's a bad driver.

Elsebeth speaks reflectively about the racialisation of her son by his context, an affluent still-white suburb in the Afrikaans-dominated northern parts of Cape Town. Arriving at the school 'the heads of the little mommies turned', she says. It is a context that produces her son as 'brown'. Her son's difference makes her family different, a difference that allows Elsebeth a critical distance from the 'little mommies', as she calls her peer group. She refuses the racialising by historicising current racism and delinking skin colour from hierarchy. However, the other respondents in the focus group are unable to rise to the occasion and instead opt for 'colour blindness', that is, the normalisation of whiteness:

> Elsebeth: He is a brown child with light people [. . .] He's said to me, 'Mommy, will my hair get straight?' And then I say, 'No, little fellow, it won't. Your nose won't change.' He's got a pretty little flat nose [. . .] In winter I grow his hair and put nice stuff in it [. . .] He's learnt about

being different. My girl [biological daughter] has also learnt about being different.

Teresa (37): In which school are they?

Elsebeth: X preparatory. There are also brown kids, black kids.

Teresa: So they are used [. . .]

Elsebeth: [. . .] but [my daughter] [. . .]

Teresa: [. . .] doesn't see it anymore.

Elsebeth: No, they see it, but [. . .] they don't have a negative connotation [with skin colour]. Whereas we grew up with, 'If you are dark [. . .] then you are less than me.'

The excerpt above shows how Elsebeth's step-by-step discursive resistance to whiteness disturbs Teresa in her 'colour blind' (read: white) world. Teresa's response about the school including children from different races ('so they're used to it') exposes the 'colour-blind' discourse's investment in an apartheid template of 'birds of a feather flock together', where not being of 'a feather' demands getting used to. Elsebeth resists Teresa's attempts at the normalisation of whiteness with her rebuttal that confirms racism as 'the particular values attached to [race] and the way those values foster and create social hierarchies' (Crenshaw 1995: 375). Elsebeth's challenge troubles Teresa's position to the extent that it provokes Teresa into an active discursive intervention to reclaim Afrikanerhood as white, and Afrikaner femininity as constituted through white, matrimonial, heterosexual relations of reproduction:

Teresa (37): I want to be an Afrikaner [. . .] I want to be married with a white Afrikaans man not with a black man [. . .] I want white children.

The gender-race dialectic of white reproduction becomes clear: a woman produces herself as white, and becomes verified as such, if she pairs up with a 'white Afrikaans man' to bring forth 'white children'.

In this section I discussed an in-the-moment demonstration of contradictory discursive manoeuvres of problematising or normalising racialisation. The pivot of these manoeuvres is reproduction, which is here shown to be a multifunctional mode employed to confirm both womanhood and whiteness.

*   *   *

This chapter situates the *volksmoeder* in the ideological context of Afrikaner nationalism and sketches its historical advance from colonialism to apartheid. The *volksmoeder* proves a remarkably pliable construct, as it was used historically to argue both *for* and *against* Afrikaner women's active political participation in the public sphere. The granting of the franchise to white women in 1930 proved a double-edged sword, marking the incorporation of Afrikaner women into the project of white supremacy in a narrowly circumscribed role of reproducer of the *volk*, corralled in the domestic sphere. This, however, does not divest the identity of political content, as these women gendered and racialised children in accordance with the heteropatriarchal and racist prescriptions of Afrikaner nationalism to entrench apartheid.

Postapartheid reports of the demise of the *volksmoeder* are premature, as it is resuscitated through its constitutive equation 'woman/wife and mother'. A particularist version of heterofemininity is construed within the disciplines of silence, service and sexuality purposed for white reproduction, resonating with the analysis of Sarielese in Chapter 2. Silence paradoxically weaponised Afrikaner women: they were the 'spiritual soldiers' and guardians of the 'inner room' of the Afrikaner home during late apartheid; in postapartheid South Africa their silence is demanded to confirm the precedence that men take in the household, in contrast to women's possible success and voice in democratic South Africa's public sphere. The ethic of service that women continue to owe the *volk* ranges from household labour to sexual passiveness, managing affect in the family, ensuring the leisure of men and reproducing white children. The gender division of labour establishes male exemption from household labour and confirms male supremacy. Silence meets service meets sex in another gender division, that of power/knowledge-ignorance, which does not only suppress knowledge of male violence, but also of female pleasure and sexual agency. The terms of postfeminist sexualisation encumber the subversion of the regime of power/knowledge-ignorance.

Therefore compulsory hetero-motherhood remains central to this ethnoracial femininity, as is also found in *Sarie* discourses. The *volksmoeder* receives an unexpected revivalist injection from postfeminism, also due to its naturalisation of motherhood and its depoliticising effects, which hinder subjects from tracing the political sources of their subjection. This includes their inability to grasp how the *volksmoeder* imaginary continues to impose compulsory motherhood in postapartheid South Africa. They are unable to link the inculcation of woman/wife-as-mother with the *volksmoeder* and instead racialise the latter due to the enduring colonial myth of black female 'fecundity'. This depoliticisation can partly be ascribed to culturally sanctioned discourses such as that of *Sarie*. Therefore, white reproduction as the key to these women's access to whiteness is legitimised and actively pursued. As with *Sarie* discourses, *ordentlikheid* is revitalised through the normalisation of the woman/wife as mother and the abjection of its racialised and sexual and gender non-conforming others.

4

'Keeping the Crown on His Head'
The Patriarchal Overseer

THE *VOLKSVADER*, OR FATHER OF THE NATION?

Nationalisms are usually understood as deploying 'woman' as the carrier of a nation's values. Consequently, in studies of Afrikaner nationalism, the *volksmoeder* looms large as keeper of racial purity and tradition, as seen in previous chapters. Formerly, Afrikaner nationalism purveyed an ethnic political project of white, bourgeois, heteromasculinist power. With Afrikaner nationalism being all but decimated, I have thus far argued for the use of the term '*ordentlikheid*' as a disciplinary regime consisting of a confluence of identity markers to grasp what remains of the Afrikaner nationalist project. The *volksmoeder* is crucial to this regime, working as a nodal category for the attachment of subjects to an ethnoracial particularity, with compulsory heterosexuality and compulsory motherhood in tow. As I have detailed so far, intensive identity work has gone into re-upholstering *ordentlikheid* after apartheid's demise tipped Afrikaner identity into an ethical crisis. The *volksmoeder* provides traction to this process, with the aid of neo-liberal and postfeminist depoliticisation and the normalisation of inequalities and subjugations. However, what are not explained are the postapartheid efforts, also by female subjects, aimed at recuperating the formerly hegemonic masculinity of Afrikaner identity.

In this book, the postapartheid identity work in relation to manhood seems the clearest, most direct attempt at resurrecting specifically 'the Afrikaner'. I argue that white Afrikaans-speakers' recurring return to manhood in identity work is the result of a gender division that exists in the representation of 'the Afrikaner'. I concur that nationalisms allocate as 'women's work' the maintenance of racial boundaries and therefore the protection of sexual 'purity' and the intergenerational transmission of associated mores. However, my contention is that the *volksvader* functions in Afrikaner nationalism as the overall keeper of the mores and traditions of the *volk*. Therefore, I argue that the pre-eminent symbolisation of Afrikaner nationalism has historically been masculine. 'Man' as symbol serves as the most crucial point of attachment for Afrikaner identity, which would explain the flurry of activity to resurrect this particular manhood after its fall from apartheid 'grace'.

In the analysis of the women's magazine *Sarie* in Chapter 2, I argue that a panoptical masculinity inscribes, surveys and polices the borders of *Sarie*'s *volksmoeder* as the most revered, or hegemonic, femininity. This masculinity double-marks the *Sarie* subject position: as feminine and as Afrikaans. Manhood is a normalised and constant standard legitimating the *Sarie* version of Afrikaner womanhood, which is always already heterosexual. The discourse analysis of *Sarie* finds a heterofemininity yoked into a chain of meanings with dependence, weakness, suffering, emotionality, immaturity, self-sacrifice and selflessness. Its superior co-construction is a masculinity hooked into a signifying chain with father, protector, God, adviser, leader and 'the one who knows'.

The discourse analysis of the research interview texts surfaces iteratives that constitute *volksmoeder* heterofemininity: service, silence and sexual accessibility purposed for white reproduction, or what I call 'white sex'. These iteratives construct the most revered or hegemonic form of womanhood for subjects who are Afrikaans, white and female. Subjects abide by, but also challenge, these *volksmoeder* directives. The rule is sometimes exposed in the resistance to it. The analysis of the *volksmoeder* affirmed the unequal co-construction, time and again, of masculinity and femininity, as these iteratives always aim to establish the relation man/woman.

The analysis of the *volksmoeder* unpacked the implications for womanhood in co-construction with manhood. Apart from explaining the postapartheid work to resurrect Afrikaner manhood, the second question that arises is: what are the co-generative implications for manhood if silence, service and white sex are *volksmoeder* iteratives? Therefore, in this chapter, the examination moves to the discursive possibilities for manhood in the ethnosexual compound of Afrikaner identity, as generated by the subjects under review. Extrapolating from the analysis on the loaded relationality of man/woman in the 'Afrikaner' sex-gender system, the marked term of 'woman' is just one pole in a hierarchical but reciprocally constructed binary. Bringing sexuality to the fore, heteromasculinity as the primary term is wholly dependent for its content on the exclusions that generate the secondary and marked term of heterofemininity. This chapter further brings into visibility the other gender pole of the 'Afrikaner', as it emerges in the discourses of Afrikaans white women. What are the discourses flowing from female subjects about the possible postapartheid permutations of white Afrikaans manhood? What are the configurations and operationalisations of this ethnic heteromasculinity in female subjects' discourses? In other words, in this chapter I trace the performatives for manhood in discourses emanating from female-bodied subjects in the production of the 'Afrikaner' sex-gender system. In some cases I revisit interview excerpts cited before, but do so in order to examine the implications of women's constructions of manhood, in particular.

Masculinity is of interest because postapartheid identity work reveals it to be indispensible to *ordentlikheid*. It would seem the symbolic investment is such that the achievement of *ordentlikheid* hinges on the restoration of white Afrikaans manhood. I discern a neo-nationalist configuration of masculinity after the collapse of official apartheid, when seen from the vantage point of this masculinity's feminine other. Female subjects' talk surfaces the most dominant or revered form of Afrikaner heteromasculinity – here termed the patriarchal overseer of the *volksmoeder*. The postapartheid identity work attempting to buff this particularist masculinity to its former 'glory' reveals the extent of its organising force field for subjects interpellated as 'Afrikaners'.

HEGEMONIC MASCULINITY AS PREDICATED ON ITS CONSTITUTIVE OUTSIDE

The product and purveyor of the patriarchal family is hegemonic masculinity (Peterson 2000: 60). This phrase, conceptualised by R.W. Connell (1987), has been problematised as obscuring the variations in power among males and the institutional arrangements that produce the dominance of males as a group over females as a group (Ratele 2008). This study takes on board Connell and James Messerschmidt's (2005: 832–3) subsequent revisions of the concept, firstly, because it foregrounds historicity and, second, while only a minority of men might perform hegemonic masculinity, it operates normatively, indicating 'the currently most honoured way of being a man', requiring men 'to position themselves in relation to it' and legitimating the subordination of women. In the Gramscian sense, therefore, the emphasis is on *hegemony as consent* rather than coercion and on hegemony as animated by *change* rather than totalisation. As Robert Morrell (2001: 9) puts it: 'Hegemonic masculinity does not rely on brute force for its efficacy but on a range of mechanisms which create a gender consensus that legitimates the power of men.' This book adopts Stephen Whitehead and Frank Barrett's (2001: 17–18) focus on 'localised and culturally specific signifying practices' that teach men to be masculine and where 'dominant discourses of masculinity connect with other forms of power, for example, class, ethnicity, race, age, religion, culture and nationhood'.

Homing in on South Africa, Belinda Bozzoli (1983) contends that not one but multiple systems of male rule – 'a patchwork quilt of patriarchies' – obtained during apartheid. Morrell (1998: 614–20) argues that settler masculinity 'provided cultural ideal types and a patriarchal order which distributed power unevenly between men and women' during apartheid. I disagree with Morrell's position that continuities in indigenous gender regimes from pre-colonial pasts demonstrate that settler masculinity did not attain hegemony across all spheres of life. Settler masculinity is here regarded as hegemonic because, at the very least, it organised all other genders in relation to itself and held sway over this organisation, even as it constantly adjusted the terms thereof in response to resistances, particularly from the late nineteenth century onwards. This analysis concurs with Aletta Norval's (1996) observation, employing a Laclauian lens, that apartheid achieved hegemony and arranged *all* social relations. In this gendered order, settler masculinity prevailed over all apartheid's others. 'Thus, key to apartheid was the entrenchment of white male entitlement through the regulation of everybody's life' (Shefer and Ratele 2013: 190). Settler, or white, masculinity was the hegemonic masculinity in the 'patchwork quilt of patriarchies'. As indicated above, this does not preclude the manifestation of countervailing forces: subjects defied white masculinity's impositions and innovated at the interstices with race, class, culture and other differences to escape its strictures or to wield these very strictures in their own favour. With Afrikaner nationalism gaining traction as a modernising force during the twentieth century, white masculinity bonded the two competing settler masculinities of English-speaking and Afrikaans-speaking white men (Morrell 2001: 15, 23; 1998: 618–19).

To avoid 'collaps[ing] males onto masculinities' by assuming that 'being of the sex one has already achieved masculinity' (Ratele 2008: 520), this book aligns itself with poststructuralist thinking in analysing how discourses engender inequality (Whitehead and Barrett 2001: 17). Following Judith Butler (1997), this allows for an analysis of masculinities as works in progress, continuous iterations attempting accomplishment – attempts that are never fully realised. In taking up the symbolic authority of masculinity, males associate with other males while pitting definitions of manhood in opposition to others – females and 'different' males (Whitehead and Barrett 2001: 20; Kimmel 2001: 267).

In the sex-gender complex, heteronormativity as the 'institutionalisation of exclusive heterosexuality' (Steyn and Van Zyl 2009: 3) assumes a gender binary. Every identity depends on the exterior that both denies it and produces its conditions of possibility (39) – which is why Ernesto Laclau and Chantal Mouffe's (1985) term 'constitutive outside' is apposite for the relation of femininity to masculinity. In 'presuming and enacting' its difference/exclusion/antagonism from other identities (Butler 2000: 12, 31), masculinity is 'inherently relational', as it 'does not exist except in contrast with "femininity"' (Connell 2005: 68). Masculinity is culturally defined as 'not feminine' (70; see also Kimmel 2001: 272–4; Whitehead and Barrett 2001: 16). Following David Bell and Gill Valentine (1995: 146), masculinity's demarcation in generative relation to the other reveals the 'rules of the game', a regulatory gender regime. Therefore, masculinity is analysed here as 'a structured representation which only achieves its positive though the eye of the negative' (Hall 1997a: 21) – that is, through Afrikaner femininity as its constitutive outside. In the next section, I explore where men fit in nationalism's regulatory gender regime.

FIGURING THE *VOLK*/NATION: THE AFRIKANER NATIONALIST FAMILY

Despite women's prominence in actively advancing or resisting Afrikaner nationalist discourse, as shown in the previous chapters, few investigations of Afrikaner nationalism either admit women as agents into their narratives or approach Afrikaner men and masculinities critically and as distinct objects of study. Some exceptions are Albert Grundlingh and Bill Nasson (2014), Sandra Swart (2001) and Kobus du Pisani (2001). The use of gender-neutral categories invisibilises the operations of femininities *and* masculinities. My contention is that 'figures of gender' anchor the 'affective conditions' that knit disparate groups into self-identified nations (Heng 1997: 31). Concurring with Nira Yuval-Davis (1997), the argument here is that the nation is imagined through both feminine and masculine forms. While Thembisa Waetjen's (2000) caution not to overstate the cohesion between nationalism and masculinity is noted, nationalisms enjoy productive relationships with dominant masculinities. Masculinity is a 'centrepiece of all varieties of nationalist movements', with nationalist politics serving as the accomplishment of masculinity by making available scripts 'by men, for men and about men', in which men determine women's roles as 'supporting actors' (Nagel 1998: 243–51).

Anne McClintock (1993: 71) posits that men in Afrikaner nationalism represented the 'political and economic agency of the *volk*' while women were the keepers of tradition and of the moral and spiritual mission, a gendered division of labour signified by the *volksmoeder*. Nevertheless, her analysis of the 1938 re-enactment of the 'Great Trek' as a showpiece of Afrikaner nationalist historiography reveals the significance of Man as symbol in this imaginary: the ox wagons were named after great male leaders to project each of the individual treks 'as a family presided over by a single epic male patriarch' (69; see also Curtin 1999: 69–70). In contrast, naming one wagon 'Woman and Mother' accentuated women's national identity as strictly circumscribed. Extending Helen Bradford's (2000) description of the fledgling Afrikaner *volk* in the late nineteenth century as masculine-gendered, I posit that in Afrikaner nationalism the most revered form of the nation is masculine. When measured against Floya Anthias and Yuval-Davis's (1989) functions of women in relation to national and ethnic collectivities, it is argued here that men in Afrikaner nationalist ideology occupy an equally pertinent position to women as 'reproducers of ideologies and transmitters of culture'. Insofar as the 'Afrikaner woman' occupied a symbolic role, it pertained to 'racial purity' while discourses exalting 'the patriarchal family tradition' positioned the patriarch as the overall keeper of the mores and tradition of the *volk* and thus as the overseer of the *volksmoeder*. While Marijke du Toit (2003) challenges the notion of 'Afrikaner as male', she also acknowledges that Afrikaner nationalist 'men were at pains to demarcate female territory' (166) or, as Elsie Cloete (1992: 49–50) asserts, Afrikaner nationalist men 'herded' women 'into the new laager of nationalism'. The patriarch's purchase strengthened in the period before and after the Afrikaner nationalist capture of state power in

1948. However, it is the concurrent crumbling of apartheid and Afrikaner nationalism that foreground the symbolic investment in masculinity, as demonstrated by the disproportionate postapartheid identity work aimed at rehabilitating the 'Afrikaner man'. In making sense of Afrikaner male identity historically, I propose in the next section a loose categorisation of hegemonic and dissident Afrikaner masculinities.

FIGURATIONS OF FOUR DOMINANT AFRIKANER MASCULINITIES – AND ONE DISSIDENT

Reviewing and interpreting the relevant literature, I group the most revered, or hegemonic, Afrikaner masculinities distributed over space and time under the following descriptions: 'noble patriarch', 'divine agent', 'organisation man' and 'man of the world'. One dissident figuration emerges: the 'Promethean Afrikaner'. The elements constituting these exalted and dissident Afrikaner masculinities shift over time, according to changing historical conditions.

The terms of the noble patriarch are set out in a text by influential Afrikaner nationalist ideologue Geoffrey Cronjé. The first version was a book chapter titled 'Die huisgesin in die Afrikaanse kultuurgemeenskap' (The family in the Afrikaans cultural community), published in 1945, a few years before the National Party victory at the white polls. It formed part of the intensive cultural production of Afrikaner nationalism at the time, featuring in a book with a telling title, reflecting the burgeoning ambitions of the cultural entrepreneurs of the time: *Kultuurgeskiedenis van die Afrikaner: Die eerste beskrywing van die Boere-volkslewe in al sy vertakkinge; Deel I* (The cultural history of the Afrikaner: The first description of the Boer people's ways in all their extensions; Part I), published by the Afrikaner nationalist Nasionale Pers. The second version of the text, with some small adjustments, appeared thirteen years later, in a co-authored book titled *Die patriargale familie: 'n Kultuursosiologiese studie* (The patriarchal family: A cultural-sociological study), published by HAUM, another Afrikaner nationalist publisher (Cronjé and Venter 1958).

While the text is ostensibly an exposition on Boer family ways of days gone past, it is here read as normative, as per J.M. Coetzee's (1991: 5–6) explanation: the nationalist intellectual conjures up a past to explain the present, with the aim of forging the ethnic collective into a nation that follows 'his' thinking. The salience of the text springs from Cronjé's position as the most eloquent of apartheid theorists (Coetzee 1991). His institutional placement demonstrates the resonance of his thoughts, as he chaired a number of commissions, including one on 'family life', between 1951 and 1960 (Pieterse 1992). His considerable popular influence (Giliomee 2004: 419) spanned four decades and multiple books, particularly on heteronormative arrangements. Addressing the 'crisis in the Afrikaans urban family life' (Cronjé and Venter 1958: 171; Cronjé 1945: 325), Cronjé's texts depart from the *volksmoeder* as a symbol of the *volk* to reactivate remnants of the frontier masculinity of the Dutch settler farmers as supreme authority, with the family as base (Bradford 2000; Curtin 1999). Cronjé lauded the noble patriarch as

> embod[ying] the highest spiritual values of the young and energetic Boer nation: [. . .] its spiritual nobility [. . .] morality, *volk* pride, racial consciousness, love of freedom [. . .] and whatever else was beautiful and noble and good in the character of the Boer nation. With the high authority vested in him [. . .] the plain Boer patriarch lent authority to the pure values and virtues of the *volk* (Cronjé and Venter 1958: 42; 163).

The noble patriarch was the 'ruler, priest, educator and manager of his family' and its 'central authority' (Cronjé and Venter 1958: 38). He ensured that his son 'maintained the mores of the *volk*' (41). The patriarchal family was the 'social cornerstone' (Cronjé 1945: 325) and 'purest *volk* inheritance' (Cronjé and Venter 1958: 159), synonymous with order and discipline, a bulwark against *volksvreemde* (alien to the *volk*) influences; its decline causing instability, permissiveness and 'spiritual-cultural impoverishment' (163). Cronjé's text issued a contradictory appeasement to 'the Afrikaner woman' as 'help to the man, even though she did not lead [. . .] her place was not inferior even though the man was of much more "acknowledged worth"' (57). This idea of lower worth connects into Protestant ideas of 'woman' as (sexually) soiled and therefore unable to sustain 'the forefathers' morals', which can be traced back to the South African War of 1899–1902. Moral aspersions were cast over Boer women due to their independent-mindedness and their ways of survival in a context of absent men during the war (Bradford 2000: 217–18; see also Smith 2014). Cronjé's judgement that the patriarch, rather than the *volksmoeder*, epitomises what is good and noble about the *volk* also ties into the gendered mind/body and culture/ nature division of Western patriarchy and colonialism.

This masculine nobility holds a divine charge. After the war, Afrikaner nationalism resurrected components of seventeenth-century Puritan morality that equated the male head of the household with the authority of the male Christian God. While T. Dunbar Moodie (1975: 102–4) does not gender his analysis of this Puritanism, in his description of the powerful, all-male Broederbond (League of Brothers), God himself assigned Afrikaner men to uphold the ideal of an eternal and separate Afrikaner nation. As priest, the most pre-eminent form of Afrikaner manhood manifests as a divine agent.

After the South African War, decades of 'bureaucratisation' followed, with a slew of interlocking and sometimes competing organisations serving Afrikaner interests across social spheres. Ascension to state power in 1948 consolidates 'the Afrikaner as organisation man', as Frederik van Zyl Slabbert (1975: 6) unselfconsciously genders 'the Afrikaner'. Public positions were specifically reserved for Afrikaner men (Du Pisani 2001; Vincent 1999). The organisation man was still guided by the puritan ideal, as personified by the 'race-conscious' rural Boer patriarch vigilantly warding off the *volksvreemde*. Puritanism retained its purchase well into the 1950s, despite large-scale Afrikaner urbanisation (Du Pisani 2001).

In the wake of apartheid state capitalism, Afrikaner corporate interests converged with those of white English-speaking capitalists (Van der Westhuizen 2007). A new Afrikaner male persona emerged in the form of the 'man of the world' (Du Pisani 2001: 161). Greater affluence oriented Afrikaners to consumerism and materialism to signify success (158–61). Given the increased exposure to American cultural influences, the Afrikaner man of the world is akin to Michael S. Kimmel's (2001: 270–1) American 'marketplace man', the capitalist who demonstrates his manhood with accumulation and homosociality with other 'real men'. At this time, the 1960s, a class- and culture-based division between '*verligtes*' (enlightened) and '*verkramptes*' (reactionaries) arose. Du Pisani (2001) argues that the *verligte* man of the world was a 'new man', quoting businessman Anton Rupert: 'I am a man with a Christian conscience, a child of Christian civilisation. I am Afrikaner-born. I am a South African. I belong to the Western world. I am a world citizen' (161). Rather than the novelty one would expect from a 'new man', however, one finds in this excerpt the elements enumerated above: the noble patriarch, the divine agent and the organisation man. The tenets of colonial whiteness undergird the man of the world, as drawn on by Afrikaner nationalists in their aspiration to ascend to Western verification. Rupert's aspiration contains the colonial conflation of Christianity with (white) civilisation, which is then extended as an Afrikaner claim on civilised status and expands to citizenship of 'the Western world'. The 'male role of breadwinner' and 'man as priest' continues, along with conformity to the group's rules, abidance by leaders' authority, 'a self-image of moral superiority', the abjection of difference, and militarism (165).

The last category and the only dissident form is the 'Promethean Afrikaner', as described by former South African president and African National Congress (ANC) leader Thabo Mbeki (2004) and elaborated on by David Johnson (2012). Promethean Afrikaners during apartheid sacrificed their positions as members of the dominant and ruling group, with its associated power and privilege, to pursue an agenda to embrace diversity that would result in the ending of exactly that power and privilege, argues Mbeki (2004). Johnson (2012: 137) criticises this construction as an incorporation into the current ANC government's nationalist project. However, his analysis runs into confusion because of his own expansion of the category of Promethean Afrikaner to include unidentified 'businessmen, politicians, intellectuals'. Most Afrikaner businessmen, intellectuals and politicians cannot be included in this category. Indeed, 'new men' such as Afrikaner businessman Rupert who rose to fabulous wealth, especially after the end of official apartheid, and was embraced by the ruling African nationalist elite, would not qualify according to Mbeki's narrow definition. This can also be discerned in Mbeki's specification of anti-apartheid theologian and activist Beyers Naudé as an example of a Promethean Afrikaner.

As can be seen, the noble patriarch shows remarkable longevity, extending over time and overlapping with other forms of masculinity made available for men who identify as Afrikaners.

(POST)APARTHEID AFRIKANER MASCULINITY: 'KEEPING THE CROWN ON HIS HEAD'

After apartheid and Afrikaner nationalism, public ruminations seek answers to the 'crisis' of Afrikaner masculinity. In an angry letter to an Afrikaans newspaper that sparked months of debate, as well as a popular play and book (Louw 2001), a journalist vented the intergenerational distress of 'the little brothers' who defended the apartheid state in the 'border war', but were denied the fruits of power that the older brothers enjoyed.[1] The use of 'brother' references the Broederbond, which is an organisational example of the *volk* as fraternity or brotherhood. In 2006, a song calling for the return of Boer general Koos de la Rey and bemoaning the loss of Afrikaner male leadership captured the popular white Afrikaans imagination, provoking public anxiety about an anti-democratic backlash from Afrikaners (Groenewald 2007). Ditto intermittent reports of right-wing Afrikaner men setting up military training camps for boys and forming organisations to defend themselves against 'black anarchy' (Van Gelder 2012). In another move, religion is mobilised at mass rallies to address 'social decay' by reinstating Afrikaner males as 'mighty men' and the 'kings and priests' of their homes, the latter resonating with the noble patriarch and the divine agent, as described above (Nadar 2009: 21–2).

These rumblings are reactions to the stigmatisation of 'the Afrikaner' as the creator and prime beneficiary of apartheid. Apartheid spurred Afrikaner political, economic and social ascendancy, but left the identity ethically spoilt; hence all the activity to refurbish *ordentlikheid*. Afrikaner nationalism crumpled along with official apartheid. With masculinity presupposed as unnamed norm, 'the Afrikaner' is always already male. As argued above, the particularist permutation of hegemonic masculinity represented all that was good about Afrikaner identity. After apartheid, the identity remains masculine: Afrikaner men were deeply implicated in the elaboration and entrenchment of apartheid because of their 'public' visibility, as opposed to Afrikaner women, whose political work was hidden in the domestic sphere of the home (Du Plessis 2010). Because of the tight fit between Afrikaner identity and Afrikaner masculinity, cleansing the identity and reinstating *ordentlikheid* necessarily involves the reinvention of Afrikaner masculinity. The focus is again on resurrecting 'the ideal Afrikaner man', in a reiteration of early Afrikaner nationalist discourse (Bradford 2000).

In this section, the analysis is extended to explore the constitution of Afrikaner masculinities in discourses emanating from white Afrikaans women, which represent views from the side of the co-constitutive feminine other. Four discourses emerge that delineate this particularist settler masculinity. These are: 'noble patriarch', 'consuming Afrikaner', 'victim of democracy' and 'messiah'. Three of these discourses, 'noble patriarch', 'consuming Afrikaner' and 'messiah' are not discrete, but overlap, both in content and across time, and can be traced during and after apartheid. 'Victim of democracy' is a postapartheid construction.

My research shows that while contestation does occur, enduring elements of Cronjé's noble patriarch still hold the fort in household spaces. The discourse of the noble patriarch is elaborated through three sub-modalities: 'the one who knows', father-husband and (violent) protector. These modalities resonate with the findings on *Sarie* magazine as a normative discourse sanctioning man as 'the one who knows', father, protector and (gateway to) God, while naturalising and submerging male violence.

Discourse I: The noble patriarch as 'the one who knows'

In Cronjé's 'familialism' (Cronjé and Venter 1958), the patriarch only ever acts in the best interests of the family, which he 'knows', to the exclusion of other family members. The patriarch determines the values of the family, as he does in the *volk* as family. He is a possessor of 'the truth', fitting into a network of masculine authorities linked through disciplinary technologies, such as religion, education and medicine. Female subjects are interpellated in relation to a male 'one who knows' who sets the norms:

> Ansie (57): One is taught to look up to your dad and that you have to respect older men, the principal, teachers. It is just a remnant of how we were taught [during apartheid] to think about men specifically. Specifically this cornerstone of our community could not have feet of clay. These were always guys that you put on a little throne.

> Katrien (42): [There were the] teacher, preacher, doctor and dentist that tell you, 'This is the truth.'

Men's public status, denied to Afrikaner women in the apartheid era, verified them as possessors of the truth and thus as those who know. The idea of the 'Afrikaner man' as the cornerstone of the community shows the central role awarded not only to men as active political agents, but also to an idealised form of manhood that could serve as 'cornerstone', ethically and ideologically. The reference to a throne is yet another association between manhood and kinghood, while 'feet of clay' references biblical gods, implicitly linking this manhood to divinity – even if of the faltering variety.

After the democratic transition, men's authority as the possessors of knowledge and the determinants of action persists, but in a fragmented form:

> Andriette (56): My dad said what happens and how it happens. I see with my children's generation it becomes easier mutually not to have those control issues, even though it is still there, but not in the patriarchal sense of 'the dad has to be respected', 'the dad is the breadwinner', 'the dad is the one determining the values'.

To iterate the patriarch as 'the one who knows' requires muting others across hierarchies of gender and age. As argued previously, silence serves as one of the most persistent iteratives in the formation of the *volksmoeder*, adapted to changing demands of Afrikaner nationalism during the twentieth century. To mute woman, knowing man speaks. He cannot be denied or opposed, an entitlement reasserted in the democratic era:

> Leah (49): You are seen at a table and never heard. We did not grow up where you speak at the table. [It's] quite strict. Dad speaks.

> Katrien (42): [My brother (46)] is a typical Afrikaans man. When he speaks, the woman stays quiet because he's speaking.

Sexuality works as disciplinary micro-power (Foucault 1998: 145–7). Masculine knowing includes sexual licence for men, as a counterpart to the regime of sexual ignorance and lack of sexual agency for women, as described in previous chapters:

> Ansie (57): The day a man marries, he doesn't want someone with experience. He's looking for a chaste, respectable girl. I always believed my mom. There were strict rules. The stereotype is men can be looser. They are more accommodated because a man's needs are different, they are more physically oriented.

> Emma (46): [My mom of 70+ years old] says [. . .], 'If your husband has to have sex, my child, then you have to [oblige].'

After apartheid, sex is still something that Afrikaner men do to, and define for, women (see research by Spies 2012: 38). This power/knowledge-ignorance regime further bolsters the patriarchal position through the persistence of the 'familialist' injunction of 'an *unceasing* aspiration to create a family' (Cronjé and Venter 1958: 98, 101; emphasis added). Voice, knowledge, sex, reproduction and 'choice' mesh to produce male domination/female submission. The maintenance of man as decision-maker and woman/wife-as-mother who accepts his decisions, gets a postfeminist boost in the form of neo-liberal 'choice':

> Katrien (42): Men are very insistent that ultimately they make the decisions. They want prettier, more supportive women who won't take them on on their opinions. He doesn't want to arrive at home in the evening and be questioned. My friends [. . .] compromise to reach their dream [of having children]. [They] don't give their opinion, but it's okay because they have chosen that someone looks after them.

The public/private dichotomy is resurrected: men slot into breadwinner ('arrive at home in the evening'), with related associations of public agency, and women slot into motherhood, with related associations of relegation to the private sphere. Conversely, fatherhood or male parenting does not feature.

Discourse II: The noble patriarch as father-husband

The constitutive outside to the patriarch is a self-deprecatory and infantilised femininity that 'tiptoes around his chair' and cannot be seen to be 'confrontational', as can be gleaned from the research interviews. Diminution inaugurates a hierarchy of father/child between men and women:

> Louise (43): Only after my dad's death did [my mom] say she always felt like one of four children.

> Andriette (56): There's probably a part of you that will always remain a child, where you carry these fears and respects within yourself [. . .] the *ooms* [uncles . . .] My husband is also an *oom*, but [. . .] I unconsciously fall back in this hole of "'scuse me, I'm the little girl' [. . .] of 'listen to

the *oom'*. It is difficult for me to contradict them. I did not grow up like that where you just take them on and say, 'Oh, really?'

The father-husband modality draws on man as 'the one who knows' to silence 'Mommy', an entitlement transferred intergenerationally:

> Andriette (56): I married into a [. . .] 1950s-type family where the man is the breadwinner [. . .] My mother-in-law was dependent [on her husband] her whole life. She simply fell in with everything he said [. . .] That kind of position of power I hoped to overcome [. . .] in my own marriage [. . .] but at times my husband sees it as I don't respect him if I differ from him [. . .] The man makes the decisions. My father-in-law said, 'Don't worry, Mommy' and patted [my mother-in-law] like this.

Discourse III: The noble patriarch as (violent) protector

Underpinning the silence is the threat of violence – ever-present, though hidden. David Theo Goldberg (2009: 301, 303) describes how apartheid encompassed all spheres of sociality and produced 'limitless violence [. . .] against the perceived forces of debilitation'. White men exercised this mandate in everyday circumstances. Goldberg does not gender his analysis. However, a dissident subject in my research highlights that public violence performed by white men did not only exert discipline over black people, but also over white female spectators:

> Andriette (56): In Stellenbosch, a very white enclave [. . .] I was so angry and upset [. . .] Schoolboys [. . .] threw acorns at a coloured man. I experienced it as extremely humiliating. Who gives them the right? [Another time] when a coloured man climbed over the rope, guys pulled it and he fell. It was so humiliating, in front of everybody. My dad said, 'Hold yourself in' because I wanted to reprimand them.

Frantz Fanon (2001: 215–16) writes about the reciprocity between the public and private violences of white colonial masculinity. Violence also embedded male petty dictatorship *inside* the white apartheid home (see Russell 1997 for case studies). A co-generative relation exists between men as violent enforcers of apartheid hierarchies in the public sphere and men enforcing patriarchal domination within the white family, under the guise of 'protection':

Andriette (56): When her dad asked, 'Where's my hat?' the whole household stood still and everybody searched [. . .] Everybody knew now life is blue and everyone made themselves small and stayed in their tracks because they feared his angry moods and outbursts and things.

The exacting male continues after apartheid:

Nerina (32): If my mom does not execute my dad's instructions exactly, then he absolutely freaks out.

A discourse of denial buttresses intra-family violence, including the use of euphemisms and women insisting that their own bodies are violation-free, which accords with findings elsewhere on white women denying domestic violence (Dobash and Dobash 1992: 52). In contrast, corporal punishment of children is freely admitted to, in line with the colonial normalisation of the violent reinforcement of the adult/child hierarchy (Nandy 1983). The protector is entitled to mete out random violence, as this description of an incident during childhood suggests:

Pieta (35): I had a beating. My dad was so humiliated. It was one of those 'just grab and hit'.

During apartheid, a masculine sexual prerogative with implicit violence was normalised, as in this text from a book of instruction for Afrikaner women: 'Man cannot understand when woman alleges that she is unconscious of encouraging him. He can also not understand why she looks over her shoulder when she runs away from him' ('Dr Goedhart' 1972: 369). As argued previously, compulsory male sexual access is co-produced with female sexual submission:

Andriette (56): The submission expected of women [. . .] sexual types of things [. . .] you had to kiss all the *omies* [uncles] and tolerate if they touched you. What standing did you have if you said, 'This *omie* is touching me'? Many women were too scared to say anything.

A shroud of silence muffles sexual and domestic violence, encumbering scrutiny. Public exposure of domestic violence from the 1960s onwards disturbed the 'good father' projection of the patriarch (Du Pisani 2001: 164). After apartheid, public resistance against the Afrikaner/white male sexual prerogative increased markedly, particularly in well-publicised court cases, such as *E. van Zijl v. I.M. Hoogenhout* and *State v. B. Hewitt*, regarding child sexual assault between 1958 and 1967, and in the 1980s, respectively. Another postapartheid outlet for Afrikaner women to air sexual assault is popular writing, such as the record-breaking bestselling Afrikaans book *Dis ek, Anna* (Lötter 2004) (translated in 2005 as *It's Me, Anna*), an autobiographical tale about child sexual assault in a white Afrikaans family during apartheid.

Violence, as an intergenerational method of correction, not only places women in submission, but also creates hierarchies for men. Cronjé proffers a normative 'description' in which a father should be 'unapproachable' and a son should harbour a 'deference for his father [that] borders on fear' (Cronjé and Venter 1958: 42, 66). Narratives surface in my research that normalise intergenerational male fear and, implicitly, violence: for example, sons who are 'more scared' of their fathers than 'of the devil'. During apartheid, conscription militarised Afrikaner masculinity, a mechanism nostalgically remembered in contemporary South Africa for its chastening effects on men:

> Pieta (35): [My father always says] military service is the best thing for a young guy because they cut you down to size [. . .] If you're a little spitfire [. . .] they get you right quickly and you also learn how to iron and do all manner of things.

> Nerina (32): Dads [. . .] transmit [the culture of violence] to their sons [as in] 'I went through it, so you have to go through it.'

After apartheid, private paramilitary camps and violent pursuits, such as hunting, are employed to 'toughen up' men and boys, in lieu of conscription:

> Nerina: [My son's cousin] for his fourth birthday got a .22 [rifle]. The hunting culture is very close to the military [culture]. That little [cousin] has a knife. He doesn't think twice about hitting someone to get his way.

Non-conforming male-bodied others are feminised, including by accusations of 'being gay', which provokes refutation by even dissident subjects:

> Nerina: There is a world of difference between that little boy and my little son [. . .] the little buck with the blood upset [my son] so much [. . .] He's a soft child, but not gay.

The counterpart to this disciplining of recalcitrant males is the disciplining of recalcitrant females. In this narrative by a dissident subject, female-bodied others were masculinised to mark their non-conformism in the apartheid gender order:

> Nita (61): My girls must just know the world is there for them. They are not bound by anything because they are women. [They] were not known as the most refined girls. In those [apartheid] years' terms [they were called] 'tomboys'. They could climb trees, ride bikes, they could do what they wanted in terms of gender.

Thus, hierarchising efforts within Afrikaner masculinity are carried out in direct relation to women and femininity. A complex deployment of feminisation and masculinisation moves between male-bodied and female-bodied subjects. Cronjé's 'feared father' is transferred intergenerationally and across genders. No stigma attaches to the violence implied as the basis of this terror. Instead, the terrifying father is revered as 'a formidable old man' in the discourse that emerges in this research, conforming to Cronjé's prescription that the younger generations (of men) should believe that the feared patriarch was a 'remarkable man' (Cronjé and Venter 1958: 42). Men positioned as inferior when younger subsequently become patriarchs in their own right to claim power over women and (younger) male inferiors, as shown below.

Discourse IV: Consuming 'Afrikaner'

Another lens is the thoroughly gendered pursuit of leisure through consumption, buoyed by the accelerated shift towards materialism in Afrikaner nationalist culture in the 1960s. White middle-class women, due to their class and race status, lay claim to leisure, but differently to white men. Bozzoli (1983) contends that white middle-class women remained cloistered in the home despite black women relieving their domestic burden. It could be argued that the increased objectification of Afrikaans white middle-class women from the prosperous 1960s onwards as ornaments denoting their husbands' material status stemmed gains from the burgeoning second wave of feminism at the time. It counteracted their class- and race-based privileges, such as leisure time on their own terms. Middle-class Afrikaner women are rendered tokens of hegemonic Afrikaner masculinity, bodies commandeered for the display of Afrikaner male success:

Pieta (35): It is little show-off things. [. . .] The new Audi they bought. They're sending the wife to Paris for a little break.

In this narrative, the unspecified 'they' refers to men who assert their material status through 'the wife' consuming services and objects. The middle-class woman's leisure activities denote her husband's status. As Antjie Krog (in Cloete 1992: 53) remarked already in the 1980s: 'The more idle their [Afrikaner men's] wives, the more successful they obviously must be.'

Middle-class white women are relieved from the worst pressures of the nuclear family gender order by becoming managers of black female labour, rather than performers of domestic labour (Bozzoli 1983: 161). This racial division of women's household work is hidden by the idealised configuration of the white heterosexual union as service relationship, of white women 'ruling the domestic roost' – 'rulers' in service of white men.

Therefore, white women do not escape household labour altogether, even if they are middle class. After all, the *volksmoeder* historically proffered a femininity that is of service to *volk* and family. Transnationally, part of women's work is to service men (Jackson 1999), which means that postfeminism will also not provide an escape. This research finds that traditional household labour, such as cooking, remains not only outside men's purview, but older women (60–75 years old) are engaged in daily regimens of feeding husbands, from early morning breakfasts to special weekend meals.

In (post)apartheid contexts, my research finds that white women's household labour shifts to activities that reflect changes in the economy towards the consumption of leisure services by the middle classes. A convergence can be discerned between gender, class and race, as leisure is a sign shared by masculinity, middle-classness and whiteness. If masculinity is leisure, femininity is service behind middle-class doors. Both are enacted through consuming objects and experiences, whether cars or holidays:

> Nerina (32): [My dad] phones my mom. 'You have to do this and that' and my mom says, 'Yes' [as if she is] his personal assistant. His hobby is cars, but he doesn't do anything. My mom does it all. Holidays, they go where he wants to go. He loves 4x4 driving. Then they go for a week and my mom says, 'Never again'. A month later they're going again.

These leisure activities are highly gendered and therefore serve to entrench social gender divisions, which in turn again reinforce a labour gender division (see Chapter 3 on the *volksmoeder* for a fuller elaboration on gender labour divisions).

Discourse V: Victim of democracy

Opposition to the postapartheid problematisation of 'the Afrikaner' identity mobilises a discourse of 'patriarchal masochism', as respondent Nita (61) names it, in which 'the Afrikaner man' is staged as a victim of democracy: humiliated, broken and 'down and out' as a result of 'his loss of political power'. This casting paves the way for the conclusion that the renovation of *ordentlikheid* is predicated on the restoration of white Afrikaans manhood. Hegemonic Afrikaans white femininity, drawing on remnants of the *volksmoeder*, is enlisted in the resuscitation of hegemonic Afrikaner masculinity as a symbol of Afrikaner identity in relation to its male others: black men's occupation of what used to be Afrikaner men's hallowed halls of state power and white English-speaking South African (WESSA) men's continued occupation of the heights of the economy. Restoration involves re-elevation and occurs at multiple levels. Engaging the national imaginary, it is aimed at recouping *ordentlikheid*, specifically the moral authority of white Afrikaans men, by eradicating the blot of the abomination of apartheid from the identity. This is done primarily through white recalibration of apartheid violations as 'exaggerated', alongside resuscitated colonial equivalences between whiteness as order and blackness as disorder (Van der Westhuizen 2017).

The notion that restoring Afrikaner manhood restores *ordentlikheid* contains a gender ploy directed at the subjection of women, in particular, and femininised others, more generally. With Afrikaner identity compromised, its gender hierarchies are under pressure, a process accelerated by resistance from unruly women drawing on democratic discourses, as seen in Chapter 3 on the *volksmoeder*. Female unruliness in postapartheid South Africa dislodges the *volksmoeder* as prop to the patriarch:

> Emma (46): The Afrikaans men I know have huge issues. They were promised the world and, whoops, they didn't have it anymore [. . .] They don't see their own privilege. Women are running out from underneath them. They are a very uncertain group and politically bitter.

> Leah (49): The woman has become so strong in the family. She juggles a job and the kids. It's just go, go, go. She doesn't have time to also pamper the husband. So he deteriorates systematically.

Male 'deterioration' occurs at a psychological level (hence 'patriarchal masochism') and coincides with the improvement in status and ascendance of their white female counterparts in the public sphere in the democratic era – quite removed from the service ethic of the *volksmoeder*. Male 'deterioration', therefore, seems to be a reactive discourse pushing back at postapartheid women's empowerment. Women's discourses of dissidence against hegemonic Afrikaner masculinity problematise male entitlement, typified as 'all or nothing'. In a paradoxical reversal, dissident women subvert the historical discourse to infantilise men, instead of women:

> Nita (61): [I told my husband], 'You have nothing to complain about. We are still in the pound seats. I won't feel sorry for you.' It's almost like a child who complains about the few toys that have been taken away, instead of playing with what you've got.

The collective noun 'we' reveals the entanglement of the fortunes of white Afrikaans women and men. While dissident subjects problematise white and masculine privilege, normative subjects fear the loss of that shared and entangled privilege.

The trope of 'victim of democracy' also serves to erase that not all Afrikaner men benefited equally from Afrikaner nationalism (Waetjen 2000). Indeed, it papers over the differences among white Afrikaans men and presents all as suffering under democracy. Within this obfuscation, hegemonic Afrikaner masculinity and its apartheid benefits remain undifferentiated, as are the advantages of democracy for feminised male others. In other words, dominant men attempt to hold on to their position by claiming injury to *all* men, papering over inter-male differences and thus appealing to white male solidarity to reassert patriarchal authority and whiteness.

The concealed motive of the trope of victim of democracy is to halt the shifts in power in this particularist gender order. Coetzee's (1991: 5) comment is apposite: in lieu of a larger citizenship, ethnicism serves as 'next-best vehicle of a closed-off community [. . .] to develop their own version of stratification, as well as an apparatus of government in which their merits will be rewarded'. The loss of the apparatus of government and therefore the racist dream of *Blank Suid-Afrika* (White South Africa) shrunk hegemonic Afrikaner masculinity's political horizon from the national imaginary to localised spaces. Politically, the identity reoriented itself to the micro-level, which is frequently still racially segregated as a result of white, neo-nationalist enclaving strategies and the endurance of apartheid geographies (see Chapter 5). A network of Afrikaans white spaces, with the family as touchstone, becomes the locus for the re-installation of 'true' Afrikaner masculinity.

The idealised Afrikaner set of gender relations is so intimately imbricated with its racial relations as to come as a package. The internal gendered and external racial divisions of this version of settler whiteness are organised complementarily:

> Ansie (57): Maybe it is just natural selection that you just talk about [. . .] If you as a woman go and stand among the men and start talking about children, your conversation won't last long. Just like this whole thing of apartheid. Maybe one should just sometimes relax a bit because things have a natural flow. Once we were invited by a little black guy to his wedding. The normal talk was between people who knew each other and it was coincidentally the black people who knew each other. People spoke across [groups], but in the end you still grouped with the people to whom you had the most to say, who had the most subjects in common.

These matching modes of essentialising identification are normalised as dehistoricised 'coincidence' and social Darwinist 'natural selection', with its implicit hierarchy. They draw on the apartheid dictum of 'birds of a feather flock together', while recentring masculinity and whiteness and eliding apartheid's repercussions altogether. With these moves, defensive hegemonic femininity attempts a recuperation of the Afrikaner identity, reasserting the 'natural' flow of racism and sexism. It employs terms associated with democracy to legitimise patriarchal relations, similar to the New Right reappropriation of anti-racist rhetoric to justify racism (Van der Westhuizen 2013):

> Ansie (57): Among my friends, everyone acts as equals, except that the man necessarily takes the final decision and the responsibility.

This postfeminist-inflected reinvention of 'equality' still asserts that 'he' has the final say, 'necessarily'. This innovation enables the reactivation of gender positionalities reminiscent of Cronjé's prescriptions for day-to-day heteronormativity: the patriarch 'needed [his wife's] help and advice and although she regarded him with deference and respect, and he was the bearer of authority and took leadership upon himself, she was a comrade for him that had great influence on his actions' (Cronjé and Venter 1958: 57).

This configuration of power is reiterated in contemporary South Africa in the everyday trope of 'man-as-head' to 'woman-as-neck'.

> Pieta (35): My dad will definitely think he is is the head of the household, but my mom makes him think so [. . .] He is the head and my mom is the neck, she turns him where she wants him.

In Chapter 3, I argue that this trope could be read as a strategic self-minimisation to claim derived power. One could analyse it as hegemonic femininity reworking the heteropatriarchal formula under pressure from postapartheid egalitarian discourses. Thus, the trope is recast as femininity deftly navigating around Afrikaner masculinity to extend women's agency. Still, the trope serves to normalise hegemonic masculinity as domination/ hegemonic femininity as submission.

If she is 'strong', she has to minimise herself to 'keep the crown on his head', especially when postapartheid changes displace men from their 'natural role' as provider. Transnational discourses of biological determinism make available another 'natural role', that of protector:

Willemien (33): I am the main breadwinner. If you take away [tradition] and you just look physiologically how men and women work differently, I didn't marry a terribly traditional man, but he has a need to protect his home, his wife.

This continued organising power confirms that hegemonic Afrikaner masculinity still retains its purchase, albeit in a weakened form.

To conclude this section on victimology, the postapartheid discourse of male victimhood unfurls the banner of 'keep the crown on his head', a performative for white Afrikaans women to enact. This is a performative packed with contradictory elements, to the extent that it:

- obscures hegemonic masculine authoritarianism and foregrounds 'male disempowerment';
- denies its patriarchal underpinnings *and* disavows feminism;
- apologetically posits women as 'stronger' than men while questioning whether this favours them, as 'strength' means assuming responsibility;
- grafts the neo-liberal and postfeminist elements of 'opportunity' and 'choice' to gender dualism and essentialism for refurbishment;

and, in an unlikely manoeuvre, rearticulates elements of egalitarian and democratic discourses to naturalise gender inequality.

Discourse VI: Messiah

As argued previously, terrestrial and heavenly masculinities are interchangeable in this sex-gender system, with the blurring of distinctions between 'man as husband', 'man as father' and 'God the Father'. In Sarielese, the patriarch appears as the family's interlocutor with 'our heavenly Father'. Other contemporary samples of this discourse are found on blogs of Christian churches, such as the affluent and influential Moreleta Park Dutch Reformed Church, situated in a sprawling complex of buildings in the capital city of Pretoria. In this Afrikaans poem, a bridegroom merges with Jesus in a sexualised encounter with an infantilised woman:

'My Bridegroom'
'I hear Thee whisper, feel Thy breath against my cheek

[. . .] Thou take me in Thine arms [. . .] Our hearts beat as one and
my being screams and shouts, JESUS, I LOVE THEE . . .
[. . .] Forever I want to be with Thee [. . .] Until the fairies and the
dwarves don't play on the mushrooms anymore [. . .]
Until the lion and the lamb lie with each other [. . .].[2]

In my research, narratives emerge of women's reverence for manhood as
godly. Mother-in-laws welcome their sons' visits in ways akin to biblical
'calves being slaughtered', or would 'carry' sons 'from the car', in one story.
These responses are normalised as 'what mothers do' – 'doesn't matter
which language they speak'.

In a major postapartheid renovation, hegemonic Afrikaner masculinity
is articulated with 'Madiba', an insertion of Nelson Mandela, the first
president of postapartheid South Africa. In the national imaginary, Mandela
attained messianic status for his stance of reconciliation (Nixon 1991).

Pieta (35): He's really amazing with [our daughter . . .] He tells her,
'How pretty you look!' then everything is all right [. . .] He's really the
head of the household. He dominates nobody, he's just this Madiba.
He's an inspiration in how he handles people, how clearly he can think
without getting emotional.

In this narrative, Mandela's colloquially used clan name 'Madiba', which
references 'father of the nation', is yoked with masculinity-as-rationality. The
effect is to re-legitimise 'man as head of the household' in a heteronormative
arrangement, while validating an ornamental femininity. In a show of
postapartheid appropriation, hegemonic Afrikaner masculinity's historical
equivalence with the divine is reactivated through articulation with messianic
postapartheid black masculinity.

* * *

The findings in this chapter are complementary to those in the previous
chapter on the *volksmoeder*. The intention here is specifically to illuminate
the possibilities for men's identifications as manufactured in female
subjects' discourses, as well as in relation to the *volksmoeder* directives of
silence, service and white sex. I also seek to understand the phenomenon

of intensive postapartheid work on Afrikaner male identity, as the most obvious attempt at resurrecting 'the Afrikaner'.

A Gramscian emphasis is adopted, which approaches hegemonic masculinity as not totalising, but rather a power formation operating through consent to organise all other gender configurations in relation to itself. Following this line of thinking, white settler masculinity is understood as hegemonic during colonialism and apartheid. Distinguishing the particularist permutation of Afrikaner masculinity from that of WESSA identity, it is posited that Afrikaner manhood was hegemonic at the height of Afrikaner nationalism and apartheid. It is here analysed in its co-constitutive dynamic with Afrikaner womanhood, configured as an ethnic heteromasculinity in female subjects' discourses.

In investigating the intensive identity work underway in democratic South Africa, I argue that the resurrection of the 'Afrikaner man' promises to decontaminate Afrikaner identity after the mor(t)al blow of apartheid and to allow the reinstatement of *ordentlikheid*. This is because, instead of 'woman' figuring the 'values' of Afrikaner nationalism, it is 'man' that represents all that is noble and good about Afrikanerdom. Interpreting the relevant literature, the following categorisations of masculinity are developed to aid the analysis: the 'noble patriarch', 'divine agent', 'organisation man' and 'man of the world'. One dissident figuration is found: the 'Promethean Afrikaner'.

The analysis of discourses generated in this book aims at tracing the (post)apartheid performatives in the white Afrikaans sex-gender system that female subjects produce for men. From the vantage point of the female gaze, four overlapping discursive positions are found: noble patriarch, consuming Afrikaner, victim of democracy and messiah. The discursive possibilities for 'Afrikaner' men emanating from female subjects in this book do not include dissident subject positions. The Promethean Afrikaner is not to be found. Instead, the possibilities all converge on constructions in service of hegemonic masculinity.

I find that, albeit more patchy in its postapartheid power effects, the formerly despotic noble patriarch is a resilient creation, adding to its traction through the sub-modalities of 'the one who knows', 'father-husband' and '(violent) protector', while shifting away from its formerly revered despotic inclinations. The consuming Afrikaner and the messiah ameliorate the loss of state power. The consuming Afrikaner male's mode is through leisure, with accompanying manly tools (4×4 vehicles, hunting rifles) and manly pursuits (Kalahari sand dune driving). In contrast, women's (wives') focus is on ornamentalising their bodies as signs of their men's success, or pursuing feminine leisure activities such as shopping in 'romantic' Paris.

In an innovative move of appropriation that confirms the desperate search for ways to refresh *ordentlikheid*, Afrikaner masculinity articulates with messianic postapartheid black masculinity, as personified by Mandela. Along with 'victim of democracy', the constructions of 'messiah' and 'consuming Afrikaner' collude to recoup the entitlement enjoyed by the noble patriarch in epochs past. The attempted restoration of male Afrikaner moral authority contains an internal gender ploy: to counteract the upheavals that democracy brings to the white Afrikaans sex-gender regime. The symbolical conflation of Afrikaner manhood with Afrikaner identity rigs the gender contestations, making even dissident female subjects prone to reconfirming feminine others as 'less'. This confirms an abjection of sexually and gender-non-conforming men, an iterative process that starts with boys and involves the legitimation of 'real' men's violence against humans and animals. Comparing the discourses in this chapter to those in the chapter on the *volksmoeder*, the gender ploy in the moral restoration of the 'Afrikaner' also serves to re-entrench colonial and apartheid gender divisions. Masculinity is positioned as unavoidably and justifiably violent, while femininity is reaffirmed as self-sacrificing. No discourses similar to those re-enforcing compulsory heterosexual matrimony and compulsory motherhood for women, such as in *Sarie*, can be found in relation to men. The discourse on fatherhood is of an identity focused on male hierarchy, using age and underpinned by violence.

The internal gendered and external racial organisation of this version of settler whiteness hinges on similar, overlapping inclusion/exclusion dynamics. After the collapse of official apartheid, significant identity work happens on the home front, with gender contestation intensifying. White Afrikaans heteromasculinity's horizon shrunk from the nation-state to localised territories and the personal has become explicitly political: the home is central and the family is a centre point in male actualisation. With that, the family and the household become primary sites for the refurbishment of *ordentlikheid*. The next chapter pursues this line of enquiry in greater depth.

5

'There is a Certain Closure'
Afrikaner Neo-Nationalist Enclaves

ABANDONING WHITENESS AS A SPATIAL MODE OF EXCLUSION?
What might be the broader aims of the pursuit of *ordentlikheid*, as assisted by subjects' mobilisation of discourses associated with the *volksmoeder* and the patriarchal overseer? Deprived of Afrikaner nationalism and the nation-state as its object, does *ordentlikheid* encompass spatial ambitions? Where would the *volksmoeder* directives of silence, service and white sex, of being 'good to yourself by being good to (white) others', be enacted? Is the surveillance of the patriarchal overseer focused on a spatial location? Have the subjects of the formerly hegemonic identity of apartheid abandoned whiteness as a spatial mode of exclusion? How might race interact with other social categories, such as gender, class and sexuality, in postapartheid spaces? And, what does this mean for the family? In short, does becoming *ordentlik* again manifest in space?

In answering these questions, it is necessary to situate this discussion.[1] South Africa's transition to democracy coincided and interlinked with massive global shifts. The fall of the Soviet Union and the end of the Cold War sparked the rise of Western capitalist triumphalism (Terreblanche 2012). Late capitalism operates through paradoxical global-local dynamics: in its processes of commodification, late capitalism both universalises identities and expands local particularities (Hall 1997a, 1997b). At this postmodern juncture, time-space is reconfigured and anchorages become dislocated (Rattansi 1994). Populations are more mobile – including South Africans, as the country is re-inducted into global circuits. Apartheid's geographical divisions have proved to be enduring, but they are also resisted. South

Africans have to contend with both navigating a global flux in identities *and* making sense of their dislocated identities after the collapse of apartheid certainties.

From the above observations, it is clear that identity is spatially organised (Hall 1997b: 43). Moreover, space is political (Massey 2005), as exemplified in South Africa, where apartheid power relations manifested in racial geographies. The 'Afrikaner' was a product of Afrikaner nationalism that projected its imagined community (the *volk*, in this instance) onto a vaunted nation-state as territory. The object of the National Party's version of Afrikaner nationalism after achieving state power in 1948 was *Blank Suid-Afrika* (White South Africa), to be spatially crafted by segregating people on the basis of race. Apartheid, as white minority rule, served as an operationalisation of Afrikaner nationalism. As described in earlier chapters, with the collapse of minority rule and the loss of the nation-state, turmoil besets the white Afrikaans identity. What are the post-nation-state permutations of this identity, including spatially? In refuting that nationalism requires the nation-state as a necessary object, Mariana Kriel (2012: 428) insists that nationalism can also have 'lower-order forms of power' as its objective. According to Brendan O'Leary, the core drive of nationalism can amount to having the nation 'collectively and freely institutionally expressed' (in Kriel 2006: 57). This would fit with a casting of nationalisms without states as focused on *cultural, economic* and *social* autonomy while accepting the political framework of the state where they occur (McCrone 2000: 126). Apart from institutional expression, nationalism without a state may be channelled through symbolic articulations to preserve a cultural community (Kriel 2006: 61). In a convincing argument, Kriel cautions that cultural nationalism is no less political because it is cultural. According to David McCrone (2000: 128), one of the hallmarks of neo-nationalisms – nationalisms without states – is a 'complex relationship between cultural and political nationalism'. Neo-nationalisms are characterised by an ambiguity with regard to their aims, specifically about whether self-determination is sought (129). This ambiguity is true of postapartheid politics, where the Solidariteit (Solidarity) Afrikaner 'rights' movement hints at self-determination as a political goal, but instead opts to use the constitutional regime to protect and extend Afrikaner rights and structures. Territorial projects building on principles of self-determination, such as Orania and Kleinfontein, have failed to attract significant interest from white Afrikaans-speaking South Africans (Van Wyk and Sharp 2016).

While agreeing that a preponderance of white Afrikaans-speakers has abandoned Afrikaner nation-state ambitions, I trace whether other remnants remain of Afrikaner nationalism's spatial aims. The postapartheid politics of Afrikaner identity is here approached as adopting a neo-nationalist form, as it satisfies McCrone's (2000: 128) point of departure that neo-nationalism may be analogous to mainstream nationalism, but possesses a distinctly different character and place in history. The loss of the nation-state literally cut Afrikaner identity's primary ideological vehicle down to size and relegated its reach to that of a minority nationalism, which in fact it is (Keating and McGarry 2001). As described in this chapter, alongside the strategy of disappearing into whiteness incognito, discussed in Chapter 1, stands a simultaneous possibility for the recuperation of 'the Afrikaner': the privatisation of *Blank Suid-Afrika*, re-created on microcosmic scale in white, Afrikaans enclaves.

Moving from the position that nationalism does not necessarily have the nation-state as its aim, but involves a quest for cultural, social and economic autonomy, including through institutional and cultural expression, this chapter is structured as follows. First, Afrikaner identity is placed in relation to other South African identities. Its postapartheid embattlement occurs in the context of two contemporary global-local strategies for identification: either working with the retrogressive elements of the 'global postmodern' or with the defensive mode of 'the return to the local' (Hall 1997a) to elaborate entitlements. I show how Afrikaner nationalist fragments are drawn together to reclaim ethnic privileges, using the neo-nationalist strategy of what is here called 'inward migration'. Inward migration is a wielding of ethnicity (Afrikanerhood) to withdraw from shared national spaces while whitening its 'own spaces' (Blaser and Van der Westhuizen 2012: 386). Twenty-three years into democracy, an Afrikaner neo-nationalism arises that shifts the perspective from the nation-state to smaller locales, targeted to be made 'homely' again. This phenomenon is here called Afrikaner enclave neo-nationalism. Therefore, in addition to Kriel's identification of institutional and symbolic expressions as vehicles for a postapartheid Afrikaner nationalism, my research finds a remaining territorial dimension, albeit at a much reduced scale when compared to the erstwhile Afrikaner nationalist attempt at creating a white nation-state. The theoretical framing is sketched in the next section, followed by research that substantiates the above assertions.

AFRIKANER IDENTITY AND POSTMODERN GLOBAL-LOCAL DYNAMICS

The fall of official apartheid re-inducted South Africa into global circuits of meaning-making at a time of seismic upheavals in identities. Cultural theorist Stuart Hall (1997a: 25) warns that the decline of the nation-state is a 'dangerous moment' as beleaguerment gives rise to narrow and defensive exclusivist national identities. He describes these vast changes compellingly. The hold of 'great collective social identities' over individuals slips, along with their impression of homogeneity (1997b: 44–5). Worldwide struggles for voice bring 'new subjects, new genders, new ethnicities, new regions, new communities' to the fore (1997a: 34). With the apartheid imaginary faltering, South Africans joined the fray.

Hall (1997a: 22) contends that this conjuncture involves the disruption of the projection of a national cultural identity as standing for a national formation. The 'nation' cloaks a 'subset of identifications' that relates to other identities, also *within* the nation (Peterson 2000: 55). Afrikaner nationalism was operationalised by apartheid, which was hegemonic in providing individuals with the material of meaning-making, drawing on ever-adapted race, gender and other categories (Norval 1996). As the centre weakens, so the differences pull away (Hall 1997a: 37). In the wake of the collapse of apartheid certainties, new locals arise in a proliferation of identities. The shift is away from singular entities of power to decentralised social and economic organisation. Hall notes that shifts are met with counter-shifts. What are the moves aimed at stemming the fragmentation of apartheid identities?

Globally, instead of the disappearance of nationalist sentiment, the state system has been racked by transnational pressures from above and insistent cultural and territorial identities from below (Keating and McGarry 2001). Hall (1997a) coins the term 'the global postmodern' to encapsulate two contradictory moments. The first is the overconcentrated capitalist economic power that paradoxically works as a homogenising force while also living through cultural particularism and pleasure as consumption. The second is the enclosed, defensive national cultural identity, which is nostalgic about nationalism (32–3). In contrast to the global postmodern, 'a return to the local' is a finding of languages about the past and hidden histories, local roots that are knowable against the standardising of the global postmodern and its 'flux of diversity' (35). This reaching for grounding involves a rediscovery of ethnicity. Similar to the global postmodern, it is a contradictory terrain and can adopt an outward- or inward-moving posture. Outward postures remember the positioning of the particular within a discourse to avoid mistaking it for a universal identity, and to think of ethnicity as a continuous process, filled with contradictions. In contrast, inward postures can usher in a withdrawal into self-protective, exclusivist enclaves, resisting modernity in a turn towards fundamentalism. Similar to Hall's argument, Peter Geschiere and Birgit Meyer (1998) suggest that greater flows are met with greater efforts at fixing. Culturally homogenising globalisation provokes culturally heterogenising localisms. Global reconfigurations render locality more uncertain, provoking 'determined efforts towards boundary-making and closure, expressed in terms of belonging and exclusion' – processes termed 'autochthony' (Geschiere and Nyamnjoh 2000: 425). The 'autochthonic dream' is of a ' "pure" otherless universe' (Yuval-Davis 2011).

Against this background, I apply Doreen Massey's (2005: 9) description of space to explore Afrikaner neo-nationalist manifestations. She describes space, firstly, as produced through interrelations ranging from the global to the 'intimately tiny'; secondly, as potentially a sphere for 'co-existing heterogeneity' and, thirdly, as 'always in the process of being made'. Are we seeing an autochthonous 'return to the local', or an embrace of greater heterogeneity and fluidity, or a nostalgic reaching for nationalism, and how are the contradictory effects of simultaneously heterogenising and homogenising global capitalism navigated?

In this book, identities are analysed as constructed in particular historical and institutional sites, produced by subjects (individuals) through discursive formations and practices by 'specific enunciative strategies' and within 'the play of specific modalities of power' (Hall 1996: 17). The decision in this study to target both Johannesburg and Cape Town was based on the sociopolitical contrast between the cities, as comparative research found an emphasis on 'shared lifestyles' in Johannesburg, in contradiction to cultural and class compartmentalisation in Cape Town, where demands for cultural homogeneity at neighbourhood level extended to the level of the city and the country (Bekker and Leildé 2006: 155–8).

As per Massey's observation of the production of space as a continuous process that also happens at the level of interpersonal intimacies, I sought to detect micro-level, taken-for-granted constructions. This approach is fruitful when studying race and racism, as the apartheid state relied on 'common-sense' understandings of race to deploy apartheid in everyday situations (Posel 2001a). This focus on the everyday resonates with Michael Billig's (1995) notion of 'banal nationalism' produced through ordinary and repetitive practices.

INWARD MIGRATION: ETHNICITY AND CULTURE AS TROJAN HORSES FOR RACISM

My research finds whitening to be the form that the constant making of Afrikaans spaces takes in some metropolitan areas. These areas are situated at a distance from the main urban centres, but with a sufficient concentration of infrastructure and capital to be secondary nodes of the large cities of Cape Town and Tshwane (Pretoria). Durbanville is an upper-middle-class area in the predominantly Afrikaans northern suburbs behind Cape Town's *boereworsgordyn* – a term meaning literally a 'curtain' made of a sausage associated with Afrikaners, used by Capetonians to refer to the geographical language and racial divide in the city.[2] The other white enclave is similarly positioned in the suburban sprawl between the metropolitan centres of Johannesburg and Pretoria: Centurion is a middle-class-to-affluent urban area that enjoyed independent municipal status during apartheid, when it was called Verwoerdburgstad after Bantustan architect H.F. Verwoerd. It has subsequently been incorporated into the greater Tshwane, which includes the country's capital of Pretoria. Colloquially, it is also referred to as 'behind the *boereworsgordyn*', to indicate the historical divide between 'English' Johannesburg and 'Afrikaans' Pretoria. This divide hails back to the founding of Johannesburg after the discovery of gold on the Witwatersrand, attracting foreigners from particularly Britain, as opposed to the founding of Pretoria as capital of the then Boer republic, the Zuid-Afrikaansche Republiek (South African Republic).

The potential for spaces crafted from heterogeneous coexistence, as suggested by Massey, is thwarted by the operation of race in interpersonal relations under the guise of culture, as emerges in the following text, generated in an interview with a subject identified as dissident because of her critical stance on the dominant form of Afrikaner identity. In this narrative, the subject's initial opprobrium of white English-speakers in an Afrikaans space drops away and is replaced with 'warmth'. The allowances made in respect of ethnicity (deviating from the rule of 'speaking Afrikaans') do not apply to race, however:

Katrien (42): In the Durbanville area there is a certain [. . .] closure. Our people, our language, our tradition, our way of doing [. . .] In the restaurant [where I work] there are two or three English waiters. Afrikaans people's first comment will be, 'Oh, but it's an English waiter.' It takes them twenty minutes to get used to the English waiter [. . . only] then [do] they become spontaneous and warm [. . .]

Researcher: And if you were to appoint a black waiter?

Katrien: Everybody knows it won't work in this specific area [. . .]

Researcher: Is there a specific decision not to appoint black people?

Katrien: It's never been said black on white [in writing], but it's pretty much the story behind the story, which is ridiculous to me. You get black people nowadays who speak such good Afrikaans.

Researcher: Many coloured people speak Afrikaans.

Katrien: Exactly. It is interesting how there are still contexts that get stuck.

Researcher: Let's say hypothetically you appointed a black person or a coloured person. What kind of reaction do you expect?

Katrien: [Among the waiters] we have a little Indian guy who sometimes wears a beanie [woollen cap. . .] If he does one thing wrong, it's immediately, 'This guy doesn't know what he's doing, he's acting like a clown [. . .] What's that beanie on his head?' [. . .] But there's another waiter with tattoos, whose hair hangs in his eyes, but there are never complaints about his appearance [. . .] [The beanie] is neat and clean, you know.

The 'waiter with tattoos' is white, but the respondent omits race in describing him, confirming whiteness as the unmarked normative position in this context. The borders of the ethnic whiteness under discussion have been enlarged to include previously unacceptable white bodies, such as tattooed ones (Bell and Valentine 1995). Apposite to the analysis here is Cheryl Harris's (1995: 281, 283) observations on whiteness as a 'proposition imposed through subordination' and as an identity marker that is not 'inherently unifying', but constituted through exclusion from privileges of those deemed 'not white'. The narrative above reveals the adjustability of the parameters of the ethnic whiteness being discussed here: first, to admit English-speaking whites and, second, to allow aesthetically non-conforming white bodies. Race overrides ethnicity as a determinant of the terms of access to Afrikaans 'warmth', as English-speaking whites are (eventually) allowed in.

The same allowances are not made for others racialised as black, as exclusivity enhances the value of whiteness. White supremacy is reproduced though social interactions with black others degraded as socially inferior (Harris 1995: 283), confirmed by the respondent's use of the dimunitive to describe the Indian waiter in the story. Whiteness awards the power to whites to pronounce on black others. The messaging marking black bodies flows among 'whites' (white clients to white waiters to white proprietors). This is a signature manoeuvre in which white inclusion is effected through the incorporation of unmarked white bodies implicitly positioned as 'neat and clean'. The respondent's emphasis on the 'beanie' being 'neat and clean' suggests that this is an 'exception' from a rule that rests on a racialised and classed binary. Ditto the references questioning the Indian waiter's competence and rationality. The narrative operationalises class as vehicle for racism. The 'pathos of inequality' (Pieterse 1992) between race and class emerges strongly in the use of the 'beanie' as a marker of otherness. These associations reveal the mutual reinforcement and interwovenness of race and class. Neatness and cleanliness are properties that the white and bourgeois subject claims as inherent to its race and class position and this is what sets it apart from the black/working-class/unemployed position. Therefore, in the co-constructive dualism conjured in the narrative quoted above, racialising and classing others in social interactions serves as a reiteration of white (bourgeois) supremacy in a particular space. Through micro-injustices blended into familiar practices (Essed 2002: 207–8), white selves and white spaces are produced against racialised interlopers.

Another effect is the regulation of black bodies in white spaces. The 'beanie' is not only a mark of otherness. A resistant claiming of otherness by the 'Indian waiter' can also be read here, using Ghassan Hage's (2000: 70) theorisation that the other 'exhibits too much will' independently from the white nationalist and thus threatens the dominance the white nationalist requires to make her/his space 'homely'. In the above excerpt, the 'beanie' therefore signifies an unruly black body. Hage's analysis applies to the Australian national context, but is also apposite for the Afrikaner neo-nationalist localisation of Afrikaans whiteness in South Africa. Disciplining the wearer of the 'beanie' through the 'clown' and 'incompetence' attributions thus aids a contrasting white self-constitution as the rational, effective, 'all-powerful nationalist' in the fantasy space of the 'homely nation'. Reaffirming the other as 'object of exclusion', white nationalists can imagine themselves as masters of a territory (48), in this case the white enclave of Durbanville.

The next excerpt references Centurion in an operationalisation of culture to sidestep explicit racism:

> Pieta (35): In Centurion everybody [. . .] is quite respectable [. . .] They will really never use a crude [racist] word, never mind a swear word [. . . But] they assume you are semi-racist [. . .] They say they aren't [. . . My husband's] brother is an engineer [. . .] He'll say, 'We are doing a project again with the Groenewalds [Afrikaans surname], so it is taking long.'
> Researcher: Meaning?
> Pieta: That is the black people. Green [stands] for Groenewald [. . .]

The respondent confirms that racism has become stigmatised, but then describes new racist encoding. In this cultural twist, an Afrikaans surname cloaks a reference to black people: the Afrikaans word *groen* in the surname Groenewald means 'green'. The use of the term 'Groenewald' foregrounds skin colour as the most salient characteristic. This construction hinges on an understanding of race as a skin-based property that belongs to black people, as opposed to white people whose lighter skins render them race-less and therefore as representing the unmarked normative standard of humanness. White superiority is confirmed through its implicit differentiation from a hidden blackness (greenness), set as equivalent with 'slowness' in time, wit and competence.

The next text confirms that ethnicity and culture are thin veils masking the entrenchment of a micro-apartheid, using methods of ethnic cleansing to whiten space. When prompted about the inclusion of coloured people who speak Afrikaans, Ansie claims 'shock' at a racist action undertaken in her white suburb. Again, race trumps ethnicity, as speaking Afrikaans does not qualify subjects for inclusion. Race remains pivotal, if hidden:

> Ansie (57): A very prominent brown [an Afrikaans postapartheid term for coloured] family got a nasty letter [. . .] that they don't belong here [. . .] The chairperson of the residents' association [. . .] said [. . .] the [male head of the coloured family] felt really very shocked and

offended by the whole tenor of the letter [. . .] Everybody is shocked and disappointed because they are really nice people and he holds a high position. [Their presence] is to the benefit of our community. It was really bad for us because a guy doesn't know where it is coming from [it is an anonymous letter] because then you could act accordingly [. . . You] feel disempowered [and] shocked to say there are people among you that hold these kinds of views.

In a performance of anti-racism and white innocence, the subject denies a shared white stance by repeatedly registering 'shock' that people exist 'among you that hold these kinds of views'. This denial is contradicted by the ostensible 'inability' to take action, with the anonymity of the attack as excuse. There is no suggestion of lodging the attack with the law enforcement agencies, despite South Africa's 1996 Constitution and new legislation providing a basis for such action. Ignorance emerges as a strategic white disposition, as per Charles W. Mills's (1997: 18) description of 'an inverted epistemology, an epistemology of ignorance, a particular pattern of localized and global cognitive dysfunctions (which are psychologically and socially functional), producing the ironic outcome that whites will in general be unable to understand the world they themselves have made'. Allowing a coloured family into their suburb – that is, being hospitable to their racial other – would call the whiteness of Ansie and her neighbours into question. Neither Afrikaansness nor class ('he holds a high position') qualify the coloured family for access to whiteness and its spaces.

The next excerpt shows the entrenchment of whiteness through a persistent refraining from questioning racial divisions and its conditions. Ignorance is iteratively installed as white buffer, even as the white subject confesses to being haunted by her black other.

Ansie (57): [My] family and friends in Johannesburg [. . .] at work level there is greater [racial] mixing, but I'm not sure people necessarily socialise together afterwards.
Researcher: Do you discuss why it is like that?
Ansie: No, actually not. We just go on with our lives [. . .] If anybody thought about it, they would not have a problem in principle to have black friends [. . .] I wish I knew where the thing lies [. . .] It is a massively upsetting realisation that we don't have black or brown people that we can invite over. It is something that haunts me.

In other words, white people would not have a 'problem' having black people as friends, but they are unaware of, and therefore do not have, such friendships. Or do they notice? A contradictory discourse is again deployed, using white ignorance and white innocence. Being haunted by the suppressed but constitutive black other is nevertheless confessed in the process.

'There are still contexts that get stuck,' in the words of respondent Katrien. This observation captures the analysis in this section, in that Afrikaner nationalism's grand design of projecting the Afrikaner identity onto a nation-state has been replaced with a projection into much-reduced spaces, made homely with micro-apartheid. The town Orania in the rural province of the Northern Cape attracts notable attention as an attempt to create an exclusive white Afrikaans space. Less noticeable are the white Afrikaans enclaves created by stealth in geographically specific suburban sites in South Africa's urban centres. This phenomenon is identified as a form of neo-nationalism, here called Afrikaner enclave neo-nationalism, a South African version of Hall's concept of a defensive 'return to the local'. Postcolonial tumult is stemmed with identity anchors that steady 'Afrikaners' in ethnoracial spaces, not unlike the laagers used by their Dutch ancestors. Laagers refer to ox wagons drawn in defensive formations during the inland advance of Dutch colonial settlement into South Africa in the nineteenth century. In the twenty-first century, new forms of migration take place. While many white Afrikaans-speakers immigrate to the United States or Europe, or to other former colonies, such as Australia and Canada, those that remain undertake what is here called inward migration, in search of white dominions. The apartheid principles of the *volkseie* (the nation's own, exclusive to the *volk*) and *eie sake* (own affairs) (Norval 1996) are reactivated and directed at smaller territories to create micro-apartheid geographies. 'Natural' apartheid divisions are, in lieu of state enforcement, privatised.

Facilitating the entrenchment of these exclusive geographies is their symbolic articulation with virtual white spaces in a plethora of cultural products, using the Afrikaans language as a vehicle.

CULTURAL ESCAPE ROUTE TO A VIRTUAL WHITE WORLD: *SARIE* WOMEN'S MAGAZINE

Hall (1997b: 29) reminds us that capitalism drives Westocentric global mass culture to 'invade' and 'weave' particularist forms into its expansion, with consumption as pleasure. Thus 'an ethnicised group of individual consumer-citizens [is] constructed through the twin operations of defensive ethnicity and neoliberalism with their shared utility of facilitating retreat from public spaces' (Blaser and Van der Westhuizen 2012: 387). The Afrikaner enclave neo-nationalists gather under the sign of consumption. This neo-nationalism hinges on the basic precept of capitalism – private property – and is enabled by the wholesale privatisation and monetisation of life under neo-liberalism (Brown 2005). Individuals become 'Afrikaners' by becoming consumers of Afrikaner space and culture. Afrikaner identity is enacted through consumption. As was the case with Afrikaner nationalism (Hofmeyr 1987), *die taal* (the language) is central. White Afrikaans subjects retreat into their white Afrikaans world through the plethora of Afrikaans-language cultural products spawned by re-invented neo-liberal Afrikaner organisations, from the media to cultural industries to trade unions (Van der Westhuizen 2015). A wholesale neo-liberalisation of Afrikaner identity occurs.

One such product is *Sarie* women's magazine, examined in Chapter 2. As identified in that chapter, to read *Sarie* is to move in a virtual white world, a result of one of the magazine's eight discursive strategies. This corresponds with Albert du Plessis's (2012) analysis that Nasionale Pers segments its target markets in accordance with apartheid boundaries.

In an implicit equivalence with blackness, *Sarie* texts produce Africa as 'unknowably other' (Chambers 1997: 189–94). An undifferentiated 'Africa' is filled with its overused colonial meaning of 'dark continent' or, alternatively, as the exotic other: 'lively' and 'colourful' (*Sarie*, Editor's Letter, January 2009). 'South Africa' is invoked with Afrikaans cultural imagery, such as Springbok rugby, or with nostalgia for a lost white, Afrikaans world. *Sarie* becomes a stand-in that offers a brief respite from the world 'out there', delivering a particular 'home' both inside and outside South Africa, as these extracts from readers' letters testify:

When *Sarie* is delivered my heart beats [. . .] pure Afrikaans [. . .] We remember the home-things (Marlein Fanoy, Stamford [Britain], April 2009).

I am [. . .] reading *Sarie* that my mom-in-law posted all the way from Graaff-Reinet [. . .] With every word I read I miss home and I think of the words 'We for you, South Africa'. I sing it softly while an excitement bubbles in me about the articles that follow. Thanks, *Sarie*, that you could let me feel so close to home in a foreign country (Jana Larson, Lourdes, August 2009).

This last letter invokes lines from the apartheid-era national anthem, '*Die Stem*' (The Voice). Nostalgia is articulated with remnants of the apartheid discourse in repeated attempts to anchor this dislocated whiteness. Its dislodgment stems from South Africa's decentring as 'home' (Steyn 2003), most obviously for Afrikaans white emigrants scattered across the globe, but also for those who remain behind. As Johanna van der Walt of Centurion (Letter of the Month, July 2009) puts it: she needs a 'GPS for the heart' to 'give me just a little indication of what direction I should go to arrive home'. *Sarie*'s 60th commemoration in 2009 created discursive opportunities for white nostalgia by stealth, as can be seen in the editions of the magazine of that year. Afrikaner nationalist signifiers such as '*Die Stem*', the 'founder' of South Africa, Vereenigde Oost-Indische Compagnie (United East India Company) employee Jan van Riebeeck and the Voortrekker Monument commemorating Dutch settlers are uncritically reaffirmed in *Sarie* as co-ordinates for inward migration.

Sarie's white space is gendered and sexualised. Inward migration is to class-based territories, where specific versions of sexuality, gender and race create an exclusive and excluding ethnic configuration, as the next section explores.

MIDDLE-CLASS HETERONORMATIVITY AS THE BEDROCK OF THE WHITE AFRIKAANS ENCLAVE

The internal economy of differences in the Afrikaner neo-nationalist enclave is as highly hierarchical as its external division of differences and reflects the external division in ways that draw on colonial intersectionalities. The institutions of commerce and religion serve as spaces to iterate and validate particularist practices of race, gender, sexuality and class. This we saw in the previous chapter discussing the attempted elevation of white Afrikaans men to godlike status. Sometimes commerce and religion conflate to reproduce these practices and associated identity formations, as is also seen in the second example in this section.

The *Sarie* editor's letter of April 2009 amplifies the workings of power at the micro-level by using the discursive reach of the magazine to carry it beyond its immediate space of enactment. The text effects a particular ethnoracial gendering. It describes a scene in a small-town hair salon, depicting the salon as a space for social reproduction: a place 'to gather, to socialise and to be made pretty'. Comments are quoted from a man that the editor's letter designates *oom* (uncle), an Afrikaans form to indicate respect when addressing an older man, which remains in use in some locales. 'Oom Jan' delivered 'his wife' for a haircut at a salon where the editor was also present. The editor's letter describes what can be called a performance of the male gaze, followed by male pronouncement on women's bodies: he 'checked out every woman' before 'thanking the hairdressers for *helping keep SA's women so pretty*'. The editor concludes in a normalising manoeuvre: 'I told you hair is important. More than that, it is a case of national interest!' The editor 'playfully' recasts masculine appropriation and policing of women as an acknowledgement of woman's role as 'national symbol'. Playfulness here serves to normalise rather than subvert because it does not problematise panoptical masculinity (Bartky 1990).[3] It circumscribes 'woman' in the patriarchal order of signification as body, object, spectacle and symbol (De Lauretis 1987: 20). Moreover, a rural hair salon with *Sarie*'s white, upper-middle-class editor as a client would exclude many, if not most, of the local women on the basis of class and race, including through racial coding of hair.[4] The column's unstated norm is of an invisibilised whiteness reminiscent of the National Party's *Blank Suid-Afrika*. 'Oom Jan' could only proclaim his appropriation of the space if it were a white, feminine, Afrikaans 'we' that 'gather, socialise and get pretty' there. Thus, a white space is produced and then claimed under the misnomer 'South African' spaces. This phantasmatic territorial claim hinges on a particularist set of racialising and gendering norms. The phantasmatic aspect is emphasised by the use of the phrase 'South Africa', conjuring a past moment when Afrikaner nationalists laid claim to the whole of the country, 'their' nation-state. The exclusion of black others is effected with white heteromasculinity's stamp of approval on white Afrikaans heterofemininity as 'the national standard', incorporating an invisibilised middle-classness.[5] This reproduction installs a particular ethnoracial heteronormative gender hierarchy as a requirement for its nostalgic micro re-enactment of apartheid to take place. Feminine self-improvement continues in service of a privatised *volk* reproduced in white Afrikaans spaces, conjured and sanctioned by *Sarie*, which also serves as a virtual space of the same order.

This book finds *Sarie*'s white Afrikaans mini-microcosm in the hair salon iterated in so-called 'cell groups', gender-segregated, postapartheid, fundamentalist church groups, which function as spaces of privatised ethno-whiteness predicated on consumerism and heteronormativity:

> Pieta (35): It is a little [. . .] show-off [. . .] People who are in cell groups they invite [. . .] the whole cell group with all their children [. . . to] children's parties that are so lavish, you can't think that child is three years old [. . .] They cost four, five thousand rand [. . . Everybody mentions] the new Audi they bought [. . .] They're sending the wife [. . .] to Paris for a little break and that is all they talk about [. . .] The one girl got engaged and she was wearing this little ring. Immediately when you see [it], you think, 'Oh, they're probably still making the ring.' [I congratulated her and her response was] immediately, 'Listen this is not my ring', but so nervous that you will think this little golden ring is her ring.

In an article proffering normative 'explanations' of Afrikaner identity, Tom Gouws (1996: 20–1) draws on neo-liberal thinker Francis Fukuyama to naturalise an 'intricate link' between 'the desire for material possessions' and Afrikaner 'cultural identity'. Accordingly, Gouws affirms as a function of material accumulation the restoration of the 'voice, cultural space and respect' of the masculine-identified Afrikaner subject. Gouws therefore approves of the neo-liberal mode of consumption as self-actualisation, but reworks it as a way to reconstitute the Afrikaner neo-nationalist collective. His rendition hides the ethnoracial heteronormative configuration that this collective historically embeds itself in. The text above surfaces this configuration as manufactured through consumption. In the narrative, the 'Afrikaner man' is an invisibilised centre, peeking out as purchaser of 'the ring' and in the odd use of the plural '*they*'re sending the wife'. The restoration of 'the Afrikaner' happens through myriad transactions, local and global, involving the institutions of matrimony and the family. Purchases generate identities at a particularist sexual-gender-class intersection. If these purchases are made by 'the children' and 'the wife', they also become commodities demonstrating affluence and therefore white bourgeois (masculine) validity. *Ordentlikheid* is restored. According to Paul Gilroy (2007), re-invented racism (or 'new racism') casts the family in a primary generative role. Ann Laura Stoler (2002b: 381) disagrees that this feature is new, as what has been posited as the 'new' prominence of the family in racist discourses was previously also a feature of colonial racisms. In the South African context, the inward migration of white Afrikaans ethnics is contingent on the family as the centrepiece of the white enclave as destination. This again exposes inward migration as neo-nationalist impulse, reinvigorating the notion of the nation as family writ large, but projected onto smaller locales, in lieu of the state. The re-creation of the lost 'White South Africa' on a micro-scale in white Afrikaans enclaves hinges on the family as much as the Afrikaner nationalist object of the *volk* did. After all, the family legitimises social hierarchy – woman to man, child to adult – 'within a putative organic unity of interests' and therefore sanctions exclusions and hierarchies (McClintock 1993: 61, 64). The neo-nationalist innovation is to conspire with neo-liberalism – in particular, consumption as a mode to generate selfhood – to reinforce this intersectional ethnoracial-class and sexual-gender matrix.

AFRIKANER ENCLAVE NEO-NATIONALISM

While Afrikaner nationalism's geographical claims to a nation-state were defeated, neo-nationalist remnants seek to reclaim Afrikaans white identities, albeit with diminished territorial purchase. Afrikaner enclave neo-nationalism emerges, taking the form of a privatised micro-apartheid in sites ranging from homes, hair salons, churches and restaurants to whole suburbs. Afrikaans media products aid inward migration and serve as extensions of these whitened locales that also exclude gender- and sexually non-conforming individuals. Drawing on a global revamping of race as a category of social subjugation, the defensive 'turn to the local' takes on a neo-nationalist spatial strategy of inward migration to white environments. Culture, ethnicity and class are deployed as Trojan horses to continually whiten spaces and reinforce racial hierarchies. Racialised others push back, upsetting the neo-nationalist phantasm of an 'other-less' universe. In an example of space produced through interrelations ranging from the global to the 'intimately tiny', the lynchpin holding these dynamics together is the heteronormative, middle-class family. Consumption is the primary generator of its white, heteropatriarchal comfort zones, drawing on the neo-liberal depoliticisation of the gendered and classed dimensions of consumption. The family's significance as an institutional basis for this neo-nationalism is amplified after the loss of the white state. Therefore, iterative efforts are redoubled to command the family as an ethno-gender compound, particularly the *volksmoeder* mode of heterofemininity that re-entrenches normative men at the pinnacle of the enclave's sexual and gender hierarchies. Such are the spaces that reinstate *ordentlikheid*.

Conclusion

'You Have Humiliated Me Terribly'

Ordentlikheid and the Transformative Potential of Shame

> One seeks to preserve oneself against the injuriousness of the other, but if one was successful at walling oneself off from injury, one would become inhuman (Butler 2005: 103).

A plethora of discourses is deployed in response to the dislocation of the formerly hegemonic identity of the 'Afrikaner', sparked by the fall of official apartheid. Afrikaner identity suffers from a double-marked whiteness: first, occupying a suspect position of lesser whiteness in relation to dominant Anglo whiteness and, second, being judged by global whiteness as morally defective because of the Afrikaner 'invention' of apartheid, the material advantage that Afrikaners drew from that system and the great human cost of apartheid to black, poor, gender- and sexually non-conforming people and women. When apartheid finally lost its hold as a social imaginary, Afrikanerness collapsed into disarray – to the extent that the identity of 'Afrikaner' is disavowed altogether. Nevertheless, longevities in the apartheid logic provide a new lease on life for the colonial and apartheid permutations of Afrikaner identity.

Of specific concern to postapartheid white Afrikaans subjects is the reattainment of moral viability, encapsulated in *ordentlikheid* and advanced by its guardians, the *volksmoeder* and her patriarchal overseer. We have seen how *ordentlikheid* is employed to reassert respectability as the mainstay of middle-class, white Afrikaans heterofemininity through various discursive strategies. These strategies are detected at two frontiers of identification: the racialised other and the white English-speaking South African (WESSA) other.

At the frontier with the racialised other, an overlapping, mutually reinforcing race-class division is deployed to normalise black poverty *and* white affluence. Afrikaans white women derive power from racialised service relations, drawing on 'natural' white entitlement to resist the gendered labour divisions of the domestic realm. The second set of discourses that organise subjects behind race as frontier adapts the colonial logic of racial binarism as dichotomous moralisations in pursuit of *ordentlikheid*. Various, sometimes contradictory, pairings are created of good whites, good blacks, bad whites and bad blacks. These permutations make available positions that allow Afrikaans whites to redirect the moral stain of racism to *all* sides, or to culturally re-encode racism to remove race altogether, while paradoxically proclaiming white supremacy. The next options consist of reversals. First, the moral reversal of the apartheid and postapartheid orders so as to cast aspersions over both the struggle against apartheid and the democratic era. Second, to shrug off apartheid as a moral burden carried by white people and reassign it to black people, as a 'chip on the shoulder'. A related innovation of whiteness is to commandeer black people to exonerate white people from apartheid guilt, while claiming white innocence, based on white ignorance in relation to apartheid. Finally, racist paternalism ('our blacks') is used to claim white innocence on the basis of a phantasmatic social affinity between black and white. In a related manoeuvre, Bantustan-style black difference is resurrected, exoticised and then accepted in a grand white gesture to again proclaim white innocence.

At the frontier with the WESSA other, the Afrikaner disposition turns from disparaging to aspirational. White Afrikaans-speakers tread a contradictory path in relation to WESSAs. The historical wound of the South African War remains close at hand to justify the Afrikaner demand for a share of the spoils of whiteness, even after apartheid. Consumption and class ascension are proffered as accomplishment qua 'Afrikaners' of equivalence with Anglo whiteness. White Afrikaans-speakers routinely cede social space to WESSAs, despite laying vociferous claim to ethnic difference through Afrikaans as a language. This relinquishing is simultaneously construed as an elevation to whiteness. The temporary abandonment of Afrikaans as the linguistic bedrock of the identity is covered over with its articulation with 'politeness' to demonstrate equality with WESSAs. *Ordentlikheid* is therefore revealed as resonating with English middle-class politeness. Being accepted by globalised Anglo whiteness opens the possibility of unmarking, of erasing the mark of an ethnic whiteness and apartheid and of disappearing into an invisibilised whiteness, called here 'whiteness incognito'. From the above, it is apparent that normative subjects still seek to reinstate *ordentlikheid* in oppressive and exclusionary racial and class terms.

Anchoring *ordentlikheid* is the *volksmoeder*. To explore the recuperation of *ordentlikheid* with the aid of the *volksmoeder*, the analysis turns to *Sarie* women's magazine, a cog in the Afrikaner nationalist media apparatus dispensing culturally sanctioned discourses, here called Sarielese. Sarielese consists of performatives for a mode of 'doing woman' at a gender-sexuality-race-class juncture where local particularity and Western 'universality' meld. Subjects are policed in accordance with the *volksmoeder* model, which addresses both the Western 'universal' of white, modernising femininity and a local ethnoracial particularity, repeatedly adapted over the decades to retain its traction since the magazine's founding in 1949. *Sarie*'s postapartheid permutation of the *volksmoeder* is an example of how global capitalism, conjoined with Western mass culture, weaves particularist forms into its expansion. Drawing on neo-liberalism and postfeminist ideas of self-actualisation, consumerism is made the gateway to accomplishing a revised version of *volksmoeder* heterofemininity, tailor-made to be *ordentlik* again. *Sarie*'s commodification of Afrikaner culture is demarcated by hegemonic masculinity that keeps this femininity white and in heterosexual check. Eight discursive strategies, listed below, are deployed in Sarielese to produce the *Sarie* subject as a self-for-others woman-as-wife/mother.

1. MODERNISING THE *VOLKSMOEDER*: WHITENESS INCOGNITO

Sarie is an instrument disseminating the Afrikaner nationalist discourse of the modernisation of a subaltern whiteness aspiring to equal status with the hegemonic and globalised Anglo whiteness of the more successful settler class in South Africa. In Sarielese, signifiers of consumerism and individualism are paradoxically hitched with the 'Afrikaner' collective. The resultant subject is devoted to 'pretty things' (including herself), meets standards of Western heterofeminine beauty and is decidedly white, middle class, maternal and hetero-monogamous.

2. CONSUMING SELF: THE COMPULSORY CHOICE OF HETEROFEMININE EMBODIMENT

Sarie has undertaken the shift in women's magazines from objectification (women reduced to body parts) to subjectification (women achieving 'self' through the consumption of commodified femininity). Its marketing in the postapartheid era is framed by the idea of 'me', drawn from neo-liberal hyper-individualism, which involves postfeminist therapeutics of self-awareness, self-realisation and self-improvement ('feel good about yourself and your world'). The 'free' *Sarie* subject is compelled to make choices and bears full responsibility for them, whatever the constraints. Accomplishment of this subject position hinges on the successful management of the excesses of the female body. Such management denotes whiteness and middle-classness. As black and working-class bodies are out of control, displaying the 'correct' body is a sign of bourgeois whiteness, synonymous with an ethical self. This is a disciplinary pursuit that is intergenerationally transferred. It is achieved through repetitions of rituals of induction and grooming into white heterofemininity by choosing to consume the right objects, starting with white Afrikaans cultural commodities such as *Sarie* itself.

3. IT'S ALL IN THE *SARIE* FAMILY: ACCESSING AN 'I' THROUGH A PATRIARCHAL 'WE'

The *volksmoeder* receives unexpected encouragement from the West in the form of postfeminism, which proclaims that gender equality has been achieved. However, it espouses a culture of the self for newly 'equal' women. *Sarie* addresses the conflict between embracing individualised agency and performing women's normalised subordination within Afrikaner gender relationality. This it does by converging the neo-liberal and postfeminist dictum of a decontextualised responsibility for the self with the *volksmoeder* dictum of women assuming responsibility for others while, as per neo-liberalism, also being solely responsible for their own failings. The ideal self can be accomplished through consumption geared towards the care of others. The vehicle is the incessantly promoted idea of *Sarie*-as-family, with the imagined community of the *volk* invoked: Afrikaner nationalist images are conjured as old familiars that need no explanation, in a reliving of white days gone by. The motto 'Give of yourself' reactivates the *volksmoeder* trope of selfless service. This is the 'we' through which the 'I' can be accessed.

4. WHITEWASHING THE BLACKOUT

Sarielese embraces the neo-liberal modes of depoliticisation, decontextualisation and desocialisation of subjects to deny structural contingencies and to maintain unequal power relations. Black people only surface from a generalised elision if they are 'good blacks' who take individual responsibility for lost 'opportunities' that are in fact the result of apartheid oppression. Apartheid as systematised oppression becomes depoliticised as 'difficult times' or 'the wrong time' and is otherwise erased in Sarielese. 'Good blacks' are allowed entry into Sarielese and authorised to speak only to shield white people from accountability for the privations that institutionalised racism brought upon black people. Moreover, 'good black women' adhere to the revered sacrificial femininity of the *volksmoeder* while also serving as stand-ins for white women's reproductive duties. 'Good black women' service normative white men unquestioningly, including by exonerating their whiteness. All other black people are exotic, culturally alien and therefore abject.

5. (SM)OTHERING CENTRE

Sarie is the playing field of homophobic othering. The *volksmoeder* reigns with discursive strategies of erasure, stigmatisation and entertainment. A blanket ban applies to lesbians, to prevent contesting sexual options from entering, so to speak, *Sarie*'s subject. This suggests a fragility to the heterosexual norm despite, or perhaps because of, the persistent iterations from page to page and edition to edition. In contrast, male homosexuality features, either as a 'problem' to be 'solved' or as entertainment. For the latter function, the popular gay Afrikaans singer-comedian Nataniël fulfils the safe role of jester who tells the 'truth' and the stereotypical role of 'the straight woman's best friend', who knows about everything from decor to love (just not politics or his own sexual exploits). Thus the *Sarie* discourse 'entertains' male feminine difference by counteracting its possible subversive postapartheid effects and using it to re-upholster *volksmoeder* elements, such as with this dictum distributed in a Nataniël-branded product with an edition of *Sarie*: 'You can never ever let yourself feel better if you don't let someone else feel better.'

6. COMPULSORY HETEROSEXUALITY: TRY AND TRY AGAIN

The flipside of the homophobic othering is compulsory heterosexuality: departure from the heteronorm can only be tolerated in extreme circumstances. The recalibration of the neo-liberal focus on the self involves steering the *Sarie* subject to self-production intent on 'heterosexual union'. Reproduction as an accomplishment of *volksmoeder* heterofemininity is projected as 'wholeness'. Male verification is central to this womanhood, whose neo-liberal self-responsibility involves being a useful wife and mother. Male infidelity and betrayal is attributed to the female subject's own shortcomings requiring self-correction. *Sarie* diverges from postfeminism by avoiding hyper-sexualisation of its female objects. Instead, the ideal *Sarie* woman is, paradoxically, simultaneously childlike *and* maternal in her sexuality. Sexually, she does not 'know', but she accepts full responsibility for all his trespasses, including violence against her.

7. PANOPTICAL MASCULINITY SURVEYING THE *VOLKSMOEDER*'S LIMITS

Hegemonic Afrikaner masculinity iteratively surveys and delimits *Sarie*'s subjects, double-marking their position as feminine and Afrikaans. The majority of columnists in *Sarie* are men who cloak the magazine's ethnoracial heteronormativity in humour and the Christian religion, with the stamp of masculine approval. Afrikaner nationalist icons and poetry are invoked in an erasure of women and a confirmation of the Afrikaner project as quintessentially about men and their status, with women as useful appurtenances. In Sarielese, women are rendered silent children at the knees of godlike father-husbands. The threat of male sexual violence is always already present and works as a masculine right and women should be grateful when it is not exercised.

8. *SARIE* AS VIRTUAL WHITE SPACE

To read *Sarie* is to move in a virtual white world. *Sarie* amplifies the workings of white power at the micro-level by using the reach of the magazine to carry its discourses beyond the immediate spaces of enactment. The text effects a particular ethnoracial heteronormative gender hierarchy as a requirement for a nostalgic re-enactment of apartheid at micro-level to take place. Feminine self-improvement continues in service of a privatised *volk* reproduced in white Afrikaans spaces, conjured and sanctioned by *Sarie*, which also serves as a virtual space of the same order.

The vision of *ordentlikheid* that emerges in Sarielese is of a subject that dodges apartheid's moral blow and reclaims her ethical self by embracing a *volksmoeder* thoroughly neo-liberalised. She actualises woman/wife-as-mother by reconfirming her devotion to white heteronormativity within the bounds of the *volk* and in reverence of hegemonic Afrikaner manhood. She shows self-reflection and self-responsibility by relentlessly repeating the rites of compulsory heterosexuality, disciplining her and her daughter's bodies, genuflecting before her husband-father, entertaining the gay male entertainer, submerging the lesbian and resolutely refusing any black people except 'good blacks' in her white, straight world.

* * *

Turning to the discourses that generate women's lives to explore the *volksmoeder* further, the reports are premature that this signifier has met its maker and is no more. This is especially so if what have been analysed as mere characteristics are understood as normative directives that manufacture, regulate and discipline subjects at the intersections of race, sexuality, gender and class to produce the 'Afrikaner woman'. Furthermore, if the analysis of the sexualisation of Afrikaner women since the 1960s is adjusted, postfeminist gendering is no longer confused with an end to the *volksmoeder*, but rather as providing the nodal category with a new lease on life.

This is borne out by the history of the *volksmoeder*, as its meanings are difficult to pin down. It has functioned as a sign of both oppression and liberation. Therefore, it is appropriate to speak of multiple *volksmoeders* generated over the past century and even earlier. Dissident subjects even create feminist *volksmoeders*. However, the conflict among, and sedimentation of, the meanings of the *volksmoeder* cause misrecognition. Discourses are discerned in which white women racialise the *volksmoeder* as an attaching node only for black women, in a racist conflation of black femininity with fecundity and reproduction. This misrecognition prevents even dissident subjects from critically discerning and debunking the continuing normalisation of heteropatriarchal unions and white motherhood as the only true signs of feminine accomplishment for white Afrikaans women.

Dissident subjects, however, do succeed in exposing that, while the 'Afrikaner' exterior of this particular whiteness might suggest its contents are homogeneous, it is predicated upon repetitive internal differentiation and hierarchisation. These are constructed in reference to its constitutive black outside, drawing on colonial divisions. White Afrikaans women are objectified and rendered equivalent to the black other *and* to the animal other, with concomitant violence, if they fail to submit to the demands of white Afrikaans men who pursue normative or hegemonic masculinity.

Dissident subjects also reveal that the failure of womanhood-as-conjugal-heteromaternity can dislocate the *volksmoeder* order. Lack of accomplishment opens a door to equivalences among differences, for example, a subject creating an equivalence between 'othering due to failure of the heteronorm', on the one hand, and 'othering due to failure of whiteness', on the other. If one stitch of the *volksmoeder* prescriptions comes undone, the whole pattern can start to fray and subjects can interrogate and resist both heteropatriarchal and racist injunctions. This would explain why *Sarie* excommunicates all subjects that could contradict its steady diet of white heteronormativity.

With the denial of political power to nascent Afrikaner nationalist feminists and the physical domestication of white Afrikaans women after white women received the vote in 1930, the home became an even more crucial political space for the reinforcement of Afrikaner nationalist gender, sexual and race normativities. Along with school and church, it was an essential space for the enculturation of children into Afrikanerhood. Small power was all that remained for Afrikaner women, kept in check by the *volksmoeder* directives of silence, service and sexuality servicing white reproduction to repetitively confirm woman/wife-as-mother. In postapartheid South Africa, the silencing of women in white Afrikaans middle-class culture unexpectedly remains a primary prop for hegemonic gender relations. Silencing is done by men and by women, including a discipline of self-silencing imbricated with self-diminution, manifested in childlikeness, in a resonance with *Sarie*'s subject. In late apartheid, silence paradoxically weaponised Afrikaner women: they were the 'spiritual soldiers' and guardians of the 'inner room' of the beleaguered Afrikaner home. In postapartheid South Africa, their silence is demanded to confirm the precedence that men take in the household, in contrast to the new possibility of women's success and voice in democratic South Africa's public sphere. Silencing enables the ethic of Afrikaans white women's service to both the family and the *volk* and of the heterosexual union as a service relationship. Men set the parameters of the service. Silence meets service meets sex in a gender division of power/knowledge-ignorance, which disallows the possibilities of pleasure for women and hides the realities of male violence.

As in Sarielese, the postfeminist trope of free female agency to self-impose compulsory feminine regimes by 'choice' bolsters the *volksmoeder*'s silence, service and white sex. It becomes 'a woman's choice to be a natural nurturer'. And, in the neo-liberal logic, it becomes like 'choosing a car to buy' if a woman 'chooses' to be silent and not challenge her husband's 'natural' authority, so as to perform heterosex and attain 'natural motherhood'. The postapartheid democratic discourse is even reworked, in accordance with New Right rhetoric, to produce unequal equality among women and men: 'Everyone acts as equals, except that the man necessarily takes the final decision and the responsibility.' Despite all these innovations, white motherhood remains the hoary aim, as delivered over decades since the first mobilisation of the *volksmoeder* in the early twentieth century. Or, rather, these innovations are all in service of white motherhood and bolster it as a directive and an objective. As with the *Sarie* discourses, *ordentlikheid* is regenerated through adherence to the *volksmoeder*'s model of women/wife-as-mother, and the abjection of its racialised and sexually and gender-non-conforming others

As I have detailed so far, intensive identity work goes into re-upholstering *ordentlikheid* after apartheid's demise tipped Afrikaner identity into an ethical crisis. However, what are not explained are the postapartheid efforts, also by female subjects, aimed at recuperating formerly hegemonic Afrikaner masculinity. Following Antonio Gramsci, hegemonic masculinity is here understood not as totalising, but rather as a power formation operating through *consent* to organise all other gender configurations in relation to itself.[1] White Afrikaans hegemonic masculinity is akin to the panoptical male identified in Sarielese, which surveys the *volksmoeder*'s operations. It is here called the 'patriarchal overseer'. While I concur that nationalisms allocate as 'women's work' the maintenance of racial boundaries, and therefore the protection of sexual 'purity' and the intergenerational transmission of associated mores, my contention is that the 'patriarch' functioned in Afrikaner nationalism as the overall keeper of the mores and traditions of the *volk*. It would seem the symbolic investment in Afrikaner manhood continues to be such that the re-achievement of *ordentlikheid* hinges on its restoration. The analysis in this book is extended to explore the constitution of Afrikaner masculinities in discourses emanating from white Afrikaans women, which represent views from the co-constitutive feminine other. Questions include: what are the co-generative implications for Afrikaans white manhood if silence, service and white sex are *volksmoeder* iteratives?

Four discourses emerge that delineate this particularist settler masculinity. These are: 'noble patriarch', 'consuming Afrikaner', 'victim of democracy' and 'messiah'. To iterate the patriarch as 'the one who knows' requires muting others across hierarchies of gender and age. The patriarch determines the values of the family, as he does in the *volk* as family writ large. The idea of the 'Afrikaner man' as the cornerstone of the community shows the central role awarded to men not only as active political agents, but also to an idealised form of manhood that could serve as 'cornerstone', ethically and ideologically. To mute woman, knowing man speaks. He cannot be argued with, an entitlement reasserted in the democratic era. Masculine knowing includes sexual licence for men, as the counterpart to the described regime of sexual ignorance and lack of sexual agency for women. Underpinning the silence is the threat of violence – ever present, though concealed. A co-generative relation exists between men as violent enforcers of racist hierarchies in the public sphere and men enforcing heteropatriarchal domination within the white family, including with sexual violence, under the guise of 'protection'. Violence as an intergenerational method of correction not only places women in submission, but also creates hierarchies among men. Dominant men's disciplining of recalcitrant females and males is mutually reinforcing. A complex deployment of feminisation and masculinisation moves between male-bodied and female-bodied subjects. Sexually and gender-non-conforming men are abjected in an iterative process that starts with boys and involves the legitimation of 'real' men's violence against animals and non-conforming individuals.

Another lens exposing masculinity is the thoroughly gendered pursuit of consumption, buoyed by the shift towards materialism in Afrikaner nationalist culture in the affluent 1960s. The objectification of Afrikaans white middle-class women as ornaments denoting their husbands' material status is continued in postapartheid South Africa: men assert their material status through 'the wife' consuming services and objects. White women's household labour shifts to activities that reflect changes in the global economy towards the consumption of leisure services by the middle classes. White middle-class women, because of their class and race status, lay claim to leisure, but in a different way to white men. If masculinity is leisure, femininity is service behind middle-class doors. Both are enacted through consuming objects and 'lifestyle' experiences, such as new cars or holidays.

Reactionary opposition to the postapartheid rearrangement of the 'Afrikaner' identity mobilises a discourse of 'patriarchal masochism', in which the 'Afrikaner man' is staged as a victim of democracy: humiliated, broken and 'down and out' as a result of 'his loss of political power'. Afrikaans white femininity, drawing on remnants of the *volksmoeder*, is enlisted in the resuscitation of hegemonic Afrikaner masculinity as symbol of Afrikaner identity in relation to its male others: black men's occupation of what used to be Afrikaner men's hallowed halls of state power and WESSA men's continued occupation of the heights of the economy. The notion that restoring Afrikaner manhood restores Afrikanerhood contains a gender ploy directed at the subjection of women, in particular, and femininised others, more generally. The trope of the male 'victim of democracy' erases the reality that not all Afrikaner men benefited equally from Afrikaner nationalism and also papers over the differences among Afrikaner men, presenting all as suffering under democracy. The advantages of the democratic dispensation for feminised (male) others are obfuscated. In other words, dominant men attempt to hold on to their position by claiming injury to *all* men, papering over inter-male differences, and thus appealing to white male solidarity to reassert heteropatriarchal authority and whiteness.

Lastly, 'the messiah' discourse makes terrestrial and heavenly masculinities interchangeable in the 'Afrikaner' sex-gender system, with the blurring of distinctions between 'man as husband', 'man as father' and 'God the Father'. In a major postapartheid renovation, hegemonic Afrikaner masculinity is articulated with 'Madiba', an insertion of the globally revered anti-apartheid icon Nelson Mandela in an attempt to elevate white Afrikaans men to the new moral heights enjoyed by some black male leaders in democratic South Africa.

With *ordentlikheid* under pressure, white Afrikaans identity work, specifically gender contestation, has intensified on the home front, re-entrenching the historical centrality of the family in the production of 'the Afrikaner'. White Afrikaans heteromasculinity's political horizon shrunk from the nation-state to localised territories. The personal has become explicitly political: the home is crucial and the family is a pivotal point in male actualisation – but not of the egalitarian variety, as we have seen. This contraction marks quite a change from 'the Afrikaner', as a product of Afrikaner nationalism, projecting his (he was male) imagined community, the *volk*, onto a vaunted nation-state as territory. A preponderance of white

Afrikaans-speakers has necessarily abandoned their Afrikaner nation-state ambitions. That said, the spatial aims have been adapted into a neo-nationalist form, involving a quest for cultural, social and economic autonomy, including through institutional expression. Alongside the strategy of disappearing into whiteness incognito, an inward migration is undertaken in a defensive 'return to the local' to smaller zones to create micro-apartheid geographies in the form of white, Afrikaans enclaves. It works as a privatisation of *Blank Suid-Afrika* (White South Africa), reactivating the apartheid principles of the *volkseie* (the nation's own, exclusive to the *volk*) and *eie sake* (own affairs), in lieu of state enforcement.

Whitening is the form that the constant making of Afrikaans spaces takes in some metropolitan areas. But the ethnic and cultural parameters of the space are adjustable, as English-speaking whites and aesthetically non-conforming white bodies are permitted to share in the Afrikaans white homeliness. The same allowances are not made for others racialised as black. Class and culture are operationalised as vehicles for racist micro-injustices, which make spaces inhospitable to black people, especially black people who challenge white racism. Ignorance emerges as a strategic white disposition, used to deny that the whitening of spaces is an active and purposive process at the everyday level through micro-hostilities. Facilitating the entrenchment of these exclusive geographies is their symbolic articulation with virtual white spaces in a plethora of cultural products, using the Afrikaans language as a vehicle, as described above with reference to *Sarie*. White Afrikaans subjects beat their retreat into a white Afrikaans world through the numerous Afrikaans-language cultural products spawned by reinvented neo-liberal Afrikaner organisations, from the media to cultural industries to trade unions.

As argued above, white Afrikaans subjects' inward migration to the destination of the white enclave is contingent on the family as the centrepiece. The re-creation of the lost 'White South Africa' on a micro-scale in white Afrikaans enclaves hinges on the family as much as the Afrikaner nationalist object of the *volk* did. After all, the family legitimises social hierarchy – woman to man, child to adult – and therefore sanctions exclusions, hierarchies and subjugating inclusions. The neo-nationalist innovation is to conspire with neo-liberalism, particularly consumption, as a mode to generate selfhood. Material accumulation restores the 'voice, cultural space and respect' of the masculine-identified Afrikaner subject.

The renovation of 'the Afrikaner' involving the institutions of heterosexual matrimony and the family happens through myriad transactions, both local and global. Purchases generate identities at a particularist sexual-gender-class-race intersection. Even if 'the children' and 'the wife' are the ones making these purchases, their physical attachment to these accoutrements render them commodities that demonstrate affluence and therefore white bourgeois male validity.

Thus, the possibilities for white, female, Afrikaans subjects in democratic South Africa remain circumscribed by the apartheid Afrikaner's enduring mesh of ethnoracial, bourgeois heteronormativity, bolstered by its latching on to neo-liberalism and postfeminism's dictates of depoliticised self-improvement and self-responsibility. *Volksmoeder* womanhood and its co-constitutive manhood-under-restoration are mobilised to reassert *ordentlikheid* as an ethnic form of respectability. More questions arise. What are the affective dimensions of *ordentlikheid* under strain? And does affect, as constitutive of identity, provide any counter-potential to resist the recuperative strategies of bourgeois whiteness and heteronormativity detailed in this book? In other words, can Mandela's challenge as posed through the figure of Ingrid Jonker be met by following an affective route that speaks to *ordentlikheid*, but not with a defensive white and heteropatriarcal posture?

In the rest of this chapter, I analyse whether emotion engaged to do political work can create transformative openings in postapartheid relations, to reimagine *ordentlikheid*.[2] Cornel Verwey and Michael Quayle (2012: 570, 573) assert that Afrikaners *shamelessly* reproduce the worst colonial and apartheid ideologies. I disagree. Rather, postapartheid uncertainties involve affective practices, particularly with regard to shame, that necessarily unsettle whiteness. I draw here on a growing body of work seeking to fill a lacuna in the understanding of emotion in social relations, approaching emotions as the 'glue' that binds people together and inspires commitment to social and cultural structures (Turner and Stets 2005: 1). Margaret Wetherell (2012) describes affective practice as referring to the domain of the emotional and the psychological. Emotion is a culturally constructed form of everyday meaning-making that is situated, involves practical activity and is infused with 'sedimented social and personal history' (96). Affect is here approached as a generative element in the formation of subjectivities, following Ernesto Laclau (2004: 326): 'Something belonging to the order of *affect* has a primary role in discursively constructing the social . . . And affect

[. . .] is not something *added* to signification, but something consubstantial with it.'

It is here argued that, among emotions, shame presents the most opportunities for transformation because it is the primary social emotion (Scheff 2000) and it makes available disruptive moments in processes of identity formation (Sedgwick 2003). Shame is understood as a collection of related emotions, such as embarassment, humiliation and feelings of failure and inadequacy (Scheff 1990, 2000). Pertinently, shame works in both inter- and intra-subjective modes, with the subject for a moment regarding herself in relation to others, but also being 'formed by the look and the presence of others' (Shotwell 2007: 128). Shame, according to Jean-Pual Sartre, is 'recognizing myself in this degraded, fixed, and dependent being which I am for the Other [. . .] I need the mediation of the Other in order to be what I am' (in Ellison 1996: 357). Hence Thomas J. Scheff's (2000) argument that shame is the emotion that situates the self in relation to the social, in contrast to guilt, an individualist emotion. Shame is about the preservation of social bonds, as individuals fear disconnection from and misunderstanding by others. Guilt is more about specific acts that harmed another (Lansky 1999). Therefore, shame holds more potential for transformation of social relations than guilt does.

Of particular significance is the differentiation between acknowledged and unacknowledged shame, first made by Helen Lewis (1971) and further developed by Scheff (1990, 2000). Unacknowledged shame activates a repetitive loop of feelings, including socially destructive anger, which can in turn re-trigger shame, while acknowledged shame averts anger and even allows the mending of the social bond. Related to this differentiation is Melvin R. Lansky's (1999: 347) understanding of shame as a 'disturbance to the status of the self within the social order', pertaining to one's standing in the social order and how one is seen before 'the eye of the other'. The next two excerpts from interviews reveal the self-reflection of a dissident subject about historical and contemporary shame. The first story took place during apartheid, while the second references contemporary South Africa:

> Andriette (56): In shame, I have to admit the woman who worked for me had a three-year-old child [and] she couldn't get enough money together to go home to see the child [. . .].[3] She had to wait a year to see her three-year-old. I said I didn't have money, but then I arrived

home with plants and I know she saw them. In retrospect I feel terrible that I didn't help her.

Andriette: [A young black man] said to me, 'You have humiliated me terribly' and I realised I had to ask his forgiveness. I was so angry I hadn't realised how much I was hurting him in front of other people.

These emotion-infused stories are examples of affective practice as 'something personally significant [that] has occurred that someone wants to mark' (Wetherell 2012: 97). The narrator's accounts feature shame in relation to shifts over time in her subject position. For Alexis Shotwell (2007: 128), shame permits changeability in seemingly static identities: 'Because one has just been something one does not want to be, the possibilities and actualities of being otherwise are manifest and foreshadowed.' In the narratives above, the subject experiences shame when she becomes aware of her degraded self – the psychosocial corrosion of coloniality referred to above – before the eye of the black other ('she saw them'; 'in front of other people'). Her acknowledgement of shame opens the door to change over time in relation to the other, as she is moved to ask forgiveness in the second story. This suggests what Shotwell (2007: 135) calls racialised shame, referring to both a refusal of a racist self, with the potential for re-identification, and the recognition of the racialised other as 'capable of shaming, hence of seeing and being seen as a person'. These dissident accounts trace a changing relationality between the white self and the social, as shame opens the door to the recognition of the black other and thus to overcoming apartheid whiteness and introducing the self into a new social bond of expansive humanness.

But if shame is unacknowledged, it is untransformative because it traps subjects into the repetitive loop described above. In opposition to the acknowledged shame of a dissident subject expanding the social bond beyond racial strictures, as described above, the following narrative from the vantage point of the dominant white Afrikaans subject position describes shame that is refused and thus unacknowledged:

Ansie (57): We Afrikaners are really under pressure postapartheid. We were really the skunks for a long time. I was a member of [Afrikaner nationalist organisations . . .] and how it really just fell apart [. . .] It was as if one [felt] not shameful, but that one was half under pressure because one could not live out the Afrikaans cultural values freely as was done previously [. . .] It is still enjoyable to attend Afrikaans festivals and [eat] *boerewors* [farmer sausage] rolls and koeksisters [sweet pastries associated with Afrikaners] and those things that define us, but I think there has also been a bit of alienation, one can't deny it [. . .] Many things changed in our country [. . .] There are different angles in our culture nowadays.

In this narrative, the word 'skunks' indicates which social bond the subject fears may be lost: it is the tie with the global white other, rather than the local black other. 'Skunks' references an expression used by white South Africans during the 1980s: that international sanctions and other forms of opprobrium turned apartheid South Africa into 'the skunk of the world', with 'the world' here implicitly referencing the white Western world.[4] This account extends the notion of 'skunk' beyond the country to Afrikaners becoming 'skunks', communicating a sense of the Afrikaans white self being shamed before its global reference point, the 'Western white'. The affective charge is deepened as Afrikaners are shamed amid feeling the enjoyment of nationalist pride – pride being the opposite of shame (Scheff 2000). The identitary purchase of nationalism (a particular set of bonds – in this case, Afrikaner nationalism) rests on a phantasm or promised fullness of enjoyment, what Jacques Lacan called *jouissance*, a pleasure of being (Stavrakakis 2010: 13). Racism can be implicated in this fullness of enjoyment, as it can be read as the disavowal of the way in which the other 'takes' their *jouissance*, in a way radically different to 'ours' (Miller 1994: 79). Nationalist enjoyment occurs through official institutions and in everyday practices, such as the culinary (Stavrakakis 2010: 13), hence the above references to food and organisations associated with 'the Afrikaner'. Regarding institutions, from the normative subject position's vantage point, the apartheid state is lost and Afrikaner nationalist organisations are 'irrelevant and half ridiculous', says a respondent. Hence, her identification is experienced as 'irrelevant'. With racism under pressure in postapartheid South Africa, the subject feels 'half ashamed and half culpable for not really thinking much about things' during apartheid. Shame is therefore also the result of the global white other's withdrawal of moral verification, thereby interrupting the promise of Afrikaner fullness and precipitating the loss of the racism-infused *jouissance* of Afrikaner nationalist belonging.

The dissident position acknowledges the loss of the pleasurable togetherness of the nationalist home:

Andriette (56): I am actually very guilty of certain things [. . .] like last night it was [an] Afrikaans [evening] at [X high school] [. . .] I felt so pleasurably at home because there were many Afrikaans people, we spoke Afrikaans and many of them, because I know them, don't fit in or slot in with the Afrikaans community anymore, but it makes you comfortable to speak in your own language.

Nevertheless, while enjoying the pleasure of speaking Afrikaans, dissenters no longer 'fit in' or 'slot in'. The phrase 'slots in' suggests even greater intimacy in belonging. For dissenters, this intimate connection is gone. The loss of apartheid as a mode of Afrikaner actualisation opens the possibility that Antjie Krog calls for: a metamorphosis 'of tongue, of voice, of being, of identity' (West 2009: 71). It is notable that the dissident subject invokes guilt rather than shame. While guilt is much less pertinent than shame in this study, and also possesses less transformatory potential (as explained above), the guilty self possesses a sense of agency focusing on ways of doing or praxis. The metamorphosis of Afrikaans whiteness contains the potential of anti-racist praxis for dislocated subjects:

Andriette: The way domestic workers were treated. You would think being a woman you'll understand another woman's position. That is why I raise colonialism. I don't have another language to explain it. You have a superiority. I see it not only with Afrikaners, but with white people and it sits inside me too. I also have to re-evaluate myself in terms of all my actions [and ask myself]: 'Am I not now thinking that I'm better, know better?'

While grief is not specifically mentioned by subjects, it is an emotion associated with the loss of a person, community or place – in this case, the *volk*. Grief leads to 'the very "I" [being] called into question by its relation to the Other [. . .] My narrative falters, as it must [. . .] We're undone by each other' (Butler 2004: 23). Through this 'disorientation and loss', the possibility arises for the 'I' to gain the 'you' (49), which is the potential opened by Andriette's radical questioning of herself: 'I also have to re-evaluate myself in terms of all my actions [and ask myself]: 'Am I not now thinking that I'm better, know better?'

The dissident position in this study resonates with the narrative of 'under African skies (or, white but not quite)' identified in Melissa Steyn's (2001) study of shifting whitenesses in postapartheid South Africa. These subjects are conscious of their whiteness and engaged in self-reflective practice. They do 'not deny personal implication in social processes of racialisation' (Steyn 2001: 115). Rather, they are engaged in a radical resignification of the term 'Afrikaner' (2004: 82), which this study finds enabled by an acknowledgment of racialised shame that involves breaking with apartheid whiteness by seeing the black other as a human being capable of shaming. Simultaneously, working with the emotions of shame and (to a much lesser extent) guilt and grief, they let go of faltering narratives of belonging circumscribed by whiteness. Instead, they pursue a metamorphosis in identity that engages in a continual self-reflective praxis of anti-racism.

Therefore, two moves are found in relation to affect in postapartheid white Afrikaans identity work. The first is unacknowledged shame, when subjects retreat into and cling to normative defensive whiteness. Normative subjects feel shame in the form of fear of loss of white belonging, especially as global whiteness withdrew its verification of apartheid whiteness and interrupted the *jouissance* of Afrikaner nationalist pride. The resulting defensive whiteness remains blind to black people's humanity. The second is acknowledged shame as enabling a deepening of humanness. White subjects' shame before the eyes of black subjects opens the possibility of restoring and creating social ties in ways that breach apartheid categorisations, as dissident white subjects work against the psychosocial degradation of whiteness to overturn the colonial denial of humanity to black people. Consequently, affective practices, particularly shame, pave ways out of apartheid whiteness, but only if acknowledged. Shame is of specific salience as it is the social emotion situating self in relation to the other and to the social. It is the emotion most associated with the protection of social ties. Unacknowledged shame ensnares subjects in repetitions of emotions, such as anger, and therefore forecloses change. Acknowledged shame opens different options, allowing recognition of the other through refusals of oppressive racial, gender and class discourses and thereby opening the potential for upending whiteness.

Recognition is here used in the way that Judith Butler (2004: 43–5) proposes: that one is recognised as human based on a set of cultural norms of recognition. Therefore, one is humanised in the eyes of the other. If it is acknowledged, shame can facilitate exactly this humanisation and, I would dare say, a *mutual* humanisation, in which white subjects humanise black others and black subjects humanise white others. Judging by South Africa's existence of just over a hundred years, its residents have been entangled in twisting coils of unacknowledged shame and anger, foreclosing humanisation. It is a truism that particularly white Afrikaans-speakers have excelled at doing unto others what has been done unto them. In early twenty-first-century South Africa, it would seem that cycle is accelerating again, as cultural brokers and other opportunists swoop in to capitalise on a growing disenchantment as a result of the failings of the postapartheid regime. New Right discourses are liberally borrowed from the Global North, with the attendant mobilisation of hostile emotions against all that seem other to white, straight selves. A white and masculinist hubris is on the rise, brazen in its intensification of oppressive including and excluding identity forms described in this book.

To counteract these recurring reruns, a politics of recognition across the old and the new social frontiers must be pursued. Despite their fresh tweaks, these tired and destructive habits of being and doing may ultimately be our collective undoing. Mutual humanisation through a consciously driven politics of recognition can open new vistas of social imagination, painfully necessary in a still relatively new South Africa that feels old before its time. As we have seen in this chapter, affect must be a part of this politics. This corresponds with Chantal Mouffe's (2005) argument for a politics that inspires passions – not in the service of white or male or heteronormative aggressions, but to advance democratic, inclusive values. In South Africa's case, these values are human dignity, freedom and equality, as contained in its first democratic Constitution. What this means for white Afrikaans people is a directed dissidence in which *ordentlikheid* is turned into a truly ethical position aligned with these values of recognition, rather than reheated dehumanising norms from yesteryear. It involves actively adopting a position opposite to the rising white heteropatriarchal hubris, a subjectivity that defies oppressive normativities and draws on uncertainty, humility and self-reflection to remake itself. In the words of Andriette:

> I also have to re-evaluate myself in terms of all my actions [and ask myself]: 'Am I not now thinking that I'm better, know better?'

Notes

NOTE TO INTRODUCTION

1. http://www.sahistory.org.za/article/state-nation-address-president-south-africa-nelson-mandela.

NOTES TO CHAPTER 1

1. *Vrye Weekblad* translates as 'Free Weekly', an independent anti-apartheid newspaper (later a magazine) that, before its demise in 1994, exposed the apartheid police hit squads.
2. I appreciate the illuminating conversations with Andries Bezuidenhout about capturing the complexities of *ordentlikheid*.
3. Subaltern studies developed in the 1980s out of a critical stance towards elitist historiography about colonial India by foregrounding subaltern groups as agents of history, particularly how in colonial India people resisted, for example, a 'politics of the people' elite domination, as opposed to a politics of the elite (Chakrabarty 2005: 472). Later critiques about the absence of gender analysis and an unproblematised acceptance of subjectivity engendered feminist and postmodern adaptations (see, for example, Spivak 1988).
4. 'Hottentots' was a derogatory term in use at the time, denoting Khoikhoi.
5. English novels of the late 1800s depicted the Boers as 'slow-witted', 'fatalistic', 'childlike' and a 'simple race'. Burghers of the Zuid-Afrikaanse Republiek were dishonest, ignorant, backward and lazy. Paul Kruger was dismissed as 'ignorant' and 'dirty' by British colonial secretary Joseph Chamberlain (Barber 1999: 18). Lord Randolph Churchill used every derogatory perception in circulation at the time: 'It may be asserted [. . .] that [the Boer] never plants a tree, never digs a well, never makes a road, never grows a blade of corn [. . .] He passes his days doing absolutely nothing beyond smoking and drinking coffee [. . .] His simple ignorance is unfathomable' (Pieterse 1992: 104). Positive stereotyping pictured Boers as hospitable, self-sufficient, peaceful, courageous and persevering.

6. While John Gabriel (1998) tracks such processes with reference to English-Irish relations, Nell Irvin Painter (2010) lays out the racialisation of subordinate whites in power contestations in nineteenth-century United States that centrifugally acted on the boundaries of whiteness in successive 'enlargements of American whiteness' to eventually include formerly barred Irish and Southern and Eastern Europeans.

7. Alongside the revamping of eighteenth-century children-of-nature analogies, Afrikaner nationalist discourses 'whitened' Afrikaners with appropriations of civilisation, industriousness, social Darwinist racial hierarchy, Christianity and racial purity (Van der Westhuizen 2007: 53–60).

8. http://www.news24.com/SouthAfrica/News/Zuma-Afrikaners-true-S-Africans-20090402.

9. Respectability was imported to South Africa amid intense contestations among Dutch and British settlers' and metropolitan concepts with African and slave knowledges about race and sexuality, unleashed by the need to transform a slave society into one based on free wage labour after 1838 (Scully 1995: 338).

10. The primary concern was about middle-class, white English women descending to the level of labour, which subverted the class hierarchy and the respectable patriarchal male's ability to be the sole provider in relation to 'his' women (Lester 1998: 520).

11. 'In 1924, 48 percent of the total manufacturing work force in Johannesburg were white women, and this figure had risen by 1935 to an astonishing 73 percent' (Hyslop 1995: 62). Social Darwinist notions confirming the intersection of class and race abounded in comments such as that those that have slipped into a lower class where race mixing is rife can, as M.E. Rothmann put it in the 1920s, 'climb up' again (Du Toit 2003: 173) and as the United Party saw it in the 1930s, the less qualified and inferior in each race would be prone to miscegenation (Hyslop 1995: 73).

12. The middle-class discourse of family prevalent in South Africa in the 1920s and 1930s prescribed a distinct masculine and feminine separation between and within the public and private spheres (Erlank 2003: 656–7).

13. All names of interviewees are pseudonyms. Interviews are my own translations from Afrikaans.

14. 'Boy' was a racist paternalistic term used during colonialism and apartheid to denote a black adult male (Pieterse 1992), appropriated for the Afrikaans language.

15. The 'tot system' on farms has persisted since colonial times. 'Coloured' labourers are 'paid' in alcohol, with widespread alcoholism and foetal alcohol syndrome as present-day consequences.

16. Translated directly as 'curtain of Boer sausage,' referring to the ethnic and geographical divide between English- and Afrikaans-speaking sections of Cape Town.

17. Sanlam was the first Afrikaner nationalist insurance company used to build a capital base for Afrikaners (O'Meara 1983).

NOTES TO CHAPTER 2

1. As elaborated later in this chapter, neo-liberalism is here understood as per Brown (2005) and Rose (1990) and postfeminism as per Gill and Scharff (2011), Budgeon (2011) and Tasker and Negra (2007).

2. The term 'second wave feminism' generally refers to the rise of liberal feminism in the West in the early 1960s, as driven by white, middle-class, heterosexual women and later including socialist and radical feminisms. A clear demarcation is difficult to make, but third wave feminism can be described as growing out of black and lesbian critiques of the exclusionary and blinkered character of the second wave from the late 1970s onwards. The concept of 'waves' of feminism is Western and has been criticised as privileging white women's resistances, or excluding black women's resistances that preceded the first wave, or that occurred in pre-colonial and colonial contexts. The terms are used here mindful of the criticism and in recognition that these 'waves' do not capture women's resistances adequately and that much more work still needs to be done in this regard, including a possible reconceptualisation of the term 'wave' itself.

3. Quotes from Maritz (2012) are translations from the original Afrikaans.

4. This problematisation by Bouwer is contradicted by *Die Vrou Deel 1* (Woman Part 1) (Van der Merwe and Albertyn 1972), an Afrikaner nationalist text published at the time that dispenses a normative Afrikaner nationalist gender discourse. The contradiction suggests discursive competition within Afrikaner nationalism about women's 'correct' position at the time.

5. The 'hero's journey' is a popular narrative of self-construction described by Joseph Campbell in *The Hero with a Thousand Faces* (published in 1949).

6. All quotations of *Sarie* texts have been translated from the original Afrikaans by the author.

7. Names in *Sarie* articles are indicated with quotation marks to emphasise that these are characters created in Sarielese.

8. The correct grammatical form in Afrikaans would be '*ek*' (I). Afrikaans grammar rules forbid the use of '-self' in certain instances while prescribing it as 'unnecessary' in others. The use of '-self' is only necessary to avoid confusion (Müller 2003: 189).

9. Skeggs (2005: 975) uses authorisation to indicate a process of validation by 'those [. . .] positioned to make judgments of other's subjectivity'.

10. Mulvey's influential article (1975) on visual pleasure in narrative cinema identifies 'the image of woman as (passive) raw material for the (active) gaze of man' as part of 'the ideology of the patriarchal order' (17–18).

11. Foucault's (2002: 58–9) panopticism is associated with the rise of bourgeois domination, organised around 'what was normal or not' and requiring continuous surveillance. It is a micropower that classifies, hierarchises and (in)validates (1991: 212).

NOTES TO CHAPTER 3

1. That said, the revisionist school's analyses exposing the class formations underpinning Afrikaner nationalism (for example, O'Meara's 1983 investigations of *volkskapitalisme*) helped to unpick liberal notions of monolithic Afrikanerdom.

2. The oppressive institution of the nineteenth-century bourgeois family sparked the rise of the first wave of feminism (Hobsbawm 2003: 279, 281).

3. The Dutch settlers (Voortrekkers) who left the Eastern Cape frontier in 1838 on what was later invented as the 'Great Trek' consisted of the following: 'The basic unit was the white family head, plus white dependents, plus servants and "apprentices" [. . .] [following] the leadership of an important man' (Curtin 1999: 69–70). This form suggests the reactivation of remnants of the frontier masculinity of the nomadic Dutch settler farmers (*trekboere*) in the late 1700s: 'Government was the informal authority of the male family head effectively ruling over his family and Khoikhoi servants, with a strict racial hierarchy of dominant whites and subordinate African servants' (49).

4. T-shirts bearing ANC struggle leader Winnie Madikizela-Mandela's image and the words 'Mother of the Nation' were for sale at the 1997 ANC Women's League national conference in Mafikeng, confirming her standing in the African nationalist imaginary.

5. This is not to deny that 'woman-as-symbol', infused with maternal symbolism, is not a stock-in-trade of nationalisms, including African nationalism in South Africa, with particular evocations of blackness in relation to heterofemininity (McClintock 1993, 1991; Hassim 1993). However, the Afrikaner nationalist *volksmoeder* is a symbol decidedly deployed to construct the 'Afrikaner woman', predicated on whiteness.

6. Freedom Front Plus politician Corné Mulder is the son of Connie Mulder, a contender for the prime ministership of apartheid South Africa in the late 1970s, who represented the *verkrampte* (reactionary) wing in the ruling National Party.

NOTES TO CHAPTER 4

1. White men were conscripted as part of the militarised reform phase of late apartheid.

2. The original Afrikaans poem is from the Moreleta Park congregation's website, http://www.moreleta.org. The poet's name is given simply as 'Rinie' and it is dated 2011.

NOTES TO CHAPTER 5

1. A version of this chapter previously appeared as an article (Van der Westhuizen 2016a) titled 'Afrikaners in Post-apartheid South Africa: Inward Migration and Enclave Nationalism' in the centenary edition of *HTS Theological Studies* 72 (4): 1–9. a3351. http://dx.doi.org/10.4102/hts. v72i1.3351. Copyright © 2016 C. van der Westhuizen. Licensee: AOSIS. This work is licensed under the Creative Commons Attribution Licence.

2. The prevalence of the term is exemplified by a December 2012 commercial holiday supplement to the English-language Cape Town newspapers featuring a page headlined 'Beyond the *Boerewors* Curtain', in which the divide is described as follows: 'The northern

suburbs are subtly separated from Cape Town's southern suburbs by what locals call "the *boerewors* curtain", an imaginary line that demarcates the predominantly Afrikaans-speaking northern suburbs from the English-speaking southern suburbs, although with the increasingly multicultural nature of suburban Cape Town this is a generalisation' (*Welcome to the Cape*, summer edition, 2012). Note the use of 'multicultural' as a code for race.

3. Foucault (1991: 212) describes panopticism as a micropower that classifies, hierarchises, validates and invalidates.

4. In 2005 the Human Rights Commission's chairperson won an Equality Court case against a hair salon after hairdressers refused to cut his hair 'because it is different to that of whites'. See also the more recent case, involving hairdresser Tanya Louw. http://www.news24.com/Archives/Witness/hairdresser-claims-not-to-know-how-to-cut-black-peoples-hair-20150430.

5. Seemingly in contrast, *Sarie* also hosts a monthly column by a gender-non-conforming Afrikaans gay white male known as Nataniël. See Chapter 2 on Nataniël as the 'good homosexual'.

NOTES TO CONCLUSION

1. See Chapter 4 for a discussion on the use of 'hegemonic masculinity' in light of criticisms.

2. A version of this section first appeared in 'Race, Intersectionality and Affect in Postapartheid Productions of "the Afrikaans White Woman"', *Critical Philosophy of Race* 4(2): 221–38 (Van der Westhuizen 2016b). Copyright ©The Pennsylvania State University Press, 2016. It is used by permission of The Pennsylvania State University Press.

3. Apartheid spatial regulation meant that the families of black people working in urban areas frequently lived in remote rural Bantustans, or 'homelands', a situation that persists in democratic South Africa, with many black people still living far from cities.

4. The pervasiveness of the use of this term was demonstrated when Nelson Mandela also referenced it in his inaugural address as the first democratic president of South Africa in 1994. http://www.africa.upenn.edu/Articles_Gen/Inaugural_Speech_17984.html.

Select Bibliography

Adhikari, M. 2005. *Not White Enough, Not Black Enough: Racial Identity in the South African Coloured Community*. Athens: Ohio University Press.

Alexander, N. 2002. *An Ordinary Country: Issues in the Transition from Apartheid to Democracy in South Africa*. Pietermaritzburg: University of Natal Press.

Als, H. 2012. 'Yael Farber's "Mies Julie"'. *The New Yorker*, 20 November. http://www.newyorker.com/culture/culture-desk/yael-farbers-mies-julie.

Althusser, L. 2008. *On Ideology*. London: Verso.

Anderson, B. 1991 [1983]. *Imagined Communities: Reflections on the Origin and Spread of Nationalism*. Revised edition. London: Verso.

Anthias, F. and N. Yuval-Davis. 1989. 'Introduction'. In *Women-Nation-State*, edited by N. Yuval-Davis and F. Anthias, 1–15. Basingstoke: Macmillan.

Attwood, F. 2009. *Mainstreaming Sex: The Sexualisation of Western Culture*. London: I.B. Tauris.

Baderoon, G. 2014. *Regarding Muslims: From Slavery to Post-apartheid*. Johannesburg: Wits University Press.

Balibar, E. 1991. 'The Nation Form: History and Ideology'. In *Race, Nation, Class: Ambiguous Identities*, edited by E. Balibar and I.M. Wallerstein, 86–106. London: Verso.

Barber, J. 1999. *South Africa in the Twentieth Century: A Political History; In Search of a Nation State*. Oxford: Blackwell.

Bartky, S.L. 1990. *Femininity and Domination: Studies in the Phenomenology of Oppression*. New York: Routledge.

Bauman, Z. 2001. 'The Great War of Recognition'. *Theory, Culture and Society* 18(2–3): 137–50.

Bekker, S. and A. Leildé. 2006. 'Class, Race and Language in Cape Town and Johannesburg'. In *Reflections on Identity in Four African Cities*, edited by S. Bekker and A. Leildé, 145–65. Cape Town: African Minds.

Bell, D. and G. Valentine. 1995. 'The Sexed Self: Strategies of Performance, Sites of Resistance'. In *Mapping the Subject: Geographies of Cultural Transformation*, edited by S. Pile and N. Thrift, 143–57. London: Routledge.

Bernard, J. 2002. 'The Husband's Marriage and the Wife's Marriage'. In *Gender: A Sociological Reader*, edited by S. Jackson and S. Scott, 207–19. New York: Routledge.

Beukes, W.D. (ed.). 1992. *Oor grense heen* [Across borders]. Cape Town: Nasionale Boekhandel.

Billig, M. 1995. *Banal Nationalism*. London: Sage.

Blackman, L. 2008. *The Body: The Key Concepts*. Oxford: Berg.

Blaser, T. and C. van der Westhuizen. 2012. 'Introduction: The Paradox of Post-apartheid Afrikaner Identity: Deployments of Ethnicity and Neo-liberalism'. *African Studies* 71(3): 380–90.

Bozzoli, B. 1983. 'Marxism, Feminism and South African Studies'. *Journal of Southern African Studies* 9(2): 139–71.

Bradford, H. 2000. 'Regendering Afrikanerdom: The 1899–1902 Anglo-Boer War'. In *Gendered Nations: Nationalisms and Gender Order in the Long Nineteenth Century*, edited by I. Blom, K. Hagemann and C. Hall, 207–25. Oxford: Berg.

———. 1996. 'Women, Gender and Colonialism: Rethinking the History of the British Cape Colony and its Frontier Zones c.1806–70'. *Journal of African History* 37(3): 351–70.

Brink, E. 2008. 'Die volksmoeder: 'n Beeld van 'n vrou' [The *volksmoeder*: A model of a woman]. In *Van volksmoeder tot Fokofpolisiekar: Kritiese opstelle oor Afrikaanse herinneringsplekke* [From the mother of the nation to Fokofpolisiekar: Critical essays about Afrikaans places of memory], edited by A.M. Grundlingh and S. Huigen, 7–16. Stellenbosch: SUN Press.

———. 1990. 'Man-Made Women: Gender, Class and the Ideology of the *Volksmoeder*.' In *Women and Gender in Southern Africa to 1945*, edited by C. Walker, 273–92. Cape Town: David Philip; London: James Currey.

Brown, W. 2005. *Edgework: Critical Essays on Knowledge and Politics*. Princeton: Princeton University Press.

Budgeon, S. 2011. 'The Contradictions of Successful Femininity: Third-Wave Feminism, Postfeminism and "New" Femininities'. In *New Femininities: Postfeminism, Neoliberalism and Subjectivity*, edited by R. Gill and C. Scharff, 279–92. New York: Palgrave Macmillan.

Butler, J. 2005. *Giving an Account of Oneself*. New York: Fordham University Press.

———. 2004. *Precarious Life: The Powers of Mourning and Violence*. London: Verso.

———. 2000. 'Restaging the Universal: Hegemony and the Limits of Formalism'. In *Contingency, Hegemony, Universality: Contemporary Dialogues on the Left*, by J. Butler, E. Laclau and S. Žižek, 11–43. London: Verso.

———. 1997. *The Psychic Life of Power: Theories in Subjection*. Stanford: Stanford University Press.

————— 1993. *Bodies That Matter: On the Discursive Limits of Sex*. New York: Routledge.

————. 1990. *Gender Trouble: Feminism and the Subversion of Identity*. New York: Routledge.

Carpentier, N. and E. Spinoy. 2008. 'Introduction: From the Political to the Cultural'. In *Discourse Theory and Cultural Analysis: Media, Arts and Literature*, edited by N. Carpentier and E. Spinoy, 1–26. New Jersey: Hampton Press.

Carton, B., J. Laband and J. Sithole (eds). 2008. *Zulu Identities: Being Zulu, Past and Present*. Pietermaritzburg: University of KwaZulu-Natal Press.

Celliers, J.F.E. 1908. *Die vlakte en andere gedigte* [The plain and other poems]. Pretoria: Volkstem-drukkerij.

Chakrabarty, D. 2005. 'A Small History of Subaltern Studies'. In *A Companion to Postcolonial Studies*, edited by H. Schwarz and S. Ray, 467–84. Malden, MA: Blackwell.

Chambers, R. 1997. 'The Unexamined'. In *Whiteness: A Critical Reader*, edited by M. Hill, 187–203. New York: New York University Press.

Charton, N. 1975. 'Afrikaners as Viewed by English-speaking Compatriots'. In *Looking at the Afrikaner Today: Views of Compatriots and Foreigners*, edited by H.W. van der Merwe, 40–51. Cape Town: Tafelberg.

Chipkin, I. 2007. *Do South Africans Exist? Nationalism, Democracy, and the Identity of "the People"*. Johannesburg: Wits University Press.

Cloete, E. 1992. 'Afrikaner Identity: Culture, Tradition and Gender'. *Agenda* 13: 42–56.

Coetzee, J.M. 1991. 'The Mind of Apartheid: Geoffrey Cronjé (1907–)'. *Social Dynamics: A Journal of African Studies* 17(1): 1–35.

Collins, P.H. 2004. *Black Sexual Politics: African Americans, Gender, and the New Racism*. New York: Routledge.

————. 2000a [1990]. *Black Feminist Thought: Knowledge, Consciousness and the Politics of Empowerment*. 2nd edition. New York: Routledge.

————. 2000b. 'Toward a New Vision: Race, Class and Gender as Categories of Analysis and Connection'. In *The Social Construction of Difference and Inequality: Race, Class, Gender, and Sexuality*, edited by T.E. Ore, 557–70. Mountain View: Mayfield Publishing Company.

Connell, R.W. 2005 [1993]. *Masculinities*. 2nd edition. Cambridge: Polity Press.

————. 1987. *Gender and Power*. Sydney: Allen & Unwin.

Connell, R.W. and J.W. Messerschmidt. 2005. 'Hegemonic Masculinity: Rethinking the Concept'. *Gender and Society* 19: 829–59.

Cornell, S. and D. Hartmann. 2007 [1998]. *Ethnicity and Race: Making Identities in a Changing World*. 2nd edition. Thousand Oaks, CA: Pine Forge Press.

Coullie, J.L. 2014. 'Remembering to Forget: Testimony, Collective Memory and the Genesis of the "New" South African Nation in *Country of My Skull*'. In *Antjie Krog: An Ethics of Body and Otherness*, edited by J.L. Coullie and A. Visagie, 1–23. Pietermaritzburg: University of KwaZulu-Natal Press.

Crenshaw, K.W. 1995. 'Mapping the Margins: Intersectionality, Identity Politics, and Violence against Women of Color'. In *Critical Race Theory: The Key Writings*

That Formed the Movement, edited by K.W. Crenshaw, N. Gotanda, G. Peller and K. Thomas, 357–83. New York: The New Press.

Critchley, S. and O. Marchart (eds). 2004. 'Introduction'. In *Laclau: A Critical Reader*, edited by S. Critchley and O. Marchart, 1–13. London: Routledge.

Cronjé, G. 1945. 'Die huisgesin in die Afrikaanse kultuurgemeenskap' [The family in the Afrikaans cultural community]. In *Kultuurgeskiedenis van die Afrikaner: Die eerste beskrywing van die Boere-volkslewe in al sy vertakkinge; Deel I* [The cultural history of the Afrikaner: The first description of the Boer people's ways in all their furcations; Part I], edited by C.M. van den Heever and P. de V. Pienaar, 309–60. Cape Town: Nasionale Pers.

Cronjé, G. and J.D. Venter. 1958. *Die patriargale familie: 'n Kultuursosiologiese studie* [The patriarchal family: A cultural-sociological study]. Cape Town: HAUM.

Curtin, P.D. 1999. 'Location in History: Argentina and South Africa in the Nineteenth Century'. *Journal of World History* 10(1): 41–92.

Dagut, S. 2000. 'Gender, Colonial "Women's History" and the Construction of Social Distance: Middle-Class British Women in Late Nineteenth-Century South Africa'. *Journal of Southern African Studies* 26(3): 555–72.

De Fina, A., D. Schiffrin and M. Bamberg (eds). 2006. *Discourse and Identity*. Cambridge: Cambridge University Press.

De Klerk, W. 1984. *Die tweede (r)evolusie: Afrikanerdom en die identiteitskrisis* [The second (r)evolution: Afrikanerdom and the identity crisis]. Johannesburg: Jonathan Ball.

De Lauretis, T. 1987. *Technologies of Gender: Essays on Theory, Film, and Fiction*. Indianapolis: Indiana University Press.

Deliovsky, K. 2010. *White Femininity: Race, Gender and Power*. Halifax: Fernwood Publishing.

Dick, A.L. 2004. 'Building a Nation of Readers? Women's Organizations and the Politics of Reading in South Africa, 1900–1914'. *Historia* 49(2): 23–44.

Distiller, N. and M. Steyn. 2004. 'Introduction: Under Construction'. In *Under Construction: 'Race' and Identity in South Africa Today*, edited by N. Distiller and M. Steyn, 1–11. Johannesburg: Heinemann.

Distiller, N. and M. Steyn (eds). 2004. *Under Construction: 'Race' and Identity in South Africa Today*. Johannesburg: Heinemann.

Dobash, R.E. and R.P. Dobash. 1992. *Women, Violence and Social Change*. London: Routledge.

Dr Goedhart [pseudonym]. 1972. 'Die andersheid van die vrou' [The difference of woman]. In *Die Vrou Deel 1* [Woman Part 1], edited by C.P. van der Merwe and C.F. Albertyn, 360–74. Cape Town: Albertyn.

Dubow, S. 1992. 'Afrikaner Nationalism, Apartheid and the Conceptualization of Race'. *Journal of African History* 33(2): 209–37.

Dubow, S. and A. Jeeves (eds). 2005. *South Africa's 1940s: World of Possibilities*. Cape Town: Double Storey Books.

Du Pisani, K. 2001. 'Puritanism Transformed: Afrikaner Masculinities in the Apartheid and Post-apartheid Period'. In *Changing Men in Southern Africa*, edited by R. Morrell, 157–75. Pietermaritzburg: University of Natal Press; London: Zed Books.

Du Plessis, A. 2012. 'Afrikaanse musiek: Eiendoms (beperk) – (Groot op gelukkige eiland)' [Afrikaans music: Property (limited) – (Big on happy island)]. *Litnet*, http://www.litnet.co.za/Article/afrikaanse-musiek-eiendoms-beperk-groot-op-gelukkige-eiland.

Du Plessis, I. 2010. 'Die familiesage as volksverhaal: Afrikanernasionalisme en die politiek van reproduksie in Marlene van Niekerk se *Agaat*' [The family saga as *volk* narrative: Afrikaner nationalism and the politics of reproduction in Marlene van Niekerk's *Agaat*]. *Litnet Akademies*, http://www.litnet.co.za/die-familiesage-as-volksverhaal-afrikanernasionalisme-en-die-politiek-van-reproduksie-in/.

Du Toit, L. 2009. *A Philosophical Investigation of Rape: The Making and Unmaking of the Feminine Self*. New York: Routledge.

Du Toit, M. 2003. 'The Domesticity of Afrikaner Nationalism: *Volksmoeders* and the ACVV, 1904–1929'. *Journal of Southern African Studies* 29(1): 155–76.

Eisenstein, Z. 2000. 'Writing Bodies on the Nation for the Globe'. In *Women, States, and Nationalism: At Home in the Nation?* edited by S. Ranchod-Nilsson and M.A. Tétreault, 35–53. London: Routledge.

Ellison, J. 1996. 'A Short History of Liberal Guilt'. *Critical Inquiry* 22(2): 344–71.

Erasmus, Z. 2005. 'Race and Identity in the Nation'. In *State of the Nation: South Africa 2004–2005*, edited by J. Daniel, R. Southall and J. Lutchman, 9–33. Cape Town: HSRC Press.

————. 2001. 'Introduction: Re-imagining Coloured Identities in Post-apartheid South Africa'. In *Coloured by History, Shaped by Place: New Perspectives on Coloured Identities in Cape Town*, edited by Z. Erasmus, 13–28. Cape Town: Kwela Books; Maroelana: South African History Online.

Eribon, D. 2004. *Insult and the Making of the Gay Self*. Durham: Duke University Press.

Erlank, N. 2003. 'Gender and Masculinity in South African Nationalist Discourse, 1912–1950'. *Feminist Studies* 29(3): 653–71.

Essed, P. 2002. 'Everyday Racism'. In *A Companion to Racial and Ethnic Studies*, edited by D.T. Goldberg and J. Solomos, 202–15. Cambridge, MA: Blackwell.

Falkof, N. 2016. 'ENG/AFR: White Masculinity in Two Contemporary South African Films'. *Critical Arts* 30(1): 15–30.

Fanon, F. 2001. *The Wretched of the Earth*. London: Penguin.

Ferguson, M. 1983. *Forever Feminine: Women's Magazines and the Cult of Femininity*. London: Heinemann.

Foucault, M. 2004. *Society Must be Defended: Lectures at the College de France, 1975–76*. London: Penguin.

————. 2002. *Michel Foucault: Power; Essential Works of Foucault 1954–1984, Vol. 3*. Edited by J.D. Faubion. London: Penguin.

————. 1998 [1976]. *The Will to Knowledge: The History of Sexuality, Vol. 1*. London: Penguin.

————. 1992 [1984]. *The Use of Pleasure: The History of Sexuality, Vol. 2*. London: Penguin.

————. 1991. *The Foucault Reader: An Introduction to Foucault's Thought*. Edited by P. Rabinow. London: Penguin.

————. 1990 [1984]. *The Care of the Self: The History of Sexuality, Vol. 3*. London: Penguin.

Fredrickson, G.M. 1981. *White Supremacy: A Comparative Study in American and South African History*. New York: Oxford University Press.

Gabriel, J. 1998. *Whitewash: Racialized Politics and the Media*. London: Routledge.

Gaitskell, D. and E. Unterhalter. 1989. 'Mothers of the Nation: A Comparative Analysis of Nation, Race and Motherhood in Afrikaner Nationalism and the African National Congress'. In *Women-Nation-State*, edited by N. Yuval-Davis and F. Anthias, 59–78. Basingstoke: Macmillan.

Gellner, E. 1964. *Thought and Change*. London: Weidenfeld & Nicolson.

Geschiere, P. and B. Meyer. 1998. 'Globalization and Identity: Dialectics of Flow and Closure; Introduction'. *Development and Change* 29(4): 601–15.

Geschiere, P. and F. Nyamnjoh. 2000. 'Capitalism and Autochthony: The Seesaw of Mobility and Belonging'. *Public Culture* 12(2): 423–52.

Giliomee, H. 2004. *The Afrikaners: Biography of a People*. Cape Town: Tafelberg.

Gill, R. 2009. 'Supersexualise Me! Advertising and the Midriffs'. In *Mainstreaming Sex: The Sexualisation of Western Culture*, edited by F. Attwood, 93–109. London: I.B. Tauris.

Gill, R. and C. Scharff. 2011. 'Introduction'. In *New Femininities: Postfeminism, Neoliberalism and Subjectivity*, edited by R. Gill and C. Scharff, 1–17. New York: Palgrave Macmillan.

Gilroy, P. 2007. *There Ain't No Black in the Union Jack*. London: Routledge.

Goldberg, D.T. 2009. *The Threat of Race: Reflections on Racial Neoliberalism*. Oxford: Wiley-Blackwell.

————. 2002. 'Racial States'. In *A Companion to Racial and Ethnic Studies*, edited by D.T. Goldberg and J. Solomos, 233–58. Cambridge, MA: Blackwell.

Goldberg D.T. and J. Solomos. 2002. 'General Introduction'. In *A Companion to Racial and Ethnic studies*, edited by D.T. Goldberg and J. Solomos, 1–11. Cambridge, MA: Blackwell.

Gouws, T. 1996. 'Postmodern Identity: History, Language and Cultural Difference or: The True Colours of the Rainbow Nation'. *New Contree* 40: 13–25.

Groenewald, Y. 2007. 'The De La Rey Uprising'. *Mail & Guardian*, 16 February. http://mg.co.za/article/2007-02-16-the-de-la-rey-uprising.

Grosz, E. 1994. *Volatile Bodies: Towards a Corporeal Feminism*. Bloomington: Indiana University Press.

Grundlingh, A. and B. Nasson. 2014. *The War at Home: Women and Families in the Anglo-Boer War*. Cape Town: Tafelberg.

Gunkel, H. 2011. *The Cultural Politics of Female Sexuality in South Africa*. London: Routledge.

Habib, A. and K. Bentley (eds). 2008. *Racial Redress and Citizenship in South Africa*. Cape Town: HSRC Press.

Hadland, A., E. Louw, S. Sesanti and H. Wasserman (eds). 2008. *Power, Politics and Identity in South African Media: Selected Seminar Papers*. Cape Town: HSRC Press.

Hage, G. 2000. *White Nation: Fantasies of White Supremacy in a Multicultural Society*. New York: Routledge.

Halberstam, J. 1998. *Female Masculinity*. Durham: Duke University Press.

Hall, S. 2006. 'Encoding, Decoding'. In *The Cultural Studies Reader*, edited by S. During, 507–17. London: Routledge.

———. 1997a. 'The Local and the Global: Globalization and Ethnicity'. In *Culture, Globalisation and the World-system*, edited by A.D. King, 19–39. Minneapolis: University of Minnesota Press.

———. 1997b. 'Old and New Identities, Old and New Ethnicities'. In *Culture, Globalization and the World-system*, edited by A.D. King, 40–68. Minneapolis: University of Minnesota Press.

———. 1996. 'Introduction: Who Needs Identity?' In *Questions of Cultural Identity*, edited by S. Hall and P. du Gay, 1–17. London: Sage.

Harris, C.I. 1995. 'Whiteness as Property'. In *Critical Race Theory: The Key Writings That Formed the Movement*, edited by K.M. Crenshaw, N. Gotanda, G. Peller and K. Thomas, 276–91. New York: The New Press.

Hassim, S. 1993. 'Family, Motherhood and Zulu Nationalism: The Politics of the Inkatha Women's Brigade'. *Feminist Review* 43: 1–25.

Haste, C. 2001. *Nazi Women*. London: Channel 4 Books.

Hattam, V.C. 2001. 'Whiteness: Theorising Race, Eliding Ethnicity'. *International Labor and Working-Class History* 60: 61–8.

Heaphy, B., C. Donovan and J. Weeks. 2002. 'Sex, Money and the Kitchen Sink'. In *Gender: A Sociological Reader*, edited by S. Jackson and S. Scott, 248–58. New York: Routledge.

Heng, G. 1997. '"A Great Way to Fly": Nationalism, the State and the Varieties of Third-World Feminism'. In *Feminist Genealogies, Colonial Legacies, Democratic Futures*, edited by M.J. Alexander and C.T. Mohanty, 30–45. New York: Routledge.

Herbert, T.W. 2002. *Sexual Violence and American Manhood*. Cambridge, MA: Harvard University Press.

Hobsbawm, E. 2003 [1975]. *The Age of Capital: 1848–1875*. London: Abacus.

Hofmeyr, I. 1987. 'Building a Nation from Words: Afrikaans Language, Literature and Ethnic Identity, 1902–1924'. In *The Politics of Race, Class and Nationalism in Twentieth-Century South Africa*, edited by S. Marks and S. Trapido, 95–123. London: Longman.

Howard, J. 2000. 'Social Psychology of Identities'. *Annual Review of Sociology* 26: 367–93.

Howarth, D. 2004. 'Hegemony, Political Subjectivity and Radical Democracy'. In *Laclau: A Critical Reader*, edited by S. Critchley and O. Marchart, 256–76. London: Routledge.

Hull, I.V. 1982. 'The Bourgeoisie and its Discontents: Reflections on Nationalism and Respectability'. *Journal of Contemporary History* 17(2): 247–68.

Hyslop, J. 1995. 'White Working-class Women and the Invention of Apartheid: Purified Afrikaner Nationalist Agitation for Legislation against Mixed Marriages, 1934–1939'. *Journal of African History* 36: 57–81.

Ingraham, C. 2002. 'The Heterosexual Imaginary'. In *Gender: A Sociological Reader*, edited by S. Jackson and S. Scott, 79–88. New York: Routledge.

Jackson, S. 1999. *Heterosexuality in Question*. London: Sage.

Jackson, S. and S. Scott. 2002. 'Introduction'. In *Gender: A Sociological Reader*, edited by S. Jackson and S. Scott, 1–29. New York: Routledge.

Johnson, D. 2012. *Imagining the Cape Colony: History, Literature and the South African Nation*. Cape Town: University of Cape Town Press.

Jørgensen, M.W. and L. Phillips. 2002. *Discourse Analysis as Theory and Method*. London: Sage.

Joseph, M. 1998. 'The Performance of Production and Consumption'. *Social Text* 54: 26–61.

Judge, M., A. Manion and S. de Waal. 2008. *To Have and To Hold: The Making of Same-sex Marriage in South Africa*. Johannesburg: Fanele.

Katz, J.N. 2000. 'The Invention of Heterosexuality'. In *The Social Construction of Difference and Inequality: Race, Class, Gender, and Sexuality*, edited by T.E. Ore, 137–49. Mountain View: Mayfield Publishing Company.

Keating, M. and J. McGarry. 2001. *Minority Nationalism and the Changing International Order*. Oxford: Oxford University Press.

Keegan, T. 2001. 'Gender, Degeneration and Sexual Danger: Imagining Race and Class in South Africa ca.1912'. *Journal of Southern African Studies* 27(3): 459–77.

Kimmel, M.S. 2001. 'Masculinity as Homophobia: Fear, Shame and Silence in the Construction of Gender Identity'. In *The Masculinities Reader*, edited by S.M. Whitehead and F.J. Barrett, 266–87. Cambridge: Polity Press.

Kipnis, L. 2006. *The Female Thing: Dirt, Sex, Envy, Vulnerability*. London: Serpent's Tail.

Kriel, M. 2012. 'A New Generation of Gustav Prellers? The *Fragmente*/FAK/*Vrye Afrikaan* Movement, 1998–2008'. *African Studies* 71(3): 426–45.

―――. 2006. 'Fools, Philologists and Philosophers: Afrikaans and the Politics of Cultural Nationalism'. *Politikon* 33(1): 45–70.

Krog, A. 2007. '". . . Between the Nose and the Mouth: Perhaps More towards the Eyes"'. In *Some Afrikaners Revisited*, by D. Goldblatt, 29–34. Cape Town: Umuzi.

―――. 1998. *Country of My Skull*. Johannesburg: Random House.

Kruger, L. 1991. 'Gender, Community and Identity: Women and Afrikaner Nationalism in the *Volksmoeder* discourse of *Die Boerevrou*, 1919–31'. Master's thesis, University of Cape Town.

Laclau, E. 2004. 'Glimpsing the Future'. In *Laclau: A Critical Reader*, edited by S. Critchley and O. Marchart, 279–328. London: Routledge.

———. 1996. *Emancipation(s)*. London: Verso.

———. 1994. 'Introduction'. In *The Making of Political Identities*, edited by E. Laclau, 1–10. London: Verso.

———. 1990. *New Reflections on the Revolution of Our Time*. London: Verso.

Laclau, E. and C. Mouffe. 1985. *Hegemony and Socialist Strategy: Towards a Radical Democratic Politics*. London: Verso.

Laclau, E. and L. Zac. 1994. 'Minding the Gap: The Subject of Politics'. In *The Making of Political Identities*, edited by E. Laclau, 11–39. London: Verso.

Lambert, J. 2012. 'Engelssprekende Suid-Afrikaners: Onseker van hul identiteit' [English-speaking South Africans: Unsure of their identity]. In *Geskiedenis van Suid-Afrika: Van voortye tot vandag* [The history of South Africa: From prehistoric times to today], edited by F. Pretorius, 525–48. Cape Town: Tafelberg.

Landman, C. 2005. '*Leefstyl-bybel vir Vroue* [Lifestyle-bible for Women]: Afrikaans-speaking Women amidst a Paradigm Shift'. *Studia Historiae Ecclesiasticae* 31(1): 147–62.

———. 1994. *The Piety of Afrikaans Women: Diaries of Guilt*. Pretoria: University of South Africa Press.

Langford, W. 2002. 'But He Said He Loved Me'. In *Gender: A Sociological Reader*, edited by S. Jackson and S. Scott, 230–1. New York: Routledge.

Lansky, M.R. 1999. 'Shame and the Idea of a Central Affect'. *Psychoanalytic Inquiry* 19: 347–61.

Lazar, M.M. 2011. 'The Right to be Beautiful: Postfeminist Identity and Consumer Beauty Advertising'. In *New Femininities: Postfeminism, Neoliberalism and Subjectivity*, edited by R. Gill and C. Scharff, 37–51. New York: Palgrave Macmillan.

Lester, A. 1998. 'Reformulating Identities: British Settlers in Early Nineteenth-Century South Africa'. *Transactions of the Institute of British Geographers* 23(4): 515–31.

Lewis, H.B. 1971. *Shame and Guilt in Neurosis*. New York: International Universities Press.

Lötter, E. 2004. *Dis ek, Anna* [It's me, Anna]. Cape Town: Tafelberg.

———. 2005. *It's Me, Anna*. Cape Town: Tafelberg.

Louw, C. 2001. *Boetman en die swanesang van die verligtes* [Young brother and the swansong of the progressives]. Cape Town: Human & Rousseau.

Mamdani, M. 1996. *Citizen and Subject: Contemporary Africa and the Legacy of Late Colonialism*. Kampala: Fountain Publishers.

Manicom, L. 1992. 'Ruling Relations: Rethinking State and Gender in South African History'. *Journal of African History* 33: 441–65.

Maritz, L. 2012. 'KODESA? Is dit 'n nuwe kopseerpil?' 'n Ondersoek na die Afrikanervrou se politieke ingesteldheid in die 20ste eeu' [CODESA? Is it a new headache pill? An investigation into the Afrikaner woman's political attitude in the 20th century].

LitNet Akademies, http://www.litnet.co.za/kodesa-is-dit-n-nuwe-kopseerpil-n-ondersoek-na-die-afrikanervrou-se-politieke/.

Massey, D. 2005. *For Space*. London: Sage.

Mbeki, T. 2004. 'Speech of the President of South Africa, Thabo Mbeki, at the Special Official Funeral of Dr C.F. Beyers Naudé, Aasvoelkop Dutch Reformed Church, Johannesburg', 18 September. http://www.dirco.gov.za/docs/speeches/2004/mbek0920.htm.

Mbembe, A. 1992. 'Provisional Notes on the Postcolony'. *Africa: Journal of the International African Institute* (62)1: 3–37.

McCall, L. 2005. 'The Complexity of Intersectionality'. *Signs* 30(3): 1771–1800.

McClintock, A. 1993. 'Family Feuds: Gender, Nationalism and the Family'. *Feminist Review* 44: 61–80.

———. 1991. '"No Longer in a Future Heaven": Women and Nationalism in South Africa'. *Transition* 51: 104–23.

———. 1990. 'The Very House of Difference: Race, Gender and the Politics of South African Women's Narrative in *Poppie Nongena*'. *Social Text* 25/26: 196–226.

McCracken, E. 1993. *Decoding Women's Magazines: From Mademoiselle to Ms.* Basingstoke: Macmillan.

McCrone, D. 2000. *The Sociology of Nationalism: Tomorrow's Ancestors*. London: Routledge.

McGroarty, P. and J. Bischof. 2014. 'Afrikaans, Often Reviled at Home, Has Tongues Wagging Abroad: Fans outside South Africa Don't Know a Word, but They Love the Beat'. *Wall Street Journal*, 19 September.

McLaren, M.A. 2002. *Feminism, Foucault, and Embodied Subjectivity*. Albany: State University of New York Press.

McRobbie, A. 2007. 'Postfeminism and Popular Culture: Bridget Jones and the Gender Regime'. In *Interrogating Postfeminism: Gender and the Politics of Popular Culture*, edited by Y. Tasker and D. Negra, 27–39. Durham: Duke University Press.

Miller, J-A. 1994. 'Extimité'. In *Lacanian Theory of Discourse. Subject, Structure, and Society*, edited by M. Bracher, M.W. Alcorn Jr., R.J. Corthell and F. Massardier-Kenney, 74–87. New York: New York University Press.

Mills, C.W. 1997. *The Racial Contract*. Ithaca: Cornell University Press.

Moodie, T.D. 1975. *The Rise of Afrikanerdom: Power, Apartheid, and the Afrikaner Civil Religion*. Berkeley: University of California Press.

Moon, D.G. 1999. 'White Enculturation and Bourgeois Ideology: The Discursive Production of "Good (White) Girls"'. In *Whiteness: The Social Communication of Identity*, edited by T.K. Nakayama and J.N. Martin, 177–97. Newbury Park, CA: Sage.

Morrell, R. 2001. 'The Times of Change: Men and Masculinity in South Africa'. In *Changing Men in Southern Africa*, edited by R. Morrell, 3–37. Pietermaritzburg: University of Natal Press; London: Zed Books.

————. 1998. 'Of Boys and Men: Masculinity and Gender in Southern African Studies'. *Journal of Southern African Studies* 24(4): 605–30.

Mosse, G.L. 1982. 'Nationalism and Respectability: Normal and Abnormal Sexuality in the Nineteenth Century'. *Journal of Contemporary History* 17(2): 221–46.

Mouffe, C. 2005. *The Democratic Paradox*. London: Verso.

Müller, D. 2003. *Skryf Afrikaans van A tot Z: Die essensiële gids vir taalgebruikers* [Write Afrikaans from A to Z: The essential guide for language practitioners]. Johannesburg: Pharos.

Mulvey, L. 1975. 'Visual Pleasure and Narrative Cinema'. *Screen* 16(3): 6–18.

Nadar, S. 2009. 'Who's Afraid of the Mighty Men Conference?' In *The Evil of Patriarchy in Church, Society and Politics*, 19–30. Cape Town: Inclusive and Affirming Ministries.

Nagel, J. 1998. 'Masculinity and Nationalism: Gender and Sexuality in the Making of Nations'. *Ethnic and Racial Studies* 21(2): 242–69.

Nandy, A. 1983. *The Intimate Enemy: Loss and Recovery of Self under Colonialism*. Delhi: Oxford University Press.

Narunsky-Laden, S. 2008. 'Identity in Post-apartheid South Africa: Learning to Belong thorough the (Commercial) Media'. In *Power, Politics and Identity in South African Media: Selected Seminar Papers*, edited by A. Hadland, E. Louw, S. Sesanti and H. Wasserman, 124–48. Cape Town: HSRC Press.

Nava, M. 1999. 'Consumerism Reconsidered: Buying and Power'. In *Feminism and Cultural Studies*, edited by M. Shiach, 45–64. Oxford: Oxford University Press.

Nixon, R. 1991. 'Mandela, Messianism, and the Media'. *Transition* 51: 42–55.

Njovane, T. 2015. 'The Violence beneath the Veil of Politeness: Reflections on Race and Power in the Academy'. In *Being at Home: Race, Institutional Culture and Transformation at South African Higher Education Institutions*, edited by P. Tabensky and S. Matthews, 116–29. Pietermaritzburg: University of KwaZulu-Natal Press.

Norval, A. 2003. 'Decolonization, Demonization and Difference: The Difficult Constitution of a Nation'. In *The Decolonization Reader*, edited by J.D. le Sueur, 256–68. New York: Routledge.

————. 1996. *Deconstructing Apartheid Discourse*. London: Verso.

————. 1990. 'Letter to Ernesto'. In *New Reflections on the Revolution of Our Time*, edited by E. Laclau, 135–58. London: Verso.

Nuttall, S. 2006. 'A Politics of the Emergent: Cultural Studies in South Africa'. *Theory, Culture & Society* 23: 263–78.

O'Meara, D. 1997. 'Thinking Theoretically? Afrikaner Nationalism and the Comparative Theory of the Politics of Identity: A Tribute to Harold Wolpe'. Paper presented to the inaugural conference of the Harold Wolpe Memorial Trust, University of the Western Cape, 1–2 April.

————. 1983. *Volkskapitalisme: Class, Capital and Ideology in the Development of Afrikaner Nationalism*. Cambridge: Cambridge University Press.

Orbach, S. 2009. *Bodies*. London: Profile Books.

Painter, N.I. 2010. *The History of White People*. New York: W.W. Norton.

Penzhorn, C. 2005. 'Participatory Research: Opportunities and Challenges for Research with Women in South Africa'. *Women's Studies International Forum* 28: 343–54.

Peterson, V.S. 2000. 'Sexing Political Identities/Nationalism as Heterosexism'. In *Women, States, and Nationalism: At Home in the Nation?* edited by S. Ranchod-Nilsson and M.A. Tétreault, 55–81. London: Routledge.

Pieterse, J.N. 1992. *White on Black: Images of Africa and Blacks in Western Popular Culture*. New Haven: Yale University Press.

Posel, D. 2010. 'Races to Consume: Revisiting South Africa's History of Race, Consumption and the Struggle for Freedom'. *Ethnic and Racial Studies* 33(2): 157–75.

———. 2001a. 'Race as Common Sense: Racial Classification in Twentieth-Century South Africa'. *African Studies Review* 44(2): 87–113.

———. 2001b. 'What's in a Name? Racial Categorisations under Apartheid and Their Afterlife'. *Transformation* 47: 50–74.

Potts, A. 2002. *The Science/Fiction of Sex: Feminist Deconstruction and the Vocabularies of Heterosex*. New York: Routledge.

Puttergill, C. and A. Leildé. 2006. 'Identity Studies in Africa'. In *Reflections on Identity in Four African Cities*, edited by S. Bekker and A. Leildé, 11–21. Cape Town: African Minds.

Quayson, A. 2005. 'Postcolonialism and Postmodernism'. In *A Companion to Postcolonial Studies*, edited by H. Schwarz and S. Ray, 87–110. Malden, MA: Blackwell.

Ratele, K. 2016. *Liberating Masculinities*. Cape Town: HSRC Press.

———. 2008. 'Analysing Males in Africa: Certain Useful Elements in Considering Ruling Masculinities'. *African and Asian Studies* 7: 515–36.

Rattansi, A. 1994. 'Western Racisms, Ethnicities and Identities'. In *Racism, Modernity and Identity: On the Western Front*, edited by A. Rattansi and S. Westwood, 15–86. Cambridge: Polity Press.

Republic of South Africa. 2004. *The Order of Ikhamanga Awards*. Pretoria: Government Printers.

Rich, A. 1979. *On Lies, Secrets, and Silence: Selected Prose 1966–1978*. New York: W.W. Norton.

Rose, N. 1990. *Governing the Soul: The Shaping of the Private Self*. London: Routledge.

Ross, R. 2009. *Status and Respectability in the Cape Colony 1750–1870: A Tragedy of Manners*. Cambridge: Cambridge University Press.

Rubin, G. 1975. 'The Traffic in Women: Notes on the "Political Economy" of Sex'. In *Toward an Anthropology of Women*, edited by R. Reiter, 157–210. New York: Monthly Review Press.

Russell, D.E.H. 1997. *Behind Closed Doors in White South Africa: Incest Survivors Tell Their Stories*. London: Macmillan.

Salusbury, T. and D. Foster. 2004. 'Rewriting WESSA Identity'. In *Under Construction: 'Race' and Identity in South Africa Today*, edited by N. Distiller and M. Steyn, 93–109. Johannesburg: Heinemann.

Samuelson, M. 2007. *Remembering the Nation, Dismembering Women? Stories of the South African Transition*. Pietermaritzburg: University of KwaZulu-Natal Press.

Scheff, T.J. 2000. 'Shame and the Social Bond: A Sociological Theory'. *Sociological Theory* 18(1): 84–99.

———. 1990. *Microsociology: Emotion, Discourse, and Social Structure*. Chicago: University of Chicago Press.

Scully, P. 1995. 'Rape, Race and Colonial Culture: The Sexual Politics of Identity in the Nineteenth-Century Cape Colony, South Africa'. *American Historical Review* 100(2): 335–59.

Sedgwick, E.K. 2003. *Touching Feeling: Affect, Pedagogy, Performativity*. Durham: Duke University Press.

Seekings, J. and N. Nattrass. 2005. *Class, Race and Inequality in South Africa*. New Haven: Yale University Press.

Shefer, T. 2010. 'Narrating Gender and Sex in and through Apartheid Divides'. *South African Journal of Psychology* 40(4): 382–95.

Shefer, T. and K. Ratele. 2013. 'Desire, Fear and Entitlement: Sexualising Race and Racialising Sexuality in (Re)membering Apartheid'. In *Race, Memory and the Apartheid Archive*, edited by G. Stevens, N. Duncan and D. Hook, 188–207. Johannesburg: Wits University Press; Basingstoke: Palgrave Macmillan.

Shefer, T., K. Ratele, A. Strebel, N. Shabalala and R. Buikema (eds). 2007. *From Boys to Men: Social Constructions of Masculinity in Contemporary Society*. Cape Town: University of Cape Town Press.

Shotwell, A. 2007. 'Shame in Alterities: Adrian Piper, Intersubjectivity and the Racial Formation of Identity'. In *The Shock of the Other: Situating Alterities*, edited by S. Hortskotte and E. Peeren, 127–36. Amsterdam: Rodopi.

Skeggs. B. 2008a. 'Making Class through Fragmenting Culture'. In *Problematizing Identity: Everyday Struggles in Language, Culture and Education*, edited by A.M.Y. Lin, 35–50. New York: Taylor & Francis.

———. 2008b. 'The Problem with Identity'. In *Problematizing Identity: Everyday Struggles in Language, Culture, and Education*, edited by A.M.Y. Lin, 12–34. New York: Taylor & Francis.

———. 2005. 'The Making of Class and Gender through Visualising Moral Subject Formation'. *Sociology* 39(5): 965–82.

Smith, A.D. 1998. *Nationalism and Modernism: A Critical Survey of Recent Theories of Nations and Nationalism*. New York: Routledge.

Smith, A.M. 1998. *Laclau and Mouffe: The Radical Democratic Imaginary*. London: Routledge.

————. 1994. *New Right Discourse on Race and Sexuality: Britain 1968–1990*. Cambridge: Cambridge University Press.

Smith, F. 2014. *Kamphoer* [Camp whore]. Cape Town. Tafelberg.

Spies, N. 2012. *Seks: Nou wat is die eintlike storie? Intimiteit in ons verhoudings* [Sex: Now what is the real story? Intimacy in our relationships]. Cape Town: Naledi.

Spivak, G.C. 1988. 'Can the Subaltern Speak?' In *Marxism and the Interpretation of Culture*, edited by C. Nelson and L. Grossberg, 271–313. London: Macmillan.

Stanley, L. and H. Dampier. 2007. 'Cultural Entrepreneurs, Proto-nationalism and Women's Testimony Writings: From the South African War to 1940'. *Journal of Southern African Studies* 33(3): 501–19.

Stavrakakis, Y. 2010. 'Discourse, Affect, *Jouissance*: Psychoanalysis, Political Theory and Artistic Practices'. Paper presented at Art and Desire Seminars, June, Istanbul.

Steinbach, S.L. 2017 [2012]. *Understanding the Victorians: Politics, Culture and Society in Nineteenth-Century Britain*. 2nd edition. London: Routledge.

Steyn, M., 2004. 'Rehybridising the Creole: New South African Afrikaners'. In *Under Construction: 'Race' and Identity in South Africa Today*, edited by N. Distiller and M. Steyn, 70–85. Johannesburg: Heinemann.

————. 2003. 'White Talk: White South Africans and the Strategic Management of Diasporic Whiteness'. Ph.D. diss., University of Cape Town.

————. 2001. *'Whiteness Just isn't What it Used to be': White Identity in a Changing South Africa*. Albany: State University of New York Press.

Steyn, M. and M. van Zyl. 2009. 'The Prize and the Price'. In *The Prize and the Price: Shaping Sexualities in South Africa*, edited by M. Steyn and M. van Zyl, 3–17. Cape Town: HSRC Press.

Stoler, A.L. 2002a. *Carnal Knowledge and Imperial Power: Race and the Intimate in Colonial Rule*. Berkeley: University of California Press.

————. 2002b. 'Racial Histories and Their Regimes of Truth'. In *Race Critical Theories: Text and Context*, edited by P. Essed and D.T. Goldberg, 369–91. Malden, MA: Blackwell.

————. 1989. 'Making Empire Respectable: The Politics of Race and Sexual Morality in Twentieth-Century Colonial Cultures'. *American Ethnologist* 16(4): 634–60.

Strange, S. 1986. *Casino Capitalism*. Oxford: Basil Blackwell.

Styhre, A. and U. Eriksson-Zetterquist. 2008. 'Thinking the Multiple in Gender and Diversity Studies: Examining the Concept of Intersectionality'. *Gender in Management: An International Journal* 23(8): 567–82.

Swart, S. 2001. '"Man, Gun and Horse": Hard Right Afrikaner Masculine Identity in Post-apartheid South Africa'. In *Changing Men in Southern Africa*, edited by R. Morrell, 75–90. Pietermaritzburg: University of Natal Press; London: Zed Books.

Swart, S.S. 2007. 'Motherhood and Otherhood: Gendered Citizenship and Afrikaner Women in the South African 1914 Rebellion'. *African Historical Review* 39(2): 41–57.

Tasker, Y. and D. Negra. 2007. 'Introduction: Feminist Politics and Postfeminist Culture'. In *Interrogating Postfeminism: Gender and the Politics of Popular Culture*, edited by Y. Tasker and D. Negra, 1–25. Durham: Duke University Press.

Taylor, N.F. 2010. 'The Personal is Political: Women's Magazines for the I'm-Not-a-Feminist-but Generation'. In *You've Come a Long Way, Baby: Women, Politics and Popular Culture*, edited by L.J. Goren, 215–32. Lexington: University Press of Kentucky.

Terreblanche, S. 2012. *Lost in Transformation*. Johannesburg: KMM Publishers.

Thomas, L.M. 2006. 'The Modern Girl and Racial Respectability in 1930s' South Africa'. *Journal of African History* 47(3): 460–90.

Torfing, J. 1999. *New Theories of Discourse: Laclau, Mouffe and Žižek*. Oxford: Blackwell.

Tuana, N. 2004. 'Coming to Understand: Orgasm and the Epistemology of Ignorance'. *Hypatia* 19(1): 194–232.

Turner, J.H. and J.E. Stets. 2005. *The Sociology of Emotions*. Cambridge: Cambridge University Press.

Van der Lingen, E.C. 1953. 'Die rol van die vrou in die politiek' [Woman's role in politics]. In *Die triomf van nasionalisme in Suid-Afrika 1910–1953* [The triumph of nationalism in South Africa 1910–1953], edited by D.P. Goosen, 142–7. Johannesburg: Impala Opvoedkundige Diens.

Van der Merwe, C.P. and C.F. Albertyn. 1972. *Die Vrou Deel 1* [Woman Part 1]. Cape Town: Albertyn.

Van der Merwe, R. 2011. 'Moulding *Volksmoeders* or *Volks* Enemies? Female Students at the University of Pretoria, 1920–1970'. *Historia* 56(1): 77–100.

Van der Merwe, S. 2011. 'Career Trajectories of White Afrikaner Women Employed in the Financial Sector of Gauteng'. Master's thesis, University of Pretoria.

Van der Westhuizen, C. 2017. 'Rejuvenating Reconciliation with Transformation'. In *Rethinking Reconciliation: Evidence from South Africa*, edited by K. Lefko-Everett, R. Govender and D. Foster, 168–92. Cape Town: HSRC Press.

———. 2016a. 'Afrikaners in Post-apartheid South Africa: Inward Migration and Enclave Nationalism'. *HTS Theological Studies* 72(4): 1–9.

———. 2016b. 'Race, Intersectionality, and Affect in Postapartheid Productions of "the Afrikaans White Woman"'. *Critical Philosophy of Race* 4(2): 221–38.

———. 2015. 'White Power Today'. Paper presented at 'A Round Table on Whiteness, Afrikaans, Afrikaners: Addressing Post-apartheid Legacies, Privileges and Burdens', Mapungubwe Institute for Strategic Reflection, Johannesburg, 5 November.

———. 2013. 'The "Comfizone" behind Red October White Angst'. *Eyewitness News*, 11 October. http://ewn.co.za/2013/10/11/OPINION-The-comfizone-behind-Red-October-white-angst.

———. 2007. *White Power & the Rise and Fall of the National Party*. Cape Town: Zebra Press.

Van Gelder, E. 2012. 'Inside the *Kommando* Camp That Turns Boys' Doubts to Hate'. *Mail & Guardian*, 24 February. http://mg.co.za/article/2012-02-24-the-kommando-camp-that-turns-boys-doubts-to-hate.

Van Rensburg, J. 2012. '*Die Boerevrou* 1919–1931: 'n Kultuurhistoriese studie oor die eerste Afrikaanse vrouetydskrif' [*Die Boerevrou* 1919–1931: A cultural-historical study about the first Afrikaans women's magazine]. Ph.D. diss., University of Pretoria.

Van Wyk, S. and J. Sharp. 2016. 'The Heart of Whiteness? An Ethnography of a Boer Afrikaner Settlement in Post-apartheid South Africa'. Paper presented at a seminar, University of Pretoria.

Van Zyl, M. and M. Steyn. 2005. *Performing Queer: Shaping Sexualities, 1994–2004*. Cape Town: Kwela.

Van Zyl Slabbert, F. 1975. 'Afrikaner Nationalism, White Politics and Political Change in South Africa'. In *Change in Contemporary South Africa*, edited by L. Thompson and J. Butler, 3–18. Berkeley: University of California Press.

Verwey, C. and M. Quayle. 2012. 'Whiteness, Racism, and Afrikaner Identity in Post-apartheid South Africa'. *African Affairs* 111(445): 551–75.

Vestergaard, M. 2001. 'Who's Got the Map? The Negotiation of Afrikaner Identities in Post-apartheid South Africa'. *Daedalus* 130(1): 19–44.

Viljoen, L. 2008. 'Nationalism, Gender and Sexuality in the Autobiographical Writing of Two Afrikaner Women'. *Social Dynamics: A Journal of African Studies* 34(2): 186–202.

Vincent, L. 2000. 'Bread and Honour: White Working Class Women and Afrikaner Nationalism in the 1930s'. *Journal of Southern African Studies* 25(1): 61–78.

———. 1999. 'The Power behind the Scenes: The Afrikaner Nationalist Women's Parties, 1915 to 1931'. *South African Historical Journal* 40(1): 51–73.

Waetjen, T. 2000. 'The Limits of Gender Rhetoric'. *Theory and Society* 30(1): 121–52.

Walker, C. 1995. 'Conceptualising Motherhood in Twentieth-Century South Africa'. *Journal of Southern African Studies* 21(3): 417–37.

———. 1990. 'Women and Gender in Southern Africa to 1945: An Overview'. In *Women and Gender in Southern Africa to 1945*, edited by C. Walker, 1–32. Cape Town: David Philip; London: James Currey.

Walter, N. 2011. *Living Dolls: The Return of Sexism*. London: Virago.

Wang, Y-J. 2008. 'The Outside inside us: Antagonisms and Identities in Taiwanese Online Gay Forums'. In *Discourse Theory and Cultural Analysis: Media, Arts and Literature*, edited by N. Carpentier and E. Spinoy, 225–44. Cresskill, NJ: Hampton Press.

Wasserman, H. and S. Jacobs. 2003. *Shifting Selves: Post-apartheid Essays on Mass Media, Culture, and Identity*. Cape Town: Kwela.

Wessels, D. 1972. 'Twee lewensfere: Beroep en gesin' [Two spheres of life: Career and family]. In *Die Vrou Deel 1* [Woman Part 1], edited by C.P. van der Merwe and C.F. Albertyn, 375–97. Cape Town: Albertyn.

West, C. and S. Fenstermaker. 1996. 'Doing Difference'. In *Race, Class and Gender: Common Bonds, Different Voices*, edited by E. Ngan-Ling Chow, D. Wilkinson and M.B. Zinn, 357–84. Thousand Oaks: Sage.

West, M. 2009. *White Women Writing White: Identity and Representation in (Post-) Apartheid Literatures of South Africa*. Cape Town: David Philip.

Wetherell, M. 2012. *Affect and Emotion: A New Social Science Understanding*. London: Sage.

Whitehead, S.M. and F.J. Barrett. 2001. 'The Sociology of Masculinity'. In *The Masculinities Reader*, edited by S.M. Whitehead and F.J. Barrett, 1–26. Cambridge: Polity Press.

Wilkins, I. and H. Strydom. 2012 [1978]. *The Super-Afrikaners: Inside the Afrikaner Broederbond*. Johannesburg: Jonathan Ball.

Willoughby-Herard, T. 2010. 'I'll Give You Something to Cry About': The Intraracial Violence of Uplift Feminism in the Carnegie Poor White Study Volume, *The Mother and Daughter of the Poor Family*'. *South African Review of Sociology* 41(1): 78–104.

Woolf, V. 2005 [1928]. *A Room of One's Own*. Orlando: Harcourt.

Worden, N. (ed.). 2012. *Cape Town: Between East and West; Social Identities in a Dutch Colonial Town*. Johannesburg: Jacana; Hilversum: Uitgeverij Verloren.

Wray, M. 2006. *Not Quite White: White Trash and the Boundaries of Whiteness*. Durham: Duke University Press.

Yuval-Davis, N. 2011. 'The Dark Side of Democracy: Autochthony and the Radical Right'. *Open Democracy*, 26 July. http://www.opendemocracy.net/5050/nira-yuval-davis/dark-side-of-democracy-autochthony-and-radical-right.

———. 1997. *Gender and Nation*. London: Sage.

Index